Hans Delbrück
& the German
Military Establishment

Hans Delbrück

HANS DELBRÜCK
& The German
Military Establishment:

War Images in Conflict

ARDEN BUCHOLZ

UNIVERSITY OF IOWA PRESS IOWA CITY

Library of Congress Cataloging in Publication Data

Bucholz, Arden.
  Hans Delbrück & the German military establishment.

  Bibliography: p.
  Includes index.
  1. Military art and science—Germany—History—
19th century.   2. Military art and science—Germany—
History—20th century.   3. Strategy—History—19th century.   4. Strategy—History—20th century.   5. Military
history—Historiography—History—19th century.
6. Military history—Historiography—History—20th century.   7. Delbrück, Hans, 1848–1929.   I. Title.
II. Title: Hans Delbrück and the German military
establishment.
U43.G3B8   1985   355′.02′0924   84–16458
ISBN 0–87745–129–X

University of Iowa Press, Iowa City 52242
© 1985 by The University of Iowa. All rights reserved
Printed in the United States of America

For Susie

CONTENTS

Illustrations

Note: Except for the frontispiece, all photographs of Hans Delbrück were furnished to the author by Frau Helene Hobe, Delbrück's daughter.

Acknowledgments

This study began under the aegis of Professor William H. McNeill of the University of Chicago. His encouragement and assistance at every step of the way have been bountiful. Dr. Alfred Vagts of Sherman, Connecticut, has aided my research for ten years. His suggestions for bibliography, insights into Germany from his own life there from 1892 to 1933, the loan of books and materials, and comments on each version of the manuscript have been a great source of inspiration. Professor Gordon Craig of Stanford University and Dr. Hans Schleier of Leipzig, East Germany, provided important suggestions at the start of research. Professor Theodore Ropp of Duke University read and commented on several versions of the manuscript. Professor Dr. Werner Hahlweg of Westfälische Wilhelms-Universität, Münster, helped with the interpretation of Clausewitz. Professor Dr. Eberhard Kessel of Johannes Gutenberg Universität, Mainz, kindly read and commented on a much earlier version of chapter 3 dealing with Schlieffen's ideas and plans.

Frau Helene Hobe, nee Delbrück, of Berlin-Dahlem, not only allowed me access to her father's papers in the Deutsche Staatsbibliothek, but graciously gave me a series of interviews, allowed me to examine the remaining Delbrück family papers in her personal possession, and made phone calls to friends throughout Germany to answer questions or verify information on the life of her father. By her hospitality she gave insights into the traditions of Prussia and of her family which were invaluable. I am greatly indebted to her.

Several groups of librarians were essential to the completion of this work. Dr. Hans-Erich Teitge, director, Diplom-Bibliothekar Horst Wolf, and Dr. Ursula Winter of the Handschriftenabteilung, Literaturarchiv, Deutsche Staatsbibliothek, Berlin, DDR (hereinafter DSB) provided fine working conditions, much extra help, and warm hospitality during two lengthy visits in 1971 and 1974. In addition they aided in sending large amounts of microfilm without which the work could not have proceeded. Officials at the Bundesarchiv, Koblenz, BRD (hereinafter BAK) rendered the same service and were especially helpful during research there in December 1976–January 1977. Librarians Norma Lawrence and Marilyn Strong of Drake Memorial Library, State University of New York College at Brockport, labored to provide me with several hundred books and articles through the national interlibrary loan system over a ten-year period.

Colleagues Lynn Parsons and Neil Johnson read and commented on the manuscript at various stages and I am indebted to their careful efforts. Colleague John Kutolowski put in many days reading, revising, and suggesting. His fine knowledge of European and military history provided a larger framework in which to view Delbrück's work. His lengthy written comments helped to liberate me from the gravitational pull of Wilhelmian German. Without his painstaking efforts, the work would not have reached completion. My colleagues Steve Ireland, Kempes Schnell, and Walter Boston nourished the spirit and maintained the necessary bureaucratic framework for scholarly work to proceed.

I am grateful for two grants from the Research Foundation of the State University of New York, Series 1974–75 and Series 1975–76, which provided funds for travel and research in Berlin and Koblenz. Colleague Robert Strayer helped to clarify the original grant proposal into a provocative paradigm which has remained in the work itself.

Dr. Ursula Brammer of the University of Pittsburgh aided in the understanding of some almost inscrutable nineteenth-century German handwriting.

Arthur Pflughaupt graciously shepherded the work along the path from manuscript into print.

Mrs. Brenda Peake typed the several drafts with precision, efficiency, and good humor.

I am grateful to Merritt, Mark, and Sue Ann Tally Bucholz for their forbearance and for time away to complete this study amid the manifold joys and responsibilities of family and community life.

To all these and many others I am deeply grateful. For the errors which remain, I alone am responsible.

Arden Bucholz
Waterport, New York
January 1984

INTRODUCTION

Hans Delbrück (1848–1929) is a major figure of Imperial Germany who remains, more than a half century after his death, largely unknown. His life was unusually complicated. As his friend Professor Friedrich Meinecke wrote, Delbrück led a double life in the university and as a political commentator.[1] Science and politics, according to another colleague, sociologist Max Weber, are two utterly different worlds—the latter the realm of myth, where prophets and saviors rule, while science, value-free and unable to guide life, is the realm of understanding.[2] The obscurity and complexity of Delbrück's life reflect the mixture of science and politics in his career.

For forty years he taught at the University of Berlin, pioneering in the study of armies and society; yet the Prussian general who said in 1901 that Delbrück's work had put an end to dilettantism in the field was corrected thirty years later. Delbrück, Eckart Kehr wrote in 1931, had failed to create a new school of military history research: he had no followers.[3] During his lifetime Delbrück's scholarship and methodology were dismissed in Germany. His military history studies were considered invalid to support promotion to full professor in 1896, and in 1921 the Berlin faculty voted not to continue his research. Yet his magisterial *History of the Art of War in the Framework of Political History* (4 volumes, 1900–1920) has been translated and published by both the USSR's People's Commissariat for Defense and the United States Military Academy at West Point.[4] Today Delbrück is internationally recognized as one of the founders of the scientific study of military history.[5]

Delbrück was actively involved in politics from 1882 until 1925. He served in the Prussian Landtag, German Reichstag, and from 1884 until after the First World War edited what Fritz Fischer has called Imperial Germany's most important journal of political commentary.[6] When he sold the *Preussische Jahrbücher* in 1921, subscribers and readers declined; it moved briefly to Switzerland and finally went out of existence. One of the authors, along with Max Weber, of the German response to the Versailles Peace Treaty, Delbrück carried on a running debate with European historians such as Alphonse Aulard and German socialists like Karl Kautsky over Germany's role in the outbreak of World War I. Member of a prominent Prussian family which included tutors to two German emperors, state secretaries under Bismarck and Kaiser Wilhelm II, and the founder of one of present-day Germany's largest banks, Delbrück was served with a family petition in 1921 asking him to recant his political position. He was a leader in the fight against what became the official Nazi interpretation of the end of the war.

Even Delbrück's personal and professional papers, saved meticulously for fifty years, were scattered by war and politics. Today librarians in the Bundesarchiv, Koblenz, West Germany, do not know the contents of the Delbrück papers in the Deutsche Staatsbibliothek, East Berlin, and no one has examined Delbrück's life in the light of both collections.

Until World War I Delbrück's dual professions in science and politics were quite separated, and therefore the first three chapters, which deal with the years 1848–1914, comprise Part I. Chapter 1 describes the nature of military history in the new German Empire of 1871 and details Delbrück's confrontation with the General Staff over the interpretation of two eighteenth-century Prussian soldiers, Frederick the Great and Carl von Clausewitz. Chapter 2 focuses on the evolution of Delbrück's historical thinking and his attempts to establish a new scholarly discipline, the scientific study of armies and society, against opposition from two bureaucracies and two dominant modes of thought: the "Prussian School" within the University and the "Schlieffen School" within the General Staff. Chapter 3 describes that symbiosis of military history and war planning which took place in the decades 1890–1914: the evolution of the Schlieffen Plan, its relationship to the General Staff educational system, and its critics, among which Delbrück became an increasingly important voice after 1908.

Part II begins in August 1914. The controversy over historical strategy and methods for the understanding of the Schlieffen Plan had apparently ended. It had been accepted, albeit with some misgivings, as Germany's plan for future war, and beginning on August 4 it was being put into operation in the battle of the frontiers. Chapter 4 finds Delbrück no longer an historian of eighteenth-century warfare but a current war commentator, applying his methods of scientific history to the first industrial mass war. By 1918 his criticism of German strategy had forced him into an isolated and misunderstood position which was exacerbated by the fact that events proved him right: Imperial Germany went down to defeat. Chapters 5 and 6 detail the origin and development of the General Staff interpretation of the World War, its relationship to politics, and Delbrück's failure to gain a hearing for his historical methods or for his correct analysis of World War I.

There is a certain risk attendant upon describing the two parts of Delbrück's double life in the same work. It may be argued that his life was too complicated and the sources for it too numerous to do justice to both aspects in a single volume. Yet, in an important sense, the two are inseparable. If this essay stimulates interest in one of the important intellectual figures of pre-Hitlerian Germany, if the outline biography, woven from equal strands of Delbrück's life and the circumstances of Imperial Germany, provokes others to investigate in more detail Delbrück's contributions as historian and as political commentator, an important purpose will have been served.

One cannot help thinking beyond Delbrück's career to the larger problem of Imperial Germany within the framework of modern European history. Transitions are always difficult. *War Images* symbolizes a particularly difficult transition in the size and technology of armies: the change from the nineteenth-century mass army to the twentieth-century million-man army, and from the cavalry charge with sabers to the large-scale use of machine gun, tank and airplane. The greatest fears as well as the most exciting hopes of the generation which came to maturity and leadership in the decades 1890–1914 were both epitomized by Dietrich Bonhoeffer from his prison cell in 1943. Something new, he wrote, was being born which was not discernible in the alternatives of the moment.[7]

NOTES

1   Friedrich Meinecke's death notice, *Chronik der Friedrich Wilhelm Universität zu Berlin*, April 1929/March 1930, 10–11.

2   Cf. especially Weber's lectures "Science as a Vocation" and "Politics as a Vocation," reprinted in *From Max Weber*, ed. H. H. Garth and C. Wright Mills (New York: Harpers, 1958), pp. 77ff.

3   Eckart Kehr, "Neuere deutsche Geschichtsschreibung" in *Eckart Kehr: Der Primat der Innenpolitik*, ed. Hans-Ulrich Wehler (Berlin: Walter de Gruyter, 1970), p. 261.

4   The Russian translation was published between the years 1936 and 1939. The English translation, by Colonel Walter Renfroe (USA-Ret.), formerly chairman of the Department of Foreign Languages, United States Military Academy, West Point, is currently being published in the Greenwood Press series Contributions in Military History, edited by Colonel Thomas Griess of the Department of History, USMA. Volume 1 was published in 1975, volume 2 in 1980 and volume 3 in 1982.

5   Theodore Ropp, in his standard survey of modern military history, called Delbrück's *History of the Art of War in the Framework of Political History (Geschichte der Kriegskunst im Rahmen der politischen Geschichte)* "the classic in the field," in *War in the Modern World* (New York: Collier Books, 1961), p. 11. European reviewers of the newest edition (4 vols., Berlin: Walter de Gruyter, 1962–66) unanimously called it the "pathbreaking standard work" and "a masterwork of German historical literature." Cf. *Historische Zeitschrift*, vol. 202, no. 3 (June 1966): 721, and vol. 196, no. 3 (June 1963): 504; *Historische Jahrbuch*, vol. 85, no. 2, 404; *Zeitschrift für Militärgeschichte* (DDR), vol. 4, (1965): 357–60; *Jahrbuch für die Geschichte Mittel- und Ost-Deutschlands*, vol. 13/14 (1965): 435; *Wehrkunde: Zeitschrift für alle Wehrfragen*, vol.

11, no. 9 (September 1962): 515, vol. 14 (March 1965): 165; vol. 15 (October 1966): 555; *Der Tagesspiegel*, (Berlin), 2 August 1963, 11; *Der Büchermarkt* (Munich), no. 3, 1962; *Der Schweizer Soldat* (Zurich), no. 10 (31 January 1963), 237–38; *Jahrbuch für brandenburgische Landes-geschichte*, vol. 13 (1962): 154–55; *Soldat und Technik*, vol. 4 (September 1964): 537–38; *Bibliotheca Orientalis* (Leiden), vol. 25 (September-November 1965): 335; *Neue Zuricher Zeitung*, 6 June 1965, 7; *Österreichische Militärische Zeitschrift* (Vienna), no. 2 (1965), 135; *Truppenpraxis* (Baden-Baden), 5 May 1967; *Deutsche Zeitung* (Köln), 14 November 1962.

6   Fritz Fischer, *War of Illusions: German Policies from 1911 to 1914* (New York: W. W. Norton, 1975), p. 39.

7   Dietrich Bonhoeffer, *Letters and Papers from Prison*, ed. Eberhard Bethge (London: Fontana Books, 1953), p. 135. Bonhoeffer, who grew up next door to the Delbrück family in Berlin Grunewald, was related to them through marriage. In his first year in prison, one of his favorite readings was Delbrück's *World History*. For original and provocative commentary on what was being born, and how, see William H. McNeill, *The Pursuit of Power: Technology, Armed Force and Society since A.D. 1000* (Chicago: University of Chicago Press, 1982), especially chapters 8 and 9.

1 / THE GRÜNDERJAHRE

PRUSSIA VICTORIOUS: THE MILITARY, SOCIETY, AND HISTORY

The wars of German unification profoundly altered the European consciousness. Austria, the leading German state in international affairs, fell before Prussian military power at Königgrätz on July 3, 1866, achieving "the Year of the Miracle" for German Nationalists. Four years later the Second French Empire also fell victim to Prussian-German might after only six weeks of field battles. A new German state suddenly vaulted into preeminence in continental affairs. The quick and decisive military victories resulted from concentration of forces in campaigns of annihilation. Nothing like this had occured in Europe since Napoleon I, and the results stunned contemporaries.

Military success and political unification preceded a remarkably rapid economic transformation. Few societies in modern history matched Imperial Germany's rapid and extensive industrialization. In the closing decades of the nineteenth century, industrial leadership in Europe passed from Great Britain to Germany, a development which might well be considered the most important event in the half century before World War I.

The relationship between military victories, political unification, and economic change needs greater emphasis than scholars have thus far accorded. Historians have noted a curious malaise in Germany in the decades before World War I, calling it cultural and economic despair, or an ideological crisis.[1] But this seems to have become important only after about 1888. A transition from the leadership of the German unification movement to the second—or Wilhelmian—generation, especially after the downfall of Otto von Bismarck, has often appeared the decisive change in modern German politics and society.[2] Our thesis, however, argues that the major turning point in Prussian-German history was 1871, highlighted by the influences of war, unification, and industrialization. Symbolized by the transition from provincial outlook to that of a national state, the change was far more than merely political or economic. The comingling and diffusion of national feeling, military victory, and growing industrial power effected a transformation of *Weltanschauungen*.

To be sure, armies are often important in new nations. As a revolutionary force they contribute to the disintegration of traditional political

1

order. As a conservative agency they aid new governments to maintain domestic tranquility and ensure national security. Transitional societies have often more easily created new armies than other modern institutions.[3] The weakening of traditional authorities raises an important question: How will a newly recruited industrial work force be incorporated into the political community of the nation? The army is one of the most rapid vehicles for acculturating people to a new national state.[4] The role of the military in the transition from provincial and dynastic to national politics has often been defined primarily in terms of its symbolic value in developing a new political identity.[5] The phrase "old societies and new nations" applies well to Germany,[6] and Ralf Dahrendorf has used the phrase "industrial feudal state" to describe that symbiosis between Prussian-German society and the industrial revolution that gave Imperial Germany so much of its character.[7]

What, then, was the relationship between the army and the new nation in Germany? It cannot be defined simply in terms of militarism: that is, those customs, interests, prestige, actions, and thought associated with armies and wars and yet transcending true military purposes.[8] Surely war involves national identity and touches on the deepest roots of legitimacy. Victory in war sustains the real and symbolic existences of the society and thereby strengthens the readiness to acknowledge the political leaders' right to rule.[9] On another level, Karl Marx proposed that the whole history of the structure of middle-class society was clearly summarized in the history of armies. Nowhere, he wrote, is the relationship between the factors of production and the structure of society more clearly illustrated.[10] Few scholars have followed up on this approach, even those who have suggested that military life affected industrialization by its leadership ideas and character formation.[11] Such lines of inquiry, however, are beyond the scope of the present essay. Let us rather suggest three specific ties between the wars of unification and the new German Reich: first in the militarization of society, secondly in the writing of history, and thirdly in the interpretation of that great writer on war, Carl von Clausewitz.

The wars of German unification had far-reaching social effect. Although Mirabeau in 1788 had remarked sarcastically that in Europe only the Prussian army had its own kingdom, by 1888 this statement seemed to verge on truth. Certainly it was natural for a generation that saw its nation founded by military power, after centuries of disunion and impotence, to honor the army as the major factor in its creation and the military estate, in consequence, as the chief element in society.[12] Theodor Schieder suggested that the military provided the social and ideological element that welded together the two ingredients of the German Reich of

1871: the power of the Prussian state and the middle-class nationalist movement.[13] Flushed with power and unity at last achieved, many Germans looked on their army as a priceless national treasure. Long-nourished resentment of Prussian militarism and drill-ground spit and polish is said to have paled and vanished among the larger part of the German bourgeois.[14] Universal military service was praised as the foundation of political liberty. The anniversary of the French surrender at Sedan became a popular holiday, the first new patriotic festival. The aristocratic officer of the exclusive guards regiment came to be the model for aspiring social classes, and the rank order of the military and military patterns of thought the standard for the prestige hierarchy.[15] Although Carl Zuckmayer's play *The Captain from Köpenick* appeared in 1930, the real life incident from which it was taken had occurred in October 1906. A man only begins to be somebody when he has got his commission, Captain von Schlettow remarks at the beginning of the play. Of course, every child knows that in Prussia the military can do anything and everything they please, says Voight in the closing scene.[16]

This militarization of society also relates to the economic changes in Germany after 1871. Significant portions of the new middle class formed in the decades before World War I, seeking an institution of refuge and permanence amid the teeming waves of change engulfing them, turned to the army. Gerhard Ritter suggests something like this by contrasting the officer class, with its firm Prussian heritage of a disciplined way of life, strict code of honor, and strong esprit de corps, with the inchoate, traditionless mass of modern industrial society.[17]

The army, then, held a unique position in Prussian-German society. It was perhaps the most visible symbol of the identity and security of the Second Reich.

A second dimension important to an understanding of Imperial Germany as a new nation was its changing attitude toward history. A new historical movement had begun more than a decade before unification among historians such as J. G. Droysen, Heinrich von Sybel, and Heinrich von Treitschke; they established the "Prussian School" of historical writing in the late 1850s. Prussia, they argued, was the preeminent German state and Frederick the Great was the eighteenth-century forerunner of nineteenth-century German nationalism. Since the fifteenth century Prussia had pursued her duty to serve the best interests of Germany as a whole.[18] Gustav Freytag, in his famous *Pictures from the German Past* of the 1860s, portrayed the king's struggles during the Seven Years War as "superhuman." Heinrich von Sybel portrayed Frederick's immortal service to Germany as the historical antecedent to Bismarck in providing unity and security.[19] The "Prussian School" of history, then, which encouraged national union under Prussian aegis, was the dominant, though by no means the only, historical tradition at midcentury.

Not surprisingly, political unification founded on military success added even more impetus to the Prussian School. Reinhold Koser, Droysen's pupil and, like him, a professor at the Berlin War Academy, began publishing a multivolume biography of Frederick in the 1880s. A new journal, the *Researches into Prussian and Brandenburg History*, was established. The *Hohenzollern Yearbook* issued a series of monographs dealing with the dynasty, and the Prussian Academy of Science began to publish Frederick the Great's political correspondence. In all of these endeavors the professors viewed Frederick as an authentic national hero, a rare creature who combined high abilities in politics, war, and letters.

The professors were not alone in their adulation of Frederick the Great. An author and philosopher, Frederick was also a strategist whom the General Staff looked upon as a paragon. Indeed, the military educational system promulgated the image of Frederick as a strategic genius. The Prussian officers corps had an intellectual as well as military tradition, dating back to the eighteenth century. The heart of this body, the Great General Staff, had been created to play an intellectual and educational role in military affairs: to plan and prepare future war and to create and teach a uniform body of war doctrine throughout the army. Like the civilian professors, General Staff officers considered themselves an intellectual elite. They were chosen by examination, educated professionally in a three-year course at the War Academy, often lectured, and wrote books and articles. They considered themselves part of the intelligentsia.

The officers, like the professoriat, had a central interest in history. Planning for future wars and executing these plans on a small scale in practical exercises entailed not only speculation about the future; it meant recapturing the military past. The Historical Section of the General Staff undertook this task. Since the early nineteenth century, history was considered essential to the education of every General Staff officer. An archive for the collection of documents and material prior to the 1850s, the Military History Section thereafter became the central workshop for military history writing within the Prussian-German army.

To help disseminate its views throughtout the army, the Military History Section sponsored an ambitious series of publications. The best known of these was the *Military Weekly News Paper (Militär-Wochen-*

blatt) created in the early nineteenth century. This official journal mir-
rored the thoughts of the General Staff on weapons, tactics, strategy, and
history. In addition, books were published dealing with both practical
aspects of military life and with military history through an arrange-
ment with the Berlin publisher E. S. Mittler & Sons—a relationship between publisher and General Staff that continued from the 1820s to the
end of the Second World War.

By the late 1860s the Military History Section had begun to publish a
history of the wars of German unification, and a decade later this work
was extended to include the Prussian wars of the eighteenth century. As
it developed, the series was written with two considerations in mind:
first, to unite the events of military history with the patriotic tradition of
the "Prussian School" of historical research; secondly, to achieve factual
accuracy by focusing on battlefield actions down to regimental level.[20]

Both academicians and officers wrote military history. But the similarities and the differences between their respective views need emphasis. As
noted, both fell under the influence of the "Prussian School": they
tended to glorify Prussia, her leaders, and her historic role in German
affairs. Yet in approaching the more limited topic of the military past,
the two bureaucratic elites pursued separate and quite separated goals.
The professors described the political causes and consequences of war
and did not attain a correctly detailed description of battlefield actions.
The officers, on the other hand, focused their attention exclusively on
combat. They described the battles and leaders in minute detail: a com-
pilation of regimental and divisional battle actions.[21] Neither professors
nor officers portrayed the important relationships between technology,
economics, and war—their armies fought and lived largely divorced
from the larger framework of human social life. Thus, increasingly after
midcentury the image of the military past tended to be divided between
two groups of specialists whose perspectives were often very different.

Such a division of labor should not surprise us, for it well reflects the
transitional period which Germany entered at this time. This increasing
specialization is well illustrated in the history of the German army
command. When Alfred von Schlieffen (1833–1913) studied at the War
Academy in the 1860s, specialists and technicians were already beginning
to overshadow that older philosophical and historical universalism
which had been the spiritual food of Helmuth von Moltke (1800–1891).
Thus Schlieffen was educated to concentrate on the technical aspects of
military problems and to ignore their political and economic impli-
cations.[22]

The wars of German unification, then, had a profound impact on the writing of history. This influence was exacerbated because it was institutionalized in university ("Prussian School") and army ("Schlieffen School").

A third significant result of the wars of German unification was their enhancement of a one-sided interpretation of Carl von Clausewitz. Clausewitz had lived through a great turning point in the history of the war: the transition from the limited war of the eighteenth century to the total war of the French Revolution and Napoleonic era. He recognized this difference, but his best-known works concentrated mainly on Napoleon's violent campaigns of annihilation. Clausewitz's writings were often impenetrable. At his death in 1831 his work was a jumble of essays, memoranda, and notes, in places repetitious and contradictory. *Vom Krieg*, his best-known work, was not a tactical or strategic handbook but a philosophical disquisition on the combined impact of democracy and nationalism on war, written in a thoroughly romantic style.[23] In spite, or perhaps because of, these difficulties, the Prussian military considered *Vom Krieg* as the highest authority on war. After 1871 it was called the "Bible of Königgrätz." To that generation Clausewitz seemed to have captured the essence of the wars of unification: war was an act of violence carried to the uttermost bounds. The destruction of the enemy fighting force by battle was the only valid goal. The strategy of annihilation was the means to this end.[24]

French and English General Staffs shared this interpretation, and so Clausewitz's emphasis on total war by battles of annihilation became the dominant model in European military thought in the half century before World War I.[25] Clausewitz's ideas and Moltke's victories appeared to reinforce each other. A generation of European officers adopted a one-sided emphasis on a single strategic doctrine.[26]

For Helmuth von Moltke, Chief of the Prussian General Staff and architect of the wars of 1866 and 1870–71, all of this was alien: he never came to believe that a single kind of strategy was a magic formula for success. Always aware that special circumstances, both military and political, had played a vital role in Prussia's victories, he reminded his officers that "in war as in art there is no general rule."[27] Recognizing that unique circumstances could not be repeated, aware of the changing diplomatic scene in Europe and cognizant of the impact of technological changes upon the instruments of war, Moltke's strategic plans from the 1870s until his retirement in 1888 were not based upon a repetition of his earlier successes. He realized that German resources would be inadequate to completely defeat France and Russia in a two-front war. Adopting a policy of limited war, Moltke planned for a strategic defense in the

west to allow for a brief "spoiling" offensive in the east, but even in the
east he did not expect battles of annihilation or a deep penetration into
Eurasia. In a famous speech before the Reichstag in 1890, Moltke warned
that the next war could last seven years or thirty years. In describing
Moltke's operation plans from 1871 to 1888, Gerhard Ritter used such
terms as "cautious" and "skeptical."[28]

In the decade after 1871 the wars of German unification became arche-
types in the military education system. Crucial in this process of image
building was the rising generation of officers who derived their military
assumptions from Moltke's campaigns but who themselves were only
indirect participants or observers in these wars. Members of this younger
generation were field grade staff officers and members of the Prussian
nobility serving in the Military History Section, and concurrently,
teaching at the Berlin War Academy. Most were soldiers who had never
seen front-line combat. Here is a critical distinction. Combat officers—
those who experienced battle first-hand, who witnessed death among
comrades and colleagues and who had been eyewitnesses to the destruc-
tive power of modern weaponry on human beings—had a different understanding of war than staff officers—those who served behind the lines
at desk jobs, marking maps, preparing reports, and carrying out administrative procedures. Remoteness from the battlefield tended to increase
the abstractness and rationalization of the "lessons" of war and their
relevance for future conflict.

These noble staff officers began to conceive ideas on strategy in the late
1870s, and by 1891 several assumed key positions of power and influence
where their mature thoughts received practical application in German
war planning. They did not share Moltke's assumptions for future war
or his limited strategic aims. Three years after Moltke's retirement, an
entirely new view had begun to emerge with his most important successor, Graf Alfred von Schlieffen, its visible representative. This "Schlieff-
en School" was both historical and policy making: it was postulated
upon the great victories of German unification, yet it encompassed the
eighteenth-century wars of Frederick the Great as well as the nineteenth-
century wars of Napoleon. Schlieffen's strategic system differed markedly from Moltke's. Perhaps it was a reaction against Moltke's failure to
establish a concrete strategic system with eternally valid "laws of war"
learned from his own achievements. Schlieffen's strategy of annihilation
was part of the second, or Wilhelmian, generation of imperial leadership, with roots in the traditional pride and presumptions of its back-
bone, the Junker elite, and in the changing diplomatic relationships of
this period.

Although this new strategic system emerged publicly only after

Schlieffen's appointment in 1891 as Chief of the General Staff, by then it represented only the tip of the iceberg. Behind it lay nearly twenty years of teaching and writing within the Prussian-German officer corps.

These three factors—the militarization of German society, particularly the enhanced prestige of the General Staff officers, the influence of the "Prussian School" of history, and the effect of the "Schlieffen School" of strategy,—all came together in a little-noted public debate which began in the late 1870s. A group of young General Staff officers debated a newly appointed University of Berlin lecturer over the history of Frederick the Great and the strategy of Carl von Clausewitz.

WAR IMAGES 1879–1889

In 1879 one of this new generation of staff officers, Major Adalbert von Taysen of the General Staff Military History Section and Berlin War Academy, published an edition of Frederick the Great's *Military Testament*.[29] To the brief main document in French, written in 1768 as advice to Prussian generals in fighting future wars, Taysen added a commentary in German. Although much of the testament concerned the technical details of military campaigns—such as provisions, conscription, fortresses, and hospitals—one section was entitled, "Regarding the Fundamental Principles of War." This section astonished Taysen. The king's strategic instructions for the next war, he remonstrated, contradicted all his previous writing on this topic. In place of that "total war" by battles of annihilation that Taysen believed Frederick had always advocated, here were directives for cautious choice of strong positions, the avoidance of battles in open country, and attempts to gain minor advantages which, taken together, might provide an overall successful outcome.[30] But this did not really contravene Frederick's standard teachings on war, Taysen reasoned; it was an exception. The king was discussing a possible war against Austria: a special case. Because of unique terrain and because the Austrians had learned Prussia's ways of war through long experience, Austria had to be treated differently than other potential opponents. Taysen concluded that even though the king urged a limited war against Austria, he would have demanded a strategy of annihilation against other opponents.

One reader of Taysen disagreed with this interpretation. Hans Delbrück, at that time completing five years as private tutor in the family of the Crown Prince of Prussia, reviewed Major von Taysen's work in the *Zeitschrift für Preussische Geschichte und Landeskunde*, a journal edited by Leopold von Ranke. The *Military Testament*, Delbrück wrote, revealed nothing new about Frederick's strategy, but Taysen's commentary obscured Frederick's basic ideas.[31] First of all, the strategy outlined in the *Military Testament* was in no way exceptional and extraordinary when compared with Frederick's other writings. Frederick had always regarded battle as an evil to be undertaken only in necessity, as Clausewitz himself had pointed out.[32] By 1756 Frederick understood that linear tactics were no longer capable of bringing victory by battle. After 1763 Frederick rejected a war of attack against the Austrians, recognizing the strength of their formidable artillery, the inaccessibility of their soldiers behind prepared positions, and their insurmountable wing extensions. The weapons of war had been brought to such perfection that the defensive had the advantage over the offensive.

Secondly, Delbrück continued, Taysen erroneously stated that Frederick's strategic ideas remained the same throughout his life. To the contrary, Frederick's thinking on war continually developed. At times the king's essays contained ideas which seemed to foreshadow the transition from the limited war of the eighteenth century to the total war of the nineteenth. But Frederick recognized that the nature of his army and its weapons would not allow a new strategy.

In Delbrück's view, Frederick's strategy had to be understood in terms of the prevailing social and technological conditions. As Frederick wrote in his *Military Testament,* the eighteenth-century soldier had to fear his own officers more than the dangers of the battlefield, or the officers would never have been able to lead him against the tempest of three hundred cannons. The social complexion of eighteenth-century armies was based on a system of discipline and fear, whereas the self-disciplined, self-willed, individual fighter was more characteristic of the nineteenth century. To change from one to the other necessitated a new period of history. New political and social structures and new ideas had to emerge before a really new art of war could be created.

Delbrück now considered the matter closed, thinking his interpretation standard. Much to his surprise, however, the debate began to generate its own momentum. Colmar Freiherr von der Goltz, later author of widely read military studies, as well as a field marshal and advisor to the Ottoman Turkish armies, in 1879 was a major in the Military History Section of the General Staff and a teacher in the War Academy.[33] Von der Goltz angrily challenged Delbrück. First, he opined that Frederick II was indeed a strategist of annihilation, the strategic forerunner of Napoleon and even of Moltke. He was shocked and indignant that anyone had said Frederick regarded battle as an evil to be avoided. Frederick and Napoleon differed only in personal idiosyncrasies, not in ideals of war.[34] Secondly, using an *ad personum* argument, von der Goltz questioned Delbrück's credentials as a civilian who presumed to "speak the language of the military," while himself not a professional soldier. In his interpretation, von der Goltz stressed strategic ideas and battlefield actions, completely excluding political, social, or technological perspectives. These two differing approaches thus quickly became basic to the conflict over war images. For the remainder of the decade, Delbrück and the officers opposed each other in various books and journals. Delbrück responded to the publications of Theodore von Bernhardi, an important military writer who had been Field Marshal von Moltke's special representative to the Austrian headquarters during the Franco-Prussian War, and to those of Majors Adalbert von Taysen, August von Caemmerer, and Dietrick von Malachowski, teachers in the War Academy and members of the Military History Section of the Great General Staff. Let us examine the arguments in detail.

Delbrück's position in the controversy rested upon two major assumptions: that armies and society were interrelated and that the historian, not the officer, was the legitimate specialist to recover the military past.

For Delbrück, the French Revolution separated two strategic periods, defined by the concepts of limited and total war. As political and social life underwent a decisive transformation after 1789, so did the military. The changed political climate meant that many who in the eighteenth century had not participated in government, and therefore had little feeling of duty toward the monarchical army, became politicized in the flow of nineteenth-century nationalism. This resulted in a vast increase in army size: Frederick crossed the Austrian border in 1756 with 117,000 men; Napoleon crossed the Russian border in 1812 with 600,000. Not only were nineteenth-century armies larger, but their motivation was different. Eighteenth- century armies were made up of beggars, bastards, the poor, and the lame. Consequently they had to fight in linear formation, held together by fear and strict discipline. Nineteenth-century armies were still disciplined, but patriotism infused their ranks; consequently they could fight in smaller, more independent units and as individual sharpshooters; they could be trusted in broken terrain, deep forests, and at night, situations which eighteenth-century commanders tried to avoid because they feared desertion or poor performance. Because of their social construction, eighteenth-century armies were regularly supplied by magazines. In an important sense, military cohesion depended as much on the satisfaction of material wants as on fear and discipline. Napoleonic armies, on the other hand, could requisition a large part of their supplies. Each of these three factors—size, social cohesion, and logistics—depended on the nature of civilian society, and each factor, in turn, affected strategy.

Delbrück wondered in what way strategy was influenced if there were 50,000 men or 150,000. He answered that numbers gained importance in relation to space, time, and geography. The distance from Berlin to Paris was the same for 50,000 men as for 500,000 men. But for every 50,000 combat troops, an additional 20,000 were needed to protect and maintain the way, to hold fortresses, and to form blockades. If five hussars went into a village to requisition, the farmers might get together and kill them, but if fifty hussars were dispatched, they would be safe. A commander who stayed within three to five days' march of his baking ovens had to restrict his strategic goals much more than one who obtained his supplies from the countryside. Finally, the army's social composition influenced the art of moving troops in battle. An army such as Napoleon's that was able to fight in broken order could readily find suitable fighting terrain. For the linear formation of the eighteenth century, flat, open land was a virtual necessity. An army, wrote Delbrück, that fought in linear formation, was bound to the magazine supply system; that army was small in size and rapidly reached its furthermost limits. With such an army the commander could not penetrate deeply into enemy territory or seize an enemy capital. Therefore, these size, space, and geographic relationships meant that, for the eighteenth-century commander, battle assumed quite another meaning than it had for Napoleon.[35]

Delbrück admitted that during the nineteenth century battle had become the most effective means for a decision in war. A victorious battle compensated for practically any mistake, and the commander who won battles appeared to understand war correctly. However, this had not always been true. There were Pyrrhic victories when the advantages were so small and the dangers so great that the commander correctly chose other means to achieve his purposes. The foundation of Frederician warfare was the realization that the means of making war did not put at the commanders' disposal the possibility of completely destroying the opposing state. Therefore commanders had to aim at peace not so much by the destruction as by the exhaustion of their opponents.

Delbrück's second assumption was that the historian, not the officer, was the legitimate professional to study the military past. To write military history, Delbrück admitted, one needed both technical military knowledge and adequate training in the methods of history.[36] Do we turn to an archeologist or a painter when we want to understand ancient vase painting, Delbrück asked? The skills of both may be needed. The problem in this case was that the officers lacked historical training, so they superimposed the strategic ideas of the present upon the previous century. They were unable to free themselves from current military doctrine. They lacked sufficient historical education and, as a result, confused operational thinking with historical reconstruction.[37] Delbrück concluded sardonically:

> The differences between the Austrian commander Daun and Frederick's strategy is not the difference of systems but the difference of individuals. In contrast to this, the difference between the strategy of Frederick and that of Napoleon is not the difference of individuals but of two different strategic systems. . . . It is important to ask how it was possible for Prussia to maintain her existence in the Seven Years War against the combined superiority of her opponents? If modern strategy was indeed possible in the 18th century, then Prussia was saved only through the accidental circumstances that the enemy side was restrained from destroying her by a false theory of war.[38]

Beyond these assumptions Delbrück was a bourgeois civilian who responded sharply to the noble officer's pretensions. For example, in *The Nation in Arms* Colmar von der Goltz had written that King Frederick Wilhelm I had named the officer corps a privileged social class because it represented the educated part of the nation. Delbrück agreed that the officer had special advantages in German society. Waiters addressed officers in the third person, "The captain wants something?" Salesmen called officers "Right Honorable Sir." The smallest military cadet was addressed formally. Officers' wives were given the title "Madam" *(gnädige Frau)* whereas civilian women were merely called *Frau Doktor* or *Frau Direktor.* Officers were greeted first and more warmly than civilians, and they received royal orders earlier in their careers. When a professor published his wedding announcement, his military rank preceded his civil position. Officers enjoyed special privileges within the military legal system and more favorable salaries than civil officials. How, then, Delbrück asked, can we explain the superiority of this particular class of state servant?

It was not, as von der Goltz wanted to think, due to their educational attainments. Public opinion regarded the officer as the embodiment of German courage but not the treasure of German education. Frederick the Great would have been horrified had anybody suggested that the Prussian officer corps was recruited on the basis of education. No, Delbrück argued, their social prestige was not based on learning. In this little-educated officer corps lived the traditions of the ancient German society which, when it went to war, sought a military leader to whom the men bound themselves with an oath. This bond was not material, but personal. Kurlander and Frenchmen served with nobles from Prussia and the Reich in a personal service relationship to the king. Only indirectly were they serving the state of Prussia. Here lies the fundamental difference between civil and military officials. The former are purely state servants, but officers, following the ancient German idea of the vassal, are the military comrades of the king. Even after the officer corps was opened up to the higher middle classes, the ancient tradition of personal service continued.[39]

Confronted by such comments, the noble officers replied imperiously. We men of the profession, they wrote, hold uniform views on Frederician strategy and we reject the interpretation of this young historian who has chosen military history as his speciality.[40] The officers maintained that their military experience qualified them to be the sole legitimate specialists on strategy. The true question, as they saw it, was what the essence of Frederick's strategy was in relationship to the strategy of the present. To deal with such a problem the practitioner was better qualified than the theorist. Even if theory might be useful, it was only formulated after repeated practical experiences.[41] How are we to decide if the Greeks rode in the same way as we do today? an officer asked. The best advice would come from someone who himself rode, who had trained horses, and who understood the development of different kinds of riding equipment. In this question officers took the advice of an intelligent stable master or circus rider with much more confidence than the work of an historian who felt himself competent on this point because of his theories.[42] A famous painter of the ancients corrected the boot of a figure in one of his pictures because a specialist shoemaker had remarked that the boot had been improperly drawn. The expert for this question was the shoemaker, not the artist. The professor could quietly paint around the shoe if he wanted to, the officer concluded.

The soldiers were incensed that a civilian should call upon Clausewitz, the greatest military authority in Germany, to buttress his error-filled interpretation. Clausewitz, they said, had no intention of developing a historical view of strategy. His sole purpose had been operational: to describe a single correct form of strategy for the future. He had no interest in the past or in historical strategies.[43]

The officers never forgave Delbrück's assertion that Frederick regarded battle as an evil. For them, war was the use of the uttermost force, a paradigm validated by the experience of their own time. Frederick had understood this truth: the destruction of the enemy fighting force was for all time the single legitimate strategy.[44] Any other conception contradicted the very nature of war.[45]

A strategy which avoided battle was incomprehensible. Outlasting an opponent, an officer wrote, could not be the basis for a legitimate military strategy. For, if this were the case, the country which went bankrupt first would lose. Material factors such as the size of the army and the supply system were important, but they were not the real essence of any historical period. If two armed peoples stood opposite each other and neither had the courage to seek a decision, the war would depend on the national credit of both sides. The ridiculousness of such a situation was self-evident.[46]

The officers believed that Frederick presaged modern strategy. With limited resources of men and material, his genius allowed him to achieve the same results in the eighteenth century that Napoleon and Moltke, with far greater resources, accomplished in the nineteenth century. In short, Frederick's strategic ideas allowed him to surmount his material conditions. One officer concluded:

> Napoleon I is looked upon by the military laity as the greatest commander of all time. Upon closer examination, however, it is clear that Napoleon's military talent was much more one-sided than that of the great Prussian king because Napoleon always had the superiority for an unlimited offensive. Frederick, on the other hand, with limited resources pursued the same strategy: that of annihilation. Therefore we must come to the unavoidable conclusion that Frederick the Great of Prussia far exceeded the French conqueror as man, prince and commander.[47]

A second summed up his position as follows:

> Frederick waged a heroic battle against as tough, persistent and powerful a ring of enemies as history has ever known. In this fight Frederick displayed a devotion without parallel to the future of his state and people. He trained them to do their duty and in doing so to discover their pride. Every heroic battle of the great king was a preparation for what has happened in our own day. Perhaps it will be a splendid and shining example for the duty which the future will bring to us.[48]

In conclusion, a series of extraordinary military victories produced a unique image of war upon a group of professional observers. In the decade 1879–89 these officers worked out their views in lectures and writings in the War Academy and the Historical Section of the Prussian-German General Staff. Surely one cannot suggest that this war image was held among all officers of this group, and it was clearly not reflected in the official operations plans of this period. It had no visible impact on the affairs of the moment. It remained a teaching within the General Staff educational system, whose assumptions and implications would have remained hidden if someone from another profession within the Prussian-German state had not challenged them. Hans Delbrück's pronouncement that Frederick the Great looked upon battle as an evil to be used only in extreme circumstances and his statement that the officers understood neither Clausewitz nor the eighteenth-century strategy provoked anger and incredulity from an officer corps which had seen itself raised to the heights of social and political prestige following the victories of German unification, which regarded Frederick the Great as the spiritual father of the new German Empire and as the true originator of the strategy of total war, and which interpreted Clausewitz as a virtual "Bible of Königgrätz."

This disagreement over strategy, however, raised a number of broader and more fundamental issues. Who was the professional in dealing with the military past, the officer or the professor? How do we know best: by experience or by knowledge? To what extent does the nature of society, politics, or technology determine military tactics and strategy? How important were material factors in evaluating military strategy?

From the outset, Delbrück's analysis was fundamentally at variance with that of the officers. Although noting the climate of political ideas differentiating the dynastic eighteenth-century army from the national nineteenth-century army, Delbrück was equally interested in economic, technological, and social factors. He focused on material and physical phenomena such as logistics and weapons technology. He delineated the social origin of soldiers and compared the difficulties of training and equipment from one era to another. Above all he understood that armies and society were parts of the same whole: both the limitations and the possibilities of armies in war were related, in one way or another, to the politics, economy, and even inventions of the general society. When social and political changes occurred, changes in tactics and strategy followed. Only comparative study uniting humanistic and technical military history would reveal this.

Why did Delbrück argue that military history was an important part of general history? How did a specialist in military history fare on a university faculty? Clues for answering such questions may be found in Delbrück's early experiences and in the formation of his historical consciousness.

NOTES

1   Fritz Stern, *The Politics of Cultural Despair* (Garden City: Doubleday, 1965); George Mosse, *The Crisis of German Ideology* (New York: Grosset & Dunlap, 1964); Fritz K. Ringer, *The Decline of the German Mandarins* (Cambridge, Mass.: Harvard University Press, 1969); Robert Gallately, *The Politics of Economic Despair: Shopkeepers and German Politics 1890–1914* (London: Sage Publications, 1974). Cf. Roberto Vivarelli, "1870 in European History and Historiography," *Journal of Modern History*, vol. 53, no. 2 (June 1981): 167–88.

2   John Röhl, *Germany Without Bismarck* (Berkeley: University of California, 1967); J.
    Alden Nichols, *Germany After Bismarck* (New York: W. W. Norton, 1958); John C. G.
    Röhl and Nicholaus Sombart, eds., *Kaiser Wilhelm II: New Interpretations. The
    Corfu Papers.* (Cambridge: Cambridge University Press, 1982).

3   John J. Johnson, *The Role of the Military in Underdeveloped Countries* (Princeton:
    Princeton University Press, 1962), pp. v, 3; Edwin Lieuwen, *Arms and Politics in
    Latin America* (New York: Praeger, 1967), p. 8; Morris Janowitz, *The Military in the
    Political Development of New Nations* (Chicago: University of Chicago Press, 1964).

4   Reinhard Bendix, *Work and Authority in Industry: Ideologies of Management in the
    Course of Industrialization* (New York: Harper, 1963), p. 441.

5   Janowitz, *The Military in the Political Development of New Nations*, p. 80ff.; Lucien
    W. Pye, "Armies in the Process of Political Modernization," in J. J. Johnson, *The
    Role of the Military in Underdeveloped Countries*, pp. 70ff.

6   From Clifford Geertz, *Old Societies and New States: The Quest for Modernity in Asia
    and Africa* (New York: Free Press, 1963).

7   Ralf Dahrendorf, *Society and Democracy in Germany* (Garden City, New York: Dou-
    bleday, 1970), p. 58.

8   Alfred Vagts, *A History of Militarism*, rev. ed. (Greenwich, Conn.: Meridian Books,
    1959), pp. 13–18; Volker R. Berghahn, *Militarism: The History of an International
    Debate, 1861–1979* (New York: St. Martin's Press, 1982), pp. 7–28.

9   An excerpt from Edward Shils, *The Intellectuals and the Powers* (Chicago: Univer-
    sity of Chicago Press, 1972), in Edward Shils, "Intellectuals and the Center of So-
    ciety," *University of Chicago Magazine* (July/August 1972), 10.

10 Marx letter of September 25, 1857, quoted in *Engels as Military Critic*, ed. W. H.
    Chaloner and W. O. Henderson (Manchester: University of Manchester Press, 1959),
    p. 228; cf. Stanislav Andreski, *Military Organization and Society* (Berkeley: University
    of California Press, 1971).

11 Cf. Christian Helfer, "Über militarische Einfluesse auf die industrielle Entwicklung
    in Deutschland," *Schmollers Jahrbüch*, vol. 83 (1963): 597ff; John Nef, *War and Hu-
    man Progress* (Cambridge: Harvard University Press, 1950); Werner Sombart, *Krieg
    und Kapitalismus* (Munich: R. Oldenbourg, 1913).

12 Michael Howard, *The Franco-Prussian War* (New York: Collier Books, 1961), p. 455.

13 Theodor Schieder, *Das Deutsche Kaiserreich von 1871 als Nationalstaat* (Köln: West-
    deutcher Verlag, 1960), p. 10.

14 Gerhard Ritter, *The Sword and the Scepter*, trans. Heinz Norden, 4 vols. (Miami:
    University of Miami Press, 1968–72), 2:97.

15 Ibid. 2:99–101; Fritz Fischer, *War of Illusions* (New York: W. W. Norton, 1975), p. 13.
    Ralf Dahrendorf, *Society and Democracy in Germany*, pass.; Ernest K. Bramsted,
    Aristocracy and the Middle Classes in Germany (Chicago: University of Chicago
    Press, 1964), pp. 233ff; Maximilian Harden liked to compare Prussia to a wool jacket;
    it scratches but it keeps you warm. In 1910 he wrote, "Whoever travels in Prussia notes
    immediately that a sharper wind blows here than elsewhere in Europe, that subordi-
    nation has become a habit and that nothing need be changed if tomorrow there was a
    mobilization. . . . Three fourths of Prussia's institutions . . . are calculated for the
    event of war. . . ." Harry F. Young, *Maximilian Harden: Censor Germaniae* (The
    Hague: Martinus Nijhoff, 1959), pp. 166–67; Eckart Kehr, "Zur Genesis des Königlich
    Preussischen Reserveoffiziers," in Hans-Ulrich Wehler, ed., *Eckart Kehr, Der Primat*

der Innenpolitik, 2nd ed. (Berlin: Walter de Gruyter, 1970), pp. 53ff; Hartmut John, *Das Reserveoffizierskorps im Deutschen Kaisserreich, 1890–1914* (Frankfurt: Campus Verlag, 1981). Arno J. Mayer, *The Persistence of the Old Regime: Europe to the Great War* (New York: Pantheon Books, 1981), pp. 3–5 and *passim*.

16   Carl Zuckmayer, *The Captain from Köpenick*, quoted in Samuel D. Stirk, *The Prussian Spirit* (London: Faber and Faber, 1941), pp. 100, 105.

17   Ritter, *Sword and Scepter*, 2:101.

18   George Iggers, *The German Conception of History* (Middletown, Conn.: Wesleyan University Press, 1968), pp. 196–209; G. P. Gooch, *Frederick the Great* (Hamden, Conn.: Archon Books, 1962), pp. 340ff; Veit Valentin, "Some Interpretations of Frederick the Great," *History*, vol. 8 (September 1934): 115–23.

19   Gooch, *Frederick the Great*, pp. 343ff.

20   Eberhard Kessel, "Moltke und die Kriegsgeschichte," *Militär-Wissenschaftliche Rundschau* (1941), 112–25.

21   This should not surprise us, since consideration of these matters was excluded from the military education system. When General Eichhorn, commander of the Eighteenth Army Corps, tried to revise the curriculum to include direct propaganda against Social Democractic ideas, a cabinet order was issued forbidding all social-political questions in military education. Wilhelm Deist, "Die Armee in Staat und Gesellschaft 1890–1918," in Michael Stürmer, ed., *Das kaiserliche Deutschland* (Düsseldorf: Droste, 1970), p. 329.

22   Hajo Holborn, "Moltke and Schlieffen," in Earle, *Makers of Modern Strategy*, p. 186. Manfred Messerschmidt, "Die Armee in Staat und Gesellschaft–Die Bismarckzeit," in Michael Stürmer, ed., *Das kaiserliche Deutschland*, pp. 103ff.

23   Vagts, *A History of Militarism*, p. 183; Ropp, *War in the Modern World*, pp. 158–60. Cf. Peter Paret, *Clausewitz and the State* (New York: Oxford University Press, 1970), pp. 431–40.

24   Peter Paret, "Clausewitz and the Nineteenth Century," in Michael Howard, ed., *The Theory and Practice of War* (London: Cassel, 1965), pp. 27ff; Jehuda Wallach, *Kriegstheorien: Ihre Entwicklung im 19. und 20. Jahrhundert* (Frankfurt/M: Bernard & Graefe, 1972), chapter 2: "Clausewitz: Der Philosoph des modernen Krieges," pp. 31ff; Hans Rothfels, "Clausewitz," in Earle, *Makers of Modern Strategy*, pp. 93ff.

25   Ropp, *War in the Modern World*, pp. 195ff.

26   Carl von Clausewitz, *Vom Kriege*, 16th ed. with critical notes by Werner Hahlweg (Bonn: Ferdinand Dümmler, 1952), pp. 395ff; Werner Hahlweg, *Carl von Clausewitz: Schriften-Aufsätze-Studien-Briefe* (Göttingen: Vandenhoeck & Ruprecht, 1966), Einleitung; Ritter, *Sword and Scepter*, 1:57–62.

27   Oberkommando des Heeres, *Gedanken von Moltke* (Berlin, 1941), p. 13.

28   Gerhard Ritter, *The Schlieffen Plan: Critique of a Myth*, trans. Andrew & Eva Wilson (London: Oswald Wolffe, 1958), pp. 17–21.

29   Major Adalbert von Taysen, *Das militärische Testament Friedrichs des Grossen* (Berlin: E. S. Mittler, 1879); for Taysen's teaching position, see Louis von Scharfenort, *Die Königliche Preussische Kriegsakademie* (Berlin: E. S. Mittler, 1910), pp. 249–50, 379.

30   Taysen, *Das militärische Testament*, p. 26.

31   Hans Delbrück, review of *Das militärische Testament Friedrichs des Grossen, Herausgegeben und erläutert von v. Taysen, Zeitschrift für preussische Geschichte und Landeskunde* (hereinafter *ZfpGul*), vol. 16 (1879): 27–32.

32   "Friedrich hat immer und zu allen Zeiten, wie das schon Clausewitz betont hat, die Schlacht als ein Übel angesehen, dem man sich nur im Nothfalle unterziehen müsse." Delbrück review, ibid., 31.

33   Hermann Teske, *Colmar Freiherr von der Goltz: Ein Kämpfer für den militärischen Fortschritt* (Göttingen: Musterschmidt Verlag, 1957), pp. 34–37; Scharfenort, *Die Königliche Preussische Kriegsakademie*, p. 379.

34   Colmar Freiherr von der Goltz, "Antikritik," *Zeitschrift für preussische Geschichte und Landeskunde*, vol. 16 (March-April 1879): 292–304. Delbrück's reply followed directly after Goltz's statement, Hans Delbrück, "Duplik," *ZfpGul* 16:305–14.

35   Hans Delbrück, "Über die Verschiedenheit der Strategie Friedrichs und Napoleons," in *Historische und politische Aufsätze* (Berlin: Walter and Apolant, 1887), pp. 324–35.

36   Hans Delbrück, "Friedrich der Grosse als Feldherr," review of Theodor von Bernhardi, *Friedrich der Grosse als Feldherr, ZfpGul* 18 (1881): 572.

37   Hans Delbrück, review of Theodor von Bernhardi, *Friedrich der Grosse als Feldherr*, von Taysen, *Zur Beurteilung des Siebenjährigen Krieges*, and August von Caemmerer, *Friedrichs des Grossen Feldzugsplan für des Jahr 1757, Historische Zeitschrift* 52 (1884): 155–59.

38   Delbrück, review of Theodor von Bernhardi's *Friedrich der Grosse als Feldherr*, in *ZfpGul*, 18 (1881): 569–70, 572.

39   Hans Delbrück, "Der preussische Offizierstand," originally published in the *Preussische Jahrbücher*, 52 (1883): 321–38, reprinted in Delbrück, *Historische und politische Aufsätze*, pp. 113–27.

40   Major von Malachowski, "Die methodische Kriegführung Friedrichs des Grossen," *Grenzboten: Zeitschrift für Politik, Literatur und Kunst*, 31 (1884): 211–20. Major von Caemmerer, *Friedrichs des Grossen Feldzugsplan für das Jahr 1757* (Berlin: E. S. Mittler, 1883), p. 4.

41   Malachowski, "Die methodische Kriegführung Friedrichs des Grossen," 219.

42   Ibid., 219.

43   Caemmerer, *Friedrichs des Grossen Feldzugsplan*, p. 31.

44   Ibid., p. 5.

45   Malachowski, "Die methodische Kriegführung Friedrichs des Grossen," 212.

46   Caemmerer, *Friedrichs des Grossen Feldzugsplan*, p. 34; Malachowski suggests the same analogy in "Die methodische Kriegführung," 212.

47   Theodor von Bernhardi, *Friedrich der Grosse als Feldherr* (Berlin: E. S. Mittler, 1881), 1:1–3.

48   Caemmerer, *Friedrichs des Grossen Feldzugsplan für das Jahr 1757*, pp. 29–30.

2 / MILITARY HISTORY, THE UNIVERSITY, AND THE ARMY, 1880–1900

Why should a young scholar oppose a group of officers over the strategy of Frederick the Great and the ideas of Clausewitz? Why would a new *Privatdozent* (lecturer) challenge the Prussian social elite? Surely the classic mold in German academic affairs was for a new entrant to mark out a tiny area of research specialization and to write a cautious and carefully detailed book for his peers to judge. Was it not strange for a new university teacher to become embroiled in controversy outside academia? To account for this, we must inquire into the life and experiences of Hans Delbrück, the status of military history in Germany, and the uniqueness of Delbrück's image of the military past.

DELBRÜCK'S EXPERIENCES AND IDEAS

Born in 1848 on the Baltic Sea island of Rügen, stemming from an old Berlin family of officials and teachers,[1] Delbrück took his *Abitur* in Berlin in 1867 and attended lectures at Heidelberg, Greifswald, and Bonn, working under the historians Karl von Noorden and Heinrich von Sybel. Under Sybel's aegis he wrote his doctoral dissertation at Bonn in 1873,[2] and was appointed to the faculty at Berlin in January 1881. To this point, there is nothing that would give a clue to Delbrück's historical insights or interests in the military.

Delbrück, however, differed from most of his contemporaries. His early interest in history, evident before he reached the university, showed an independent and critical mind. In 1867 his gymnasium teacher wrote that Delbrück's exhaustive comprehension of history was matched only by his audacious interpretations.[3] During his first semester at Heidelberg he was critical of his professors. In spite of the power of their lectures relating *what* had happened in the past, Delbrück differed in his judgment of *why* the events had taken place. Their false pathos disturbed his sense of reality.[4] When he was young, his family had introduced him to the material side of life. Scarcely past twelve years old, he received an annual allowance to purchase all his personal needs, including clothing. Delbrück's letters written from the university are filled with references to the cost of things—from food and lodging to theatre and musical

19

Hans Delbrück
1884

events. Although courted by several student corporations at Heidelberg, he never joined, writing to his closest friend that he opposed these fraternities because they were a part of the exterior facade of life which he sought to penetrate beneath.[5]

From the beginning, Delbrück joined ideas and experience and built his world view on the tension and interaction between the two. Friedrich Lange's *History of Materialism* in 1869 helped to bring a "revolution" in his thinking. To his friend William Rohde he wrote that truth itself was unknown but understanding came in the interaction of practical experience and ideas.[6] His year of service *(Einjährigfreiwilliger)* in the Royal Prussian and North German Rifle Defenders of the Fatherland in 1868–69 reinforced this sense of the relation between action and contemplation. Reading Shakespeare while on maneuvers, he was fully sensitive to the contrasts between university and military life.[7]

Delbrück's education was catholic and universal in the broadest sense. As he raised his own children on "Goethe, Goethe and more Goethe,"[8] so his reading and study were directed at the broadly humanistic tapestry of western civilization. Returning from military service in 1869, he plunged into academic work, simultaneously studying the English language, Greek tragedy, French literature, and German constitutional history. "The whole of Europe passes before my eyes," he wrote to a friend.[9]

In later years Delbrück was called a Hegelian.[10] Traces of this appear much earlier. His mother's father was Leopold von Henning, a favorite student of Hegel's who carried forward Hegelian ideas as professor of philosophy at Berlin. Delbrück, as the eldest son, was very close to his mother, especially after his father died in 1869, and it is likely that he derived a good deal of his philosophical direction from this highly creative and independent woman.[11] From Hegel came a conceptual or macrohistorical perspective and a tendency to focus on the broadest spectrum of human activity. Hegel argued that history was, of necessity, universal history. Although we apprehend the past through particulars, such as Alexander the Great, Caesar, the German Emperors, or the French kings, the real history of mankind is not the life and battles of these men, but the universals which unfold themselves in different guises in each cultural epoch.[12] For Delbrück such a focus gradually developed over many years, but even in his earliest work one can recognize a dialectical quality, in contrast to purely descriptive concerns, and that is one reason why it stands out so markedly from the work of his contemporaries. Delbrück used comparisons not only to describe a single phenomenon, such as war, in two different time periods and cultural settings, but to contrast events from distant historical settings to the practical and technical realities of his own day. He believed that what was physically impossible for modern armies was also impossible for armies in sixteenth-century Switzerland, ninth-century Germany, or fifth-century B.C. Greece. In support of these comparisons he tried to see for himself the characteristics of equipment or terrain. In May 1878, as he was writing on Napoleon's Waterloo campaign, he made a walking tour of the battlefields; it was as useful as examining the written sources.[13]

Finally, Delbrück was a Rankean. His closest mentors, Karl von Noorden and Heinrich von Sybel had both studied with Ranke. He sent all of his early essays to Ranke, and in 1900, fourteen years after Ranke's death, Delbrück dedicated the first volume of his *History of the Art of War* "to historians and friends of history in the spirit of Leopold Ranke."[14] Ranke's teachings meant above all the application of a rigorous critical methodology in understanding the past, the necessity of basing written history on primary sources, and the importance of objectivity—of separating the study of the past from the passions of the present as much as humanly possible.

By 1870, age twenty-two, Delbrück was a well-defined individual. His historical consciousness was critical not accepting, humanistic not parochial, realistic not romantic, conceptual as well as descriptive. He sought to penetrate beneath surface appearances. He was sensitive to that symbiosis between present experience and past sources from which good history often comes. Each feature of his historical consciousness was deepened during the next decade by actual war experiences, by his reading of Clausewitz and Wilhelm Rüstow, and by his first attempts at writing military history.

Eighteen months after the completion of his one year's voluntary service, the Franco-Prussian War broke out. He entered the army as a corporal, later became a reserve lieutenant in the Twenty-ninth Rhenish Infantry Regiment and experienced war firsthand. Passing over the French border amid jubilant rejoicing of the troops, Delbrück's unit marched across the battlefield at Saarbrücken, a "horrible sight," as the Prussians two days earlier had attacked the fortifications four times and lost nearly all their officers.[15]

> He was right who said that hell is falsely painted. It is a paradise in comparison to a bivouac in pouring rain and darkness with nothing to eat or drink, lying on soaking clay soil without wood or straw. In spite of great tiredness we cannot sleep. . . . I have made a strange discovery, the men openly admit they do not go into fire the second time with the same enthusiasm as the first and have even less courage the third time.[16]

The first battle passed, the terrible bullets came, but he was unscathed. Later, on a reconnaissance, sudden shooting began. Taking cover, he sat with two others, drinking wine and discussing what to do next when suddenly a bullet hit the sand between them and threw dust into their eyes. A second bullet killed a sergeant nearby. The French were nowhere to be seen.

We hurried back to our regiment, and soon the main battle began. The shells began to scream, without striking the ground, the cannons became ever more intense. Quickly we passed through a village and were out into the open fields. Here we had to expose ourselves to the most terrible shells, *mitrailleuse* and chassepot fire, running as long as we could, then resting. During the open field run our regiment became completely scattered and lost all order. In a gulley in the middle of the field many tried to remain lying down, as it was pretty safe. They could scarcely be moved to go forward. In the confusion two or three hundred men from different units became mixed together. Leadership either did not exist or it was poor and the soldiers showed no courage: it was a pitiful sight. Finally we came to the outskirts of a woods, filled with nearly impassable underbrush. Scarcely had we begun to advance forward into it than a murderous fire began against us and we had to retreat. The French stood a few hundred feet before us in a protected and prepared position and fired, without our being able to see them. Fortunately about thirty yards from the edge of the woods, there was a deep gorge, which was absolutely safe, but the bullets went showering overhead. With our small numbers an attack was unthinkable. A reserve lieutenant commanded and sent me back three times to bring more men. I had to bring them forward with sword in hand and with threats to use it![17]

The next day, after Prussian reinforcements on Delbrück's left flank had forced a French retreat, he noted that many Prussians had killed each other by accident in the darkness. His unit was hindered in its advance by the thick explosion of its own shells. Dead French soldiers lay over the battlefield as far as the eye could see, and a great many Prussians as well. In his company eleven men were dead, thirty wounded, and ten missing. From Vigneules on August 22 Delbrück wrote that there had never been such a battle as St. Privat. The first division lost seven thousand men. From four regiments of guards over half were killed or wounded.

Only discipline forces men into fire, he concluded. The same men used as a mobile guard would entirely disappear at the first shot. For these unreliable troops—the same as mercenaries in the last century—the closed line was the only possible way to attack. "Now," Delbrück wrote, "I begin to understand how 10,000 closed formation Greeks could beat 100,000 Persians and how the city of Rome could conquer the world."[18]

Delbrück's war experiences profoundly influenced his larger philosophical view of the world. As he wrote to his friend Dorn, the last piece of idle theorizing had been scraped out. His idealism was refined and strengthened. He had seen reality.[19]

Advancing toward Paris with the Sixth Army Corps, Delbrück was promoted to first lieutenant and awarded the Iron Cross, first class, but was soon forced to drop out because of a severe case of typhus. He was taken to Bonn, where a physician friend of Professor von Noorden cared for him, but it was a full year before he was able to complete his doctoral thesis.

The next year, 1873, was difficult. Delbrück did not know exactly what occupation he would pursue, yet for financial reasons he had to do something: his father was dead and his mother and her remaining children had moved back to her family home. He tried unsuccessfully to find a publisher for a book on religious wars and took a temporary job as tutor to the Swedish royal family at Neuwied. Finally, in 1874 Delbrück won appointment as tutor to Prince Waldemar, second son of Prussian Crown Prince Friedrich Wilhelm, and began nearly five years' residence with the Prussian royal family in Berlin and Potsdam, in England, Scotland, Italy, France, and Austria. This experience was crucial to Delbrück's developing interest in military affairs. The royal entourage was made up mainly of officers, many of whom had served with the crown prince in the campaigns of 1866 and 1870–71. Delbrück conducted detailed discussions with several of these men and later incorporated their ideas into his university lectures and articles. The crown prince himself gave Delbrück a copy of the works of Carl von Clausewitz.[20]

In 1875, while on summer maneuvers as a reserve officer, Delbrück read Wilhelm Rüstow's *History of Infantry*. Rüstow, a former Prussian officer, member of Garibaldi's army, and Swiss military commentator, had written a series of military works in the 1850s utilizing an entirely new approach to military history.[21] Instead of the "drum and trumpet" approach in which battles and leaders were depicted in a vacuum separate from politics and social life, Rüstow's armies reflected civil society. The Greek phalanx originated in the polis, Roman mercenaries related to Imperial politics, and the fifteenth-century Swiss infantry derived from the canton communities. Although not organized systematically, limited to a discussion of infantry, and concentrating mainly on the early modern period, one can understand how such a work could fascinate Delbrück. Rüstow's conceptual framework became a fundamental part of Delbrück's approach to military history.

Finally, a year or two after his appointment as royal tutor, Delbrück met Gräfin Hedwig Brühl, granddaughter of Graf Neidhardt von Gneisenau, one of the most famous Prussian generals of the Napoleonic

Wars. Gräfin Brühl asked him to complete the biography of her grand-father begun in the 1860s by Georg Heinrich Pertz. To accomplish this, Delbrück gained access to a massive archival collection.[22] In addition to the letters of Gneisenau, these documents contained correspondence and essays written to Gneisenau by his military colleague and friend Carl von Clausewitz. In reading this correspondence while completing the final volumes of the Gneisenau biography, Delbrück first recognized how Napoleonic warfare differed from that of the eighteenth century and realized that Clausewitz had understood this difference. In 1878 he published an essay from this archive[23] in which Clausewitz developed a clear historical distinction between limited and total war, between war in the eighteenth century and war in the time of Napoleon:

> In spite of the winged feet upon which the army moved across entire king-doms, it was finally reduced to crawling, self-armored like a turtle, from one fortress to another. In the middle of the 18th century, tents, baggage, food wagons, bake ovens, and other accoutrements stopped up the stream; for-tresses, fortified positions and other armies acted like dams in the way of vic-tory. After the development of military institutions had been badly spoiled with many abuses came the French Revolution and again made valid the law of the natural elements. With this event, the most audacious of all dare devils [Napoleon I] made his appearance and staked everything on one card: decisive battles of annihilation. Since then, all campaigns have produced such comet-like vibrations that they can scarcely be thought of as only military because they involve the whole of society.[24]

The Life of Fieldmarshal Count Neidhardt von Gneisenau, com-pleted in 1880, was Delbrück's first major work and remains the standard scholarly treatment.[25] Building upon the two masterful volumes by Pertz, and with some help from General Edward von Fransecky, who had worked with the Gneisenau papers in the 1850s,[26] Delbrück com-pleted his work in the classic nineteenth-century life and letters tradi-tion. In closing the final volume, he addressed eighteenth-century and Napoleonic strategy. In the eighteenth century, he wrote, war did not depend on the resources of the entire state; soldiers fought to fight again, forts besieged to surrender, not perish. With the enlarged armies and economic resources opened up by the French Revolution, everything intensified. The army burgeoned and the quality of troops improved as the soldier became the defender and representative of national inde-pendence. The changed social composition of armies was a symbol as well as a main motive power of the new style warfare: troops no longer welcomed officers whose only claim to leadership was a title.[27]

Delbrück contended that political revolution brought strategic changes. During the Seven Years' War, battles seldom took place because maneuver, siege, and encampment could attain the same goal. The French Revoution replaced the dual strategic conception of battle and maneuver with a single dominant idea. It was no longer sufficient to damage an opponent; every state rebounded from such loss with general conscription and by drawing upon economic reserves. Defeat had to be complete, destroying military resources as well as the opposing army. Attack had to be carried into the very heart of the enemy's land. Napoleon mastered this, subordinating everything to concentrated battles of annihilaton. In Delbrück's *Gneisenau* some of the same themes examined in chapter 1 appear, above all a distinction between two kinds of strategy based upon two different political and social systems.

In the spring of 1879, soon after Prince Waldemar had died from diphtheria, Delbrück's formal *Abschied* request to Crown Prince Friederich Wilhelm was regretfully accepted.[28] His nearly five years as a member of the Crown Prince's household had been unusually fruitful, both personally and professionally. Not only did Delbrück earn a good living, he thrived in court society, finding it replete with interesting people to whom he had access as royal tutor.[29] He moved from uncertainty about the future to a clear fascination with the military past—a logical outcome of a half decade of close association with Europe's most military ruling house. Delbrück had resolved to join the faculty of the University of Berlin to teach and write military history.

MILITARY HISTORY BETWEEN UNIVERSITY AND ARMY

With the publication in 1880 of the Gneisenau biography, Delbrück became qualified for admission to the university faculty, one of the great elite forces in late nineteenth-century Germany. He had considered a university position ever since his mentor Professor von Noorden had encouraged him a decade before.[30] It might seem that Delbrück was assured of a position as *Privatdozent*, the entering rank in the German university system, considering his family's connections in Berlin bureaucracy and society, and his acquaintances at court and within the royal family. This was apparantly not the case. Joining the faculty was difficult for reasons still not altogether clear.

There seem to have been several problems. Choosing faculty members at Berlin was highly selective, excluding most men before they could become candidates. The university had few positions available, it never underwent large-scale expansion, and professors, once appointed, tended to remain. This was especially true at Berlin, considered by many the leading German university.[31] Most important, Delbrück had certain specific disadvantages. The faculty did not like the idea of having a former royal official in their midst, especially one from the service of a prince who had tried, in the summer of 1880, to get Prussian Minister Gossler to appoint Delbrück an associate professor in military history. The minister had replied that the faculty was against this: a man had to begin at the bottom.[32]

The professoriate were part of the Prussian bureaucracy and came under the administrative supervision of the Ministry of Spiritual, Educational and Medical Affairs.[33] In this respect Berlin was unique within the German university system; it had been called the "spiritual lifeguard of the Hohenzollerns," which, although not altogether true, indicates at least the ambivalence of its position. Set across *Unter den Linden* from the palace of the crown prince, not far from the Ministry of the Interior and the Military Museum, in the main section of "official" Berlin, professors were bound both to state and academia. Preservation of faculty rights held high value even if not anything like an absolute rule. The most important problem, however, was Delbrück's academic specialty.

Prussian Minister Gossler envisioned opposition from both university and General Staff should he appoint a professor in military history. The faculty had never had someone in this specialty before. They doubted if military history properly belonged in a university curriculum. But if such a professorship were to be created, they suggested that a military specialist *(Fachmann)*, an educated officer from the Historical Section of the General Staff, would be the best candidate.[34]

The faculty considered military history a *Fachwissenschaft*, a technical science not legitimate for university teaching or scholarship. By contrast, "pure" history, concentrating on politics or the development of ideas, was considered a part of *Geisteswissenschaft*, a humanistic discipline.[35] War and military history were not viewed as important elements of culture or the proper concern of a university faculty. The professoriate, like the officers, sharply separated themselves from the rest of society. In this they may have been consciously trying to distinguish between themselves and the *Junker*-related officer corps. The former were the purveyors of cultural traditions; the latter were the bulwark of social prestige and political authority. The professors separated culture from the world of affairs: "merely practical knowledge" was rejected out of hand.[36] Knowledge of war was useful mainly to teach soldiers how to fight future battles, a practical worldly concern divorced from the intellectual purposes of higher education.

As Delbrück tried to attain a teaching position in the university, he had to defend the legitimacy of military history within the university and the validity of humanistic scholarship to the General Staff. Characteristically, Delbrück began with outspoken criticism.

He noted that among the most widely read contemporary history were the General Staff works on the wars of German unification. Thousands of laymen zealously reading these works evidenced the lively interest in military affairs far outside army circles. But this series was cumbersome and difficult to understand: even using a good map it was nearly impossible to follow the detailed movements of individual regiments or to reconstruct the nature of the war as a whole. More important, these technical "battle studies" left out the influence of politics on war. Delbrück asked about the political goals of the Danish War, the relationship of Prussia to the other great powers, and how the North German Confederation related to the smaller German states and to Denmark. These questions, if answered, might allow an understanding of the apparent weaknesses of the Prussian high command. Political goals, Delbrück concluded, ultimately determined military strategy and therefore had to be discussed.[37]

If the General Staff works lacked political perspective, Delbrück wrote, books by academic historians were filled with errors regarding technical military actions. Theodor Mommsen, the dean of German historians, in discussing Roman history overlooked the decisive turning points in such battles as Cannae and Pharsalus. Professor Max Duncker described a Greek army of eight hundred thousand men operating in a geographic area insufficient for an army a tenth its size. His own advisor Karl von Noorden's descriptions of the battles of Prince Eugene of Savoy were sometimes faulted at the militarily decisive point. After reading his doctoral mentor Heinrich von Sybel's study of Frederick the Great's campaign of 1757, Delbrück concluded that Sybel did not understand strategic fundamentals. These errors were not simply minor details: they occurred at major turning points in whole epochs and resulted from an incorrect understanding of the material realities of war.

After such stiff criticism, some of it directed against his own teachers, Delbrück outlined what was needed: histories written to mediate between technical military affairs and the humanistic world of politics and society. He cited the works of Wilhelm Rüstow and the military letters of Prince zu Hohenlohe-Ingelfingen as examples.[38] Both authors described the impact of specific military procedures on war: precise knowledge about simple, elementary tactics, the art of issuing orders for large numbers of men, the capacity of troops for different kinds of work, details of horses, equipment, weapons, and supply. Such details seldom appeared in print because they were mostly unknown to historians but were too well known to military officers to be specifically noted. Secondly, these authors commented on the broader historical background of war and used this to compare similar kinds of actions in different historical epochs, for example the use of cavalry in the eighteenth century, in 1806, and in 1866.[39] The scarcity of works such as these, Delbrück concluded, demonstrated the lack of a true specialization in military history. What, then, was needed for a professional approach to military history? He outlined four requirements.

First, historians should acquire and utilize detailed knowledge of the practical realities of military life. To study military history and to carry out war were as different as art criticism and oil painting. Training in military history did not prepare men to lead troops any more than archaeology prepared them to construct buildings. But it was impossible to describe the living phenomenon of the past without practical and technical knowledge. The artist and the art historian complemented each other as the officer and the military historian.[40]

Secondly, historians had to adopt the comparative approach. The historical sciences had developed based upon specialization—which was unavoidable but also fraught with dangers. Specialization must not only be limited to pure historical cross sections and single time periods, but should include comparisons made longitudinally, that is, between chronological blocks. Historians using a single set of standards should compare various features of one era with the same phenomena in a different time period.

Thirdly, historians had to pay more attention to the uniqueness of military actions. Strategy, which was enormously complex, was often presented either too simplistically or too aesthetically. In Theodor von Bernhardi's *Frederick the Great as Commander,* all eighteenth-century generals except Frederick were treated as such simpletons that one was amazed armies could be entrusted to their leadership.

Finally, Delbrück took a conservative, materialistic view of war. The image of the military past closest to reality was apt to be one of hemorrhaging and exhaustion, not heroism and valor. If the experiences of the last wars were any indication, victory came not to those who did the right thing but to the army which made the fewest mistakes. Delbrück's image of his own war experiences had not been dimmed by time, eroded by his exposure to the pomp and ceremony of the Prussian court, or replaced by other historians' romantic idealism.

Delbrück's developing understanding of military history was based upon the dialectic between ideas and experience. Tension between these two worlds was also quite evident in his own life in 1881, and was another reason why he was not warmly received by the university faculty. Although Delbrück pioneered in the study of armies and society, during his lifetime he was best known as a political commentator. For nearly forty years he edited the most important historical and political monthly in Prussian-Germany, the *Preussische Jahrbücher*.[41] Founded in the 1850s to promote German nationalism under Prussian aegis, it was one of the few really influential journals of politics and culture of its day. Circulation, which averaged about eighteen hundred copies monthly, included many of the "opinion makers of the ruling classes": land-owners, officers, clergy, bureaucrats, industrialists, and journalists. Its small circulation belied its wide impact: essays from *Preussische Jahrbücher* were reproduced in newspapers and often quoted by other journals. Outside Germany, it was read in Austria, Russia, England, France, Denmark, Sweden, and Norway.[42]

As a military historian who had experienced war, so Delbrück was a political commentator who entered politics. He served in the Prussian Landtag and for six years in the German Reichstag. Significantly, while trying to join the university faculty he won a seat in the Prussian Landtag by defeating Rudolf von Gneist, an old well-known Berlin Professor.[43] Political experience paralleled political commentary.[44]

Delbrück's participation in politics and his personal acquaintance with the Prussian royal family, with officials like his uncle Rudolf Delbrück, President of the Reich Chancellor's Office, Chancellors Otto von Bismarck and Leo von Caprivi, infused his writings with a sense of reality that gained him a wide following. These excursions into real life, however, aroused misgivings within the university. A journalist was not quite respectable in Imperial Germany, and thus Delbrück was always slightly suspect in the minds of his colleagues.

In any event, Delbrück finally won appointment to the Berlin faculty as *Privatdozent* in late 1880. Present evidence is insufficient to say exactly what factors were finally decisive. Details from the committee which examined his Gneisenau biography, the contents of his trial lecture, and the faculty session which discussed and voted on his appointment, all are lacking. He joined the faculty in January 1881. His inaugural lecture was entitled "The Battle of Napoleon with Old Europe". Thus began Delbrück's struggle against traditional military history which lasted for the next half century.

THE NEW MILITARY HISTORY AND ITS CRITICS:
WAR IMAGES, 1887–1900

During the next three decades Delbrück set out to define and legitimize a new scholarly specialty within the university while maintaining his controversy with the officers of the General Staff. In both cases, Delbrück faced formidable opposition from professional groups which, although counter-elites in the larger social and professional world, shared many common identities regarding the military past. They diverged most widely in their views on the relationship of past and future. The professors, of course, were past-oriented, holding to the fifty-year rule for scholarly research. The officers, however, looked mainly toward the future, and increasingly during the 1890s they rejected Delbrück's views on military strategy as dangerous, fearing his interpretation might contaminate the correct, uniform strategic view they felt necessary within the officer corps, General Staff, and War Academy. These apprehensions were based on their own professional responsibilities for operations in future war. This period saw the beginning of that well-known "encirclement psychosis" which gripped the German strategic planners tighter and tighter after 1891; it also saw the emergence of the Schlieffen School—the strategy of annihilation in a two-front war—firmly in control of the Great General Staff.

By 1900, in seminars, books, and articles, Delbrück had laid out a distinctive methodology for understanding the military past and for integrating military history into general history. In doing this he pursued two goals. One defined a unique methodology in studying the military past. The second applied concrete examples of his methods to produce distinctive research results. Both revealed a marked uniformity of development. In both methods and conclusions he increasingly separated himself from university colleagues and General Staff officers.

As we have already suggested, Delbrück's methods combined an Hegelian sensitivity to conceptual history, a Rankean appreciation of primary sources for description, with a Rüstowian concern for the details of practical military life. The foundation of historical knowledge did not lie, Delbrück said, simply in the recapitulation of a single tradition. The record of the past in the original sources had to be critically discussed and revised according to the most recent investigations. There were two problems associated with this process. One was the danger that a false tradition might be perpetuated because the material impossibilities *(Sachliche Unmöglichkeit)* were not correctly understood. Here he was referring to both scholars and officers in their view of eighteenth- century war. A second difficulty arose from the practice of transferring experience and knowledge from contemporary life into the past without sufficient attention to the differences. Here he was alluding to the image of Frederick the Great as a strategist of annihilation. To deal with these dangers, Delbrück proposed a new critical method, which he called *Sachkritik:* specific criticism of material and technical details of the subject under examination. *Sachkritik* had to go hand in hand with *Wortkritik* or rigorous philological source criticism. Each was dependent on the other. For military history, *Sachkritik* depended on detailed knowledge of the size of armies, the means of moving them, specifics of weapons and equipment, details of the supply system, and correct knowledge of tactical and strategic forms. In addition, the historian needed concrete details of the geographic, political, economic, and social context.[45]

Delbrück approached his critics boldly. To the officers he admitted that one difficulty of such a specialty as the humanistic study of war lay in the acquisition of sufficient technical knowledge. But this could be overcome:

> We believe that the historian of literature fully understands the literary process, that the art historian understands the techniques of painting or architecture, that the economic historian comprehends the actions and workings of the guilds, trade and commerce. We do not ask that these specialists themselves paint madonnas, build churches or found colonies, but when they have not done these things, the individual possessing such experience can always contend that a particular point was incorrectly stated by the historian because he had no firsthand knowledge of the matter under consideration. The historian of the art of war has the same problem and must deal with it in the same way. He must methodically study the sources, understand the material circumstances and the technical possibilities of the past events so that he controls them with full certainty.[46]

To the professors, Delbrück declared that specialized military history was an integral part of universal history, by which he meant the history of Western civilization. The progressive specialization of labor within the historical sciences had manifested itself in art and literary history, the history of religion, constitutional and legal history, but they all flowed together and reinforced each other. No specialty could be dispensed with or the understanding of the whole would suffer. The same was true for the history of the art of war.[47]

These approaches are well illustrated in his first books: *The Persian Wars Compared with the Burgundian Wars* (1887), *The Strategy of Pericles Interpreted by Means of the Strategy of Frederick the Great* (1890) and the classic four-volume *History of the Art of War* (1900–1920). They produced an always iconoclastic and often irreverent image of the military past.

Delbrück scoffed at the idea that an Athenian force had run 4,800 feet in a full charge at the Battle of Marathon (490 B.C.). Herodotus, who claimed this, and all those classical scholars who believed him failed to recognize its absolute impossibility. Prussian regular infantry, less weighted down than Greek hoplites, were forbidden by army regulations from running for more than four minutes with pack or two minutes with full field gear. At a speed of 165 to 175 steps per minute, Delbrück calculated, 350 steps was the farthest the Greeks could have run. Even if ten thousand heavily armored men could have run 4,800 feet without losing formation, when they reached the enemy they would have been too tired to fight. One had to be cautious in accepting what was possible and probable in the past. He wrote:

> A movement that is made easily by a detachment of one thousand men is an achievement for ten thousand men, a work of art for fifty thousand men and an impossibility for one hundred thousand.[48]

Herodotus wrote that the army of Xerxes numbered 4,200,000 men. Can this figure be accepted as reliable, Delbrück asked? A modern German army corps of 30,000 men with its artillery took up approximately fourteen miles of road. Counting fourteen miles for each 30,000 Persians with their baggage, a Persian army of 4,200,000 would have taken up 1,960 miles of continuous road in their line of march. If one accepted the figure of Herodotus, the lead elements of the Persians would have arrived at Thermopylae at the same time that the rear elements were just leaving Susa, east of the Tigris.[49]

Ancient historians and classical philologists were incensed at this method of comparing ancient and modern events. They were upset at Delbrück's disrespect for the literal statements of classical sources. Berlin classicist Ulrich von Wilamowitz-Moellendorff upbraided Delbrück for disregarding Herodotus: the goddess Artemis, he wrote in the *Historische Zeitschrift,* had given the Greeks sufficient strength to make the 4,800 foot run at Marathon. Wilamowitz sternly rebuked scholars who refused to accept the military contribution of the Greek gods.[50]

A second example of Delbrück's new military history was his use of paradigms to characterize different epochs of history and to relate to the broader perspective of politics, economics, and social life. We have already seen how this was applied to his comparison between the strategy of Frederick the Great and Napoleon. He applied the same model to the ancient world. In Delbrück's view, Pericles was a strategist of attrition (limited war) while Alexander the Great and Caesar were strategists of annihilation (total war).

Classical scholars criticized Pericles for following a strategy far too pusillanimous, defensive, and weak: he should have been more aggressive.[51] This was not so, Delbrück answered. Athenian strategy was limited by the Athenian state and society and by external political factors. Athens was numerically inferior to her enemies and in no way could she achieve superiority. The social system of ancient Greece precluded requisition of extensive military service from her allies in the same way that

Frederick the Great could not introduce universal military conscription: political society placed a ceiling on the size of the army. This limitation in turn influenced military strategy. Pericles, like Frederick the Great, faced a large coalition. Both commanders could inflict damage against only one opponent at a time. They had to be prepared at any time to break off action against one enemy to turn against a second or third. Consequently neither commander could hope to destroy completely a single opponent. Finally, the nature of tactics and supply and the geographic and physical barriers of fortifications in both periods circumscribed the armies' achievements. Even with a large army, which Athens did not have, the complete destruction of an ancient walled city was formidable. Neither Frederick the Great nor Pericles lacked the strength of character necessary to undertake a strategy of annihilation. To the contrary, it was their strength of character which enabled them to prevail under adverse circumstances. What they did lack was sufficient material and human resources. No great man, Delbrück continued, not Alexander, Caesar, Pericles, or Frederick could make up for a serious deficiency in material resources solely by the power of personal leadership.

> There is one school which believes that there is a single, correct strategy for all times and in all relationships. Following Clausewitz's guidance, we have seen that this is incorrect. We have argued that there is a natural doubleness in strategy. On this basis we have constructed an analogy between the similarities of two moments in military history. We have seen that the modern Napoleonic way of war is completely unsuitable for the Peloponnesian Wars. Our investigation has demonstrated that the strategy of the Athenians was the same kind as that practiced in the 17th and 18th centuries.[52]

Ancient historians of Delbrück's day, whether military or civilian, tended to treat war in a vacuum, detached and unrelated to economic, political, and social life. In their view the army of Julius Caesar succeeded not because of the Roman state, economy, or technology, but because a genius led it. For Theodor Mommsen, Caesar was the entire and perfect man. T. Rice Holmes thought Caesar the greatest man of action who had ever lived. For this generation Caesar was the apotheosis of a superman.[53] For Delbrück, Caesar did not triumph over Ariovistus or Vercingetorix but rather Roman civilization won over German civilization, culture triumphed over barbarism. *Technique* and *Technik*, he wrote, were the measure of Roman success. Not only was the organization and management of the army better, but so were the technical and material aspects of Roman culture which supported it. Roman military success came from the ability to bring a large mass together in one place, move it in formation, and supply and maintain it together for a long time. These things the Gauls could not do: this was the creation of a higher culture.[54]

The concept of a single correct and legitimate form of strategy, Delbrück believed, originated in a misinterpretation of Clausewitz. A dominant theme in Clausewitz's *Vom Kriege* was that there was essentially only one strategy, that of annihilation. In developing this idea, Delbrück believed that Clausewitz had been responding to his own contemporary circumstances. At that time, the strategy of annihilation was considered invalid; strategic writers such as Dietrich von Bülow and Henry Evans Lloyd emphasized careful, cautious, mathematical operations. To counteract this, Clausewitz placed major emphasis on the strategy of annihilation. By the end of his life, however, Clausewitz recognized that his work was incomplete and needed revision, especially in the systematic presentation of the second form of strategy, attrition. But Clausewitz nevertheless had already described it at some length in *Vom Kriege*. If the commander could not use battle, he had noted, because of limited political goals or insufficient force, then he had to try to overcome his opponent in other ways. Delbrück admitted that this "second form" of strategy appeared in Clausewitz's writings as a kind of "subordinated species" which looked strange next to the more magnificent, direct form of battle. Nevertheless Clausewitz's concept of attrition was clear: when the will and the power did not allow a decision, then strategy had to be limited accordingly. A commander who lacked the will or the power could not wage a war of annihilation.[55]

Clausewitz's insufficient historical understanding did not allow the Prussian general to comprehend the economic, social, or political reasons for the two kinds of strategy outlined in *Vom Kriege*, and therefore he could not explain his two strategic forms. Clausewitz's understanding was limited to general appearances. A war which moved from the Rhine to the Dnieper to the Seine, as Napoleonic warfare did, appeared much greater to him than eighteenth-century war, which moved year in and year out between the Erz and the Riesen mountains. Clausewitz did not grasp that size differentials had little bearing on the relative greatness of the commanders involved. Even though his opponents often missed it, Delbrück stressed that the strategic greatness of Frederick was every bit equal to that of Napoleon. Success was more difficult amid the "retarding" elements of eighteenth-century war. It was psychologically more complex to decide from one moment to the next whether to fight a battle or to use a more limited means of war. Napoleon did not confront such decisions.

Beyond Clausewitz, Delbrück mentioned several other factors which had led to a misunderstanding of strategic doctrine after 1871. Actual war experience strongly reinforced Clausewitz's emphasis on the strategy of annihilation. Under the influences of war, and because of the incompleteness of Clausewitz's writings, gradually the opinion grew that only one true system of strategy existed and that all deviations or divergencies, even in history, were either excusable or erroneous.[56]

In trying to clarify this, Delbrück took one further step. He laid out a binary definition of strategy in world history. Describing one form using the term "annihilation" *(Niederwerfungsstrategie)* he defined this by means of a single pole: battle. This strategy was carried out by commanders such as Napoleon, who had both the material means and the willpower to destroy their enemy and seize his political and economic base. All other means of war, equally valid and legitimate, he defined using the term "attrition" *(Ermattungsstrategie)*. This term was derived from the word *ermatten,* meaning to exhaust or to tire, and was related to the adjective *matt,* connoting something weak, feeble, and lifeless. This choice of terms itself aroused intense opposition: Prussian officers and bureaucrats were unable to associate Frederick the Great with such a phrase.

To illustrate more forcefully his point that Frederick the Great could not be called a strategist of annihilation, Delbrück did just this. In his *Strategy of Pericles Interpreted by Means of the Strategy of Frederick the Great,* one chapter was entitled, "Frederick the Great as Commander: A Methodological Parody." Here he criticized Frederick's campaigns of 1756 and 1757, as if they had been waged with a strategy of annihilation.

In the spring of 1756 the Prussian king could have fought a war as Napoleon did in 1805 when he beat the Austrians before they joined the Russians, or in 1806 when he beat the Prussians before the Russians arrived.[57] Before a Russian or a Frenchman appeared on the battlefield, the Austrian State might have been destroyed. Did Frederick do this, Delbrück asked? No, he waited until the time needed for an energetic campaign had been used up, the Austrians had reinforced Bohemia, and the Saxons had time to reinforce and build up Pirna. But, in spite of this, the situation was still very favorable: the Prussians outnumbered the Saxons by more than three to one. The king thought about an attack, General Winterfeld prepared a plan, but no attack was made. Instead, Frederick delayed until the Saxons gave up for lack of supplies. On October 14, when the Saxons surrendered, the king stood with 120,000 troops approximately ten miles from the Austrian army of 80,000. Still Frederick did not fight but instead went into winter quarters. Delbrück summarized the campaign of 1756 by saying that it was no particular accomplishment to pit an army of 120,000 men against another of 80,000 men and to occupy an otherwise undefended land.

Delbrück noted that the campaign of 1757, with its sudden attack into Bohemia from three sides, the battle of Prague, and the surrounding of the enemy army, was considered one of the master-strokes of the hero king: if Frederick had won the battle of Kolin he might have dictated peace beneath the walls of Vienna. Delbrück asked from whom came the much-praised strategic plan for all of this? Not from the king. Frederick laid out no fewer than four plans, all defensive: the initiative was to remain with the enemy. Delbrück quipped that a commander who understood the value of the initiative did not make decisions dependent on the actions of the enemy. Frederick's plan in no way aimed to destroy Austria, but only to weaken her so that a part of the Prussian army would suffice for further fighting on the front, while the rest could be sent against the French. It could be said of the famous battle of Prague that it was not battle at all, but only an indecisive skirmish. What about Rossbach and Leuthen? Well, they were very brave deeds; but, after all, at Rossbach Frederick attacked a miserable army under wretched leadership, while at Leuthen Frederick beat the Württembergers, who were uneasy fighting against the Protestant king of Prussia. That was the high point of Frederick's wars. The later campaigns could be passed over. After 1762 Frederick fought no more battles, whether his opponents were weak or strong.[58]

Delbrück concluded his parody with the military reputation of Frederick the Great on the ground in shreds. What remained of the great man? He was a wonderful spirit who surrounded himself with the talent of his century. He was a capable war minister who kept his army in good order. He was a decent finance minister and administrative official who did not squander state money on private affairs, and who kept the organization of his father in good working order. If he had been a great statesman, the Prussian state that he left behind would not, twenty years later, have been so easily destroyed by a single blow. It was remarkable that this weakened state could suddenly rise again by 1871 and that the memory of the great deeds of King Frederick inspired later Prussians with the courage and convictions for this rebirth. The great deeds of Frederick? As we have seen, Delbrück concluded, their magic is gone. It seems there are names which humans believe in, and once this belief has been established it is thereafter unshakable.

As a result of this parody, Delbrück was even more misunderstood. He was attacked for maligning a national hero and accused of insulting the honor of the Prussian army.[59] Few understood Delbrück's purpose or his way of argument, and he ran into massive opposition. Frederick the Great was an authentic hero, part of the national pantheon.[60] Officers and conservative journalists upbraided Delbrück: He was not a man of sword and deed, they wrote, but a *"Kathederstrategie"*—a strategist of the lectern.[61] They scoffed that with Delbrück's *"Doktoren-Strategie"* war became an art whose most important problems could be solved by any regimental secretary at the map table.[62] They refused to associate Frederick with a term *(Ermattungsstrategie)* that connoted something weak and lifeless.

Specifically, officers united on several themes in their criticism. To them, Delbrück appeared to be putting forth two basic laws of war. There were few unchangeable fundamentals of war, they replied, and these were not found in changing technology or strategy, but in moral factors such as energy and willpower. The officers did not accept Delbrück's notion that resources of men and material limited strategy. They asserted the power of ideas as the dominant force in war.[63] Frederick's writings "breathed the spirit of the offensive."[64] The officers resented Delbrück's attempt to reinterpret Clausewitz. Major Friedrich von Bernhardi, the son of the man whose book on Frederick's strategy Delbrück had criticized in 1881, was particularly incensed. Clausewitz, he wrote, had been recognized as the foremost authority in military theory since the 1830s. Since then the entire theory of war had been built on his fundamentals, and the study of Clausewitz had molded and educated the German army and the German people. Now, sixty years later, a civilian claims that our basic understanding of Clausewitz is wrong, that *Vom Kriege* is incomplete and deals primarily with only one kind of strategy. Those professional officers who have studied Clausewitz will doubt that a civilian scholar can correctly criticize such an intellectual hero. Delbrück, Bernhardi continued, confused the outer appearance of war *(Erscheinungsform)* with the inner realities *(innere Wesensbedingungen)*. Frederick, just as Napoleon, was subject to the exterior conditions of his era, and thus the superficial appearances of their wars may be quite different. In essence, however, war did not change. In salt water one swam more easily than in fresh water, but did one swim in one kind of water with a different system than in the other? asked Bernhardi. Certainly not. If Delbrück assumed differently, it was no wonder he was ignored, especially when his work went directly against the dominant view of the army, which, up to then, had never been challenged.

The officers disliked a civilian criticizing their interpretation. But their fears went deeper than mere concern that a specialist from a different royal bureaucracy was poaching on their territory. Since Delbrück lectured at the university, several officers opined, and anyone could read his writings, there was a danger that his teachings might become part of military education. Worse yet, some young men might enter university life from his seminars and carry this erroneous interpretation into their own military writings. This would not only breed error and confusion in the development of military science, but would undermine the confidence of the educated German in the army and its leadership.[65]

THE NEW MILITARY HISTORY AND GERMAN HISTORICAL SCIENCE

Delbrück's approach to the past was discordant and cacophonous not only to the officers, but also to most German university historians, and, in an important sense, was against the tide of historical ideas in his own country. Delbrück was moving toward the new and developing European social sciences, and away from the dominant line of German historical scholarship. This was a period of changing relationship between history and the older disciplines of literature and philosophy, on the one hand, and between history and the newer disciplines such as sociology and economics on the other. In France the development of history as a distinct discipline took a very different turn during this period.[66] As French historical scholarship was opening up to take cognizance of the newer, more "scientific" approaches of sociology, economics, and demography, exactly the opposite seems to have occurred in Germany. History became closed down, narrower, and more exclusive in methods and goals. The single new line of development, the history of ideas represented in the work of Friedrich Meinecke after the turn of the century, typifies many features which we have seen in the work of both officers and professors who dealt with the military past. Meinecke, following Ranke, promulgated an idealistic concept of the state as an end in itself and the highest creation of culture. Political history and the study of ideas were the only true focus of historical research. His philosophy of value rejected normative thinking. No historical action could be judged by standards external to the situation in which it arose. These men rejected conceptualized thinking, ruling out the possibility of a common human substructure subject to rational inquiry.[67]

As this suggests, the dominant mold of German historical scholarship by 1910 was historistic: it aimed to describe the past by means of empathy and individuality. Empathy implied an attempt to understand from the perspective of past individuals, to uncover their unique motivating emotions and ideas, emphasizing conscious intentions and feelings rather than statistical or timeless laws of behavior. Individuals were regarded uniquely, not as members of unhistorically abstracted classes. Past culture and epochs were seen as self-contained spiritual wholes not comparable to other epochs.[68] This approach was compatible with the creation of great historic individuals and thus flowed easily into the kind of history indentified with the "Prussian" and "Schlieffen" Schools.

The differences between history in France and Germany are related to factors which go well beyond the purposes of the present discussion. As we have seen, by 1900, Delbrück differed from most of his German contemporaries. His perspectives were more universal and comparative, on the one hand, and more material and realistic, on the other. Delbrück, then, was closer to the mainstream of European social thought. Like Max Weber and Ferdinand Tönnies, he tried to combine a recognition of the diversity of the past with a search for the constant or typically recurring elements in historical change—for patterns of development. Delbrück, unlike many of his German contemporaries, saw the need for larger interpretative historical writing. During this period many scholars believed Ranke taught that source criticism was all there was to writing history. In fact, Ranke's greatest works are interpretive histories based on careful source criticism. The same can be said for Delbrück. In this sense, Delbrück's work was a major, though unrecognized, part of a "Ranke Renaissance" taking place during these years.[69]

German historiography of this period closely reflected the monarchical state and authoritarian society. As we have suggested, the only new methodology, the history of ideas, kept the real world at a distance and did not approach social or economic realities. Those who ventured into social or economic history, even though they were staunch monarchists in every way, ran into difficulties. Gustav von Schmoller, whom Delbrück in various ways resembled, was stricken from a list of candidates being considered for the directorship of the Prussian State Archives because Kaiser Wilhelm II said that he could not entrust state documents to a socialist.[70] Schmoller, an economic historian, was anything but a socialist; however, his work associated him somehow with socialism in the Kaiser's mind. Delbrück even more than Schmoller remained alienated from the mainstream of German historical scholarship. The degree of this isolation is shown not only in the criticism he received, but also in his promotion to full professor, not in military history but in "world history." Few of his seventy-five doctoral students, all of whom wrote dissertations dealing with military history, went on to university posts; and those who did, with one exception, were recognized for contributions in fields other than military history. Official German scholarship considered Delbrück's methods and his research conclusions virtually a dead end.

Among the few who did not attack Delbrück's work, there were several degrees of understanding. By the end of the century a few foreign officers and a few retired German officers implied that Delbrück had said something of value about eighteenth-century strategy because their interpretation generally agreed with his. The most important of these was Major Max Jähns, a retired teacher at the War Academy, who in 1891 published the third volume of his massive and still well-regarded *History of War Science*.[71] Although he refused to admit it even privately, apparently not wanting to be in any way associated with Delbrück's views, Jähns essentially agreed with Delbrück's position on Frederick.[72] The youthful Frederick, he wrote, tried to carry out a new, unconventional strategy of annihilation; however, through bloody experiences in the first two Silesian Wars, Frederick found that the conditions needed to carry out such a strategy were lacking.[73]

A degree of understanding may be seen in a few scholarly reviews. Although the professors were unable to accept Delbrück's criticism of such classical sources as Tacitus and Caesar, or to fully understand Delbrück's arguments, they nonetheless found his work unique. One wrote that Delbrück illuminated not only the single appearances of war but also the continued interrelationships between war and the whole of public life.[74] Delbrück's work had no counterpart in the whole of historical literature, another reviewer noted. This raised a peculiar problem. Whether it was written for historically educated officers or for historians capable of judging military affairs, very few of either specialist existed.[75]

The clearest understanding came from the socialists such as Walter Koch and Franz Mehring. They alone not only perceived the uniqueness of Delbrück's approach to war but had a deeper appreciation. Mehring wrote that socialist ideas during the nineteenth century had partially emancipated bourgeois intellectuals, yet those writers most influenced by socialist views did not carry over their analysis into a study of military affairs. Some of the works of Friedrich Engels and Karl Burkli had begun to do this, but only incompletely and unsystematically. Delbrück's work marked an important step in the study of war. Using a comparison with the English historian George Grote, who had used his knowledge of modern English politics to reconstruct the history of Athenian democracy, Mehring wrote that Delbrück was even more radical in applying the comparative method. He satirized those bourgeois historians who attacked Delbrück's interpretation of Pericles because Pericles had not understood the fundamentals of strategy, which had been laid down by the Prussian hero Frederick the Great! Viewing Delbrück's military writings as a whole, Mehring concluded that here war and society were clearly related. Quoting the passage describing the triumph of Roman civilization over the barbarians, he said that it could not be better demonstrated that the means of production had a decisive impact in war.[76]

Delbrück was not entirely alone in his criticism of the "official" interpretation of Frederick or in his attempt to focus on comparative economic and social analysis. Others who did this had the same or worse difficulty. Professor Karl Lamprecht, who tried to write a cultural history of mankind by using insights from the newly developing disciplines of anthropology, psychology, and sociology, and by comparative analysis, was vigorously opposed by members of the Prussian School. Professor Dietrich Schäfer, a conservative student of Heinrich von Treitschke, scoffed at the "so called" cultural historians. Politics and ideas were the only proper reality for historians. Their duty was to detail the thousandfold influences of the state and of patriotic and religious ideas.[77]

Another historian not following the expected historiographical tradition was Delbrück's friend Professor Max Lehmann. Using Frederick's *Political Testament* of 1752, portions of which the Foreign Office censored, he argued that Frederick's main objective in 1756 had been the acquisition of Saxony and, therefore, the Seven Years' War could not be considered exclusively defensive. A great outcry ensued against this revision of the image of the hero. Albert Naude, civilian teacher of history at the War Academy, attacked Lehmann in the *Historische Zeitschrift*. Patriots demanded that Lehmann be punished for this heresy. In commenting on the controversy in 1894, Lehmann wrote:

> It is more than a hundred years since the death of Frederick the Great and yet historical research on his reign is still in its infancy. Like the great religious and confessional histories, the radiant myths surrounding the personality of the Prussian king are still confused with his deeds. Political orthodoxy is the same as religious: whoever holds heretical views on the king is no longer considered a good Prussian. Now the great deeds of 1866 and 1871 have separated patriotic history from its political considerations. Germany was united by Prussia and thus Prussia no longer needs to derive its claim to German responsibility from history. But this historical freedom applies yet only very little for the period of Frederick. His greatest historian, Delbrück, must endure condemning judgments raining down upon him.[78]

No one writes history today to learn and understand, another reviewer noted sarcastically, but only to glorify individuals and to construct a magnificent row of heroes. Comes someone who puts the facts above the individual, whose research places individual achievements into proper historical perspective, and he is attacked by people who only want drillmasters of public opinion.[79]

In spite of Delbrück's clear "outsider" position in German historical scholarship, he was appointed full professor in 1896, ironically enough succeeding to the chair of Heinrich von Treitschke, one of the founders of the Prussian School. Negotiations with the permanent official under whose aegis these appointments fell, Friedrich Althoff, began in 1893.[80] Gordon Craig has suggested that Delbrück's late promotion to full professor at the age of forty-eight, sixteen years after joining the faculty, was due to his discipline, military history.[81] We have seen much evidence that such prejudice existed. How effective it was in creating opposition to his promotion is difficult to say precisely. Delbrück had received and rejected several offers of full professorships at other German universities well before 1896.[82] Only because he lived in Berlin, the seat of the university, with the largest German libraries, with parliament and the center of political and economic life, could Delbrück contribute to so many spheres of activity simultaneously.[83] As we have seen, his activities outside the university were as disadvantageous to him in his relationship with his colleagues as they were advantageous in leavening his historical scholarship with practical experience and breadth of vision.

As for promotions, many men of the same age or younger were promoted ahead of Delbrück.[84] Perhaps this shows discrimination. However, it is equally possible that Berlin, the ranking German university, expanded very slowly and one simply had to wait one's turn. Some evidence indicates that the average age of full professors in the philosophy faculty was higher, both in 1890 and in 1901, than the average age of professors in other faculties and at other universities.[85] How then was Delbrück promoted? It was suggested afterwards that Althoff, who had read Delbrück's early works in the 1880s, virtually forced the appointment through.[86] If this is so, Delbrück had to pay a price. First of all he was asked to censor *Preussische Jahrbücher* articles on various sensitive political topics, a request which he was able, apparently with the support of the Prussian royal family, to turn down.[87] Secondly, the final appointment came in "world history,"[88] not military history, and Delbrück began in 1896 to give a four-semester course in world history, which after 1925 became his five published volumes under this title.[89] Althoff may have reached a compromise with the university faculty by appointing Delbrück to the status of full professor instead of creating a chair in military history.

By the 1890's, Delbrück had distanced himself from both groups of specialists to whom his work was intended as a bridge, the scholarly world of the historian and the operational world of the officer. Military history was not a recognized professional specialty, and Delbrück set out to define its boundaries and begin a legitimate break with past tradition. His opponents were wont to give ground. The professors resisted the formulation of a new area of knowledge because it did not fit into their notions of a proper humanistic discipline. The military and its conservative supporters opposed Delbrück because he appeared to criticize a national military hero, because his work confused issues which in their minds had to be uniform and doctrinaire for future application, and also because they did not like to be judged by a bourgeois academic. In trying to cut between the traditional lines of military history, as defined by the university and by the war academy, Delbrück pleased neither group and aroused the wrath of both.

Beneath the rhetoric, however, a far more important issue was at stake. Gerhard Ritter, in commenting on the controversy from the vantage point of 1936, wrote that behind the debate between Delbrück and the historical section of the General Staff lay a highly topical question.[90] Was the classic method of seeking to destroy the enemy army by offensive battle the best in all circumstances—even against a greatly superior opponent pressing forward on several fronts at once? Or was another equally valid method available, that of exhausting the enemy through continued limited actions? In such a situation as Frederick faced in the 1750s, might not this latter approach hold greater promise of success? In the decade before 1914, the analogy of Frederick the Great was used again and again by the officers of the General Staff. Let us then turn to the great German strategic debate which preceded World War I, and to an examination of Delbrück's indirect but nonetheless essential role in it.

NOTES

1   His mother was the eldest child of Leopold von Henning, professor of philosophy in Berlin, who had worked with Goethe and had been attracted from Thuringia by Georg F. Hegel. Her great grandfather Krutische had been a gardener for Frederick the Great at Sansouci. A great uncle was Justus von Liebig, pioneer in the modern chemistry of agriculture. On his father's side were scholars, officials, and businessmen. His grandfather, Friedrich Delbrück, had been tutor to the late King Friedrich Wilhelm IV of Prussia and to Emperor Wilhelm I of Germany. Rudolf Delbrück was Bismarck's state secretary and author of the imperial economic program. Other family members were connected with cement factories near Berlin and with Bankhaus Delbrück, Schickler. See "Hans Delbrück in Briefen," the unpublished memoirs assembled by Delbrück's wife, Lina Thiersch, in possession of Frau Helene Hobe, Delbrück's daughter, Berlin-Dahlem. Many in the family gathered around the home of Rudolf Delbrück, president of the Reich Chancellor's Office under Bismarck in the 1870s. He and his wife were childless, and thus they collected many of the younger Delbrück generation. Cf. Annemarie Niemeyer, *Erinnerungen und Betrachtungen aus drei Menschenalter von Theodor Niemeyer* (Kiel: Walter G. Muhlau, 1963), pp. 68–69.

2   A critical appraisal of the writings of a German chronicler of the eleventh century, Lambert von Hersfeld, whose work had long been accepted as credible by historians. *Über die Glaubwürdigkeit Lamberts von Hersfeld* (Bonn: Carl Georgie, 1873).

3   "Hans Delbrück in Briefen," p. 5.

4   Delbrück to his brother Max, 26 May 1867, ibid., p. 10.

5 Delbrück to his friend Dorn, September 1867, ibid., p. 20.

6 Delbrück to Rohde, 12 December 1869, ibid., p. 2.

7 Delbrück to Dorn, December 1868, ibid., p. 18.

8 Conversation with Delbrück's daughter, Frau Helene Hobe, July 1974, Berlin-Dahlem.

9 "Ganz Europa geht so vor mir auf und ab spazieren. . . ." "Hans Delbrück in Briefen," p. 19.

10 Agnes von Zahn-Harnack, *Adolf von Harnack* (Berlin, Walter de Gruyter, 1951), p. 138.

11 Peter Rassow, "Hans Delbrück als Historiker und Politiker," originally a speech given on the hundredth anniversary of Delbrück's birth, 11 November 1948, in the historical seminar at Köln University, then published in *Die Sammlung*, 4 (March 1949): 134. Rassow's family were relatives of Delbrück, and Rassow himself was a student of Delbrück's at Berlin.

12 Herbert Marcuse, *Reason and Revolution: Hegel and the Rise of Social Theory* (Boston: Beacon Press, 1960), p. 228.

13 "Hans Delbrück in Briefen", p. 117.

14 Hans Delbrück, *Geschichte der Kriegskunst im Rahmen der politischen Geschichte*, 4 vols. (Berlin: George Stilke, 1900−20), 1:xi.

15 Letter of 9 August 1870, "Hans Delbrück in Briefen", p. 30.

16 Letter of 11 August 1870, ibid.

17 Letter of 19 August 1870, Gravelotte, ibid., pp. 32−36.

18 Letter from camp by Chatel in front of Metz, 5 September 1870, ibid., p. 42.

19 Letter of 11 September 1870, ibid., p. 43.

20 Originally, Delbrück had been reluctant to apply for the position. His mother pushed him into trying for it. It was an opportunity, she argued, that he could learn from. Delbrück's life with the crown prince's family endowed him with personal relationships which he carried throughout his life. Crown Princess Victoria, eldest daughter of England's Queen Victoria, inspired Delbrück's early interest in English politics. Delbrück's relation with the crown prince, who ruled as Emperor Frederick III for ninety-nine days in 1888, was especially close. Had the emperor lived, there is reason to believe Delbrück might have had a political career as minister in the government. Delbrück's relationship with the eldest son of the crown prince, the later Emperor Wilhelm II, is also important. Wilhelm was fifteen when Delbrück became a tutor; he was twenty, and less than a decade from assumption of the royal authority, when Delbrück left the royal house. Their relationship was never close, but it remained cordial. Finally, there was Delbrück's relationship with members of the crown prince's suite and household, especially with the officers who largely comprised it. With some of these, Delbrück carried on extensive conversations regarding the wars of 1866 and 1871, in which the officers had held commanding positions. With others, such as General Leo von Caprivi, the later Reich chancellor (1890−94), Delbrück established relationships which proved fruitful in later years. All in all, Delbrück's five years as royal tutor was a crucial period in his life, yet few good sources exist to document it. One of his wife's memoirs, "Hans Delbrück in Briefen," contains a number of letters and reminiscences from this period. After Frederick III's death in 1888, Delbrück en-

gaged in a *Polemik* with the chief editor of the *Preussische Jahrbücher*, Heinrich von Treitschke, over Frederick's personality and character. Treitschke criticized Frederick, Delbrück defended him. Cf. Delbrück's "Persönliche Erinnerungen an den Kaiser Friedrich und sein Haus," *PJ*, vol. 62 (August 1888), reprinted in Hans Delbrück, *Erinnerungen, Aufsätze und Reden* (Berlin: George Stilke, 1902), pp. 64–68. This controversy led to Treitschke's resignation and to Delbrück assuming the position of chief editor. The controversy over Frederick III is traced in Andreas Dorpalen, "Emperor Frederick III and the German Liberal Movement," *American Historical Review*, vol. 54 (1948): 1–31; Delbrück's relationship with Treitschke in Hans Schleier, "Treitschke, Delbrück und die 'Preussische Jahrbücher' in den 80er Jahren des 19. Jahrhunderts," *Jahrbuch für Geschichte*, vol. 1 (1967): 134–79. The longest and closest relationship which remained from all of this was that of Delbrück to the Empress Frederick. Delbrück often visited her in Berlin on the death day of her husband, and they corresponded virtually every year until her death in the summer of 1901. A number of her letters to Delbrück may be found in *Nachlass Delbrück*, DSB. Some are in possession of Frau Helene Hobe, Berlin. Delbrück also wrote "Das Tagebuch Kaiser Friedrichs" (1888) and "Kaiserin Friedrich" (1901), both reprinted in Hans Delbrück, *Erinnerungen, Aufsätze und Reden* (Berlin: Georg Stilke, 1902). For an impressionistic account of Empress Frederick's life, see Daphne Bennett, *Vicky: Princess Royal of England and German Empress* (New York: St. Martin's Press, 1971).

21   Dr. Alfred Vagts and Professor Gordon A. Craig both believe Rüstow deserves research on his own. A Prussian lieutenant of democratic leanings, as Peter Paret observed, he fought under Garibaldi and ended his military career an an officer in the Swiss army. Through it all, Rüstow was writing. In the first volume of his *Geschichte der Kriegskunst*, Delbrück wrote that "the basis for the scholarly knowledge of the Greek military art is formed" from Wilhelm Rüstow and H. Köchly, *Geschichte des griechischen Kriegswesens von der ältesten Zeit bis auf Pyrrhos* (Aarau: Verlags-Comptoir, 1852), and *Griechische Kriegsschriftsteller*, 3 vols. (Leipzig: Engelmann, 1853–55). Both Delbrück and Paret pay tribute to Rüstow's own work, especially his *Geschichte der Infanterie*, 2 vols. (Zurich: Ferdinand Forstemann Verlag, 1857), and *Heerwesen und Kriegsführung C. Julius Cäsars*, 2nd ed. (Nordhausen: Förstemann, 1862). Cf. Peter Paret's comments in his *Yorck and the Era of Prussian Reform* (Princeton: Princeton University Press, 1966) pp. 280–81. Letters of Alfred Vagts to author, May 1973; letter of Gordon Craig to author, 2 July 1974.

22   Most of these may be found in the Gneisenau *Nachlass* in the Geheimes Staatsarchiv, Preussischer Kultur-Besitz, Berlin-Dahlem. About a hundred letters were given to Delbrück as a gift upon completion of the manuscript. A number of these remain in possession of Frau Helene Hobe, Berlin-Dahlem.

23   Carl von Clausewitz, "Über das Fortschreiten und den Stillstand der Kriegerischen Begebenheiten," *Zeitschrift für preussische Geschichte und Landeskunde* 4 (1878): 233–41.

24   Clausewitz, "Über das Fortschreiten und den Stillstand der kriegerischen Begebenheiten," 4. From the original manuscript in the Gneisenau *Nachlass* (PAK. 22. A31, vols. 1, 2), Geheimes Staatsarchiv Preussische Kultur-Besitz, Berlin. Cf. Peter Paret's comments in his *Clausewitz and the State* (New York: Oxford University Press, 1976), pp. 362–64.

25   *Das Leben des Feldmarshalls Grafen Neidhardt von Gneisenau* 2 vols. (Berlin: George Stilke, 1920). There were editions of 1880, 1894, 1907, and 1920.

26   See E. F. von Fransecky, "Gneisenau" *Militär-Wochenblatt* 41 (January-April 1856).

27   Delbrück, *Gneisenau* 2:229–30.

28   "Hans Delbrück in Briefen," p. 128.

29   This is in sharp contrast to his initial response to the idea, ibid., p. 120.

30   Ibid., p. 86.

31   Although students at Berlin increased from 2,219 in 1871 to 5,185 in 1891 and to 9,593 in 1914, the number of full professors in the philosophy faculty increased only from thirty-two in 1874 to fifty in 1910. Cf. Dieter Fricke, "Zur Militarisierung des deutschen Geisteslebens im Wilhelminischen Kaiserreich: Der Fall Leo Arons," *Zeitschrift für Geschichtswissenschaft* 18 (1960): 1071; Helene Tompert, *Lebensformen und Denkwesen der akademischen Welt Heidelbergs im Wilhelminischen Zeitalter* (Lubeck: Mattheisen, 1969), pp. 96ff.; see Fritz Ringer, *The Decline of the German Mandarins*, especially pp. 34–38. Specific examples of the process of *Habilitation* can be seen in John Williamson, *Karl Helfferich* (Princeton: Princeton University Press, 1971), pp. 25–53; Andreas Dorpalen, *Heinrich Von Treitschke* (New Haven: Yale University Press, 1957), pp. 47–55; James Sheehan, *The Career of Lujo Brentano* (Chicago: University of Chicago Press, 1966), pp. 1–15. Cf. Mitchell G. Ash, "Academic Politics in the History of Science: Experimental Psychology in Germany, 1879–1941," *Central European History*, vol. 13, no. 3 (September 1980), 255–86. See the unpublished essay by John E. Craig, "The Politics of University Reform in Imperial Germany," delivered at the AHA Convention, December 1973, kindness of the author.

32   Letters of 19 June 1880, and 9 September 1880, Herr von Norman to Delbrück, *Nachlass Delbrück*, DSB. See Hans Schleier, "Treitschke, Delbrück und die Preussische Jahrbücher in den 80er Jahren des 19 Jahrhunderts," *Jahrbuch für Geschichte*, 1 (1967): 157–84; Hans Werner, "Zu Hans Delbrücks 80 Geburtstage," *Berliner Steglitzer Anzeiger*, 10 November 1928.

33   Ringer, *The Decline of the German Mandarins*, p. 24.

34   Letter of 12 September 1880, von Norman to Delbrück, *Nachlass Delbrück*, DSB.

35   The distinction made by German academicians of this period between philosophical and technical knowledge, and between the sciences and the humanities, suggests that military history would fall into the category of technical knowledge. Whether it was considered a true "science" or not is hard to say, but in any event it was not a science which was considered to come under the purview of the university. See Ringer, *The Decline of the German Mandarins*, pp. 102–07; Rassow, "Hans Delbrück," p. 136; Dahrendorf, *Society and Democracy in Germany*, pp. 147–55.

36   Ringer, *The Decline of the German Mandarins*, pp. 102ff.

37   Hans Delbrück, "Das Generalstabswerk über den deutsch-dänischen Krieg," originally published in the *Preussische Jahrbücher* 59 (1887), reprinted in Hans Delbrück, *Erinnerungen*, pp. 1–12.

38   General Prince zu Hohenlohe-Ingelfingen, *Militärische Briefe, Strategische Briefe, Gespräche über Reiterei*, 5 vols. (Berlin: E. S. Mittler, 1886–87).

39   Hans Delbrück, "Etwas Kriegsgeschichtliches," *Preussische Jahrbücher* 59 (1887): 609ff.

40   Ibid., 610–11.

41   Fischer, *War of Illusions*, p. 39.

42   Schlier, "Treitschke, Delbrück und die 'Preussische Jahrbücher,'" 136.

43 Hans Werner, "Zu Hans Delbrücks 80. Geburtstage," *Berliner-Steglitzer Anzeiger*, 10 November 1928.

44 From 1882 he edited the *Staatsarchiv*, an annual collection of official and diplomatic documents, and Schulthess's *European History Calendar*, which listed the important events of the preceding year. Cf. Delbrück's own comments on the relationship of these three endeavors in his preface to Schulthess's *Europäischer Geschichtskalender* for 1887 (Nördlingen: E. H. Bech's).

45 Hans Delbrück, *Geschichte der Kriegskunst* 1:3–7; Hans Delbrück, *Die Strategie des Perikles erläutert durch die Strategie Friedrichs des Grossen* (Berlin: Georg Reimer, 1890), pp. i–iv.

46 Delbrück, *Geschichte der Kriegskunst* 1:iii–vi.

47 Ibid.

48 Ibid., 1:7.

49 Ibid., 1:10.

50 Review of *Geschichte der Kriegskunst*, *Historische Zeitschrift* 95 (1902): 1, 514.

51 Max Duncker, *Griechische Geschichte*, 5 vols. (Leipzig: Duncker & Humbolt, 1888), 5:418; Ernest Curtius, *The History of Greece*, 5 vols. (New York: Schribner & Armstrong, 1875), 3:57ff. Adolf Holm, *The History of Greece*, 4 vols. (London: MacMillan, 1895), 2:318ff.

52 Delbrück, *Die Strategie des Perikles*, p. 108.

53 Theodore Dodge, *Caesar* (Boston: Houghton Miflin, 1892), pp. 376, 750, 768. J. F. C. Fuller comments that Caesar's apotheosis as a superman took shape after the Renaissance and thereafter became an *idée fixe* in the historical imagination, in *Julius Caesar* (New Brunswick, New Jersey: Rutgers University Press, 1965), p. 12.

54 Delbrück, *Geschichte der Kriegskunst* 1:556.

55 Delbrück, *Die Strategie des Perikles*, pp. 7–12.

56 Ibid., pp. 3–4.

57 Ibid., pp. 30ff.

58 Ibid., pp. 34–36.

59 *Kreuz-Zeitung*, 26 January 1892; Gordon Craig, "Delbrück the Military Historian," in E. M. Earle, ed., *Makers of Modern Strategy* (Princeton: Princeton University Press, 1943), p. 274.

60 Cf. Gooch, *Frederick the Great*, p. 342. As we have suggested this image began in the 1860s, but it picked up considerable impetus with unification and continued strongly into the twentieth century. In a new state seeking its national identity, the image of Frederick the Great made an important contribution. In the 1880s a whole series of historical publications was announced dealing with Frederick and Prussia. A new journal, the *Researchs in Prussian and Brandenburgian History*, was established. The *Hohenzollern Yearbook* began a series of monographs dealing with the dynasty and the state of Prussia. A large-scale history of the wars of Frederick the Great was begun by the Historical Section of the Great General Staff, and the publication of Frederick's political correspondence was begun by the Prussian Academy of Science, edited by J. C. Droysen, Max Duncker of the War Academy, and Heinrich von Sybel, Official His-

toriographer of Prussia. Reinhold Koser, a student of Droysen's and, like him, a professor at the War Academy, began publishing his four-volume *Wars of Frederick the Great* in 1886. Gustav Freytag, who in his famous *Pictures from the German Past* of the late 1860s had portrayed the struggles of the great king in the Seven Years' War as "superhuman," symbolized the general approach if not the exact conclusions of many members of this school.

61   *Norddeutsche Allgemeine Zeitung,* 4 February 1892; cf. Otto von Moser, *Ernsthafte Plaudereien über den Weltkrieg* (Stuttgart: Chr. Belser, 1925), p. 6.

62   *Die Reichswehr,* 14 February 1892.

63   *Literarisches Beiblatt zum Militär-Wochenblatt,* 1900, Nachlass Delbrück, Faz. 92.

64   Major August von Rossler, "Die Angriffs-Pläne Friedrichs des Grossen in den beiden ersten Schlessischen Kriegen," *Militär-Wochenblatt,* 1891; "Die Verteidigungspläne Friedrichs des Grossen in den beiden ersten Schlesischen Kriegen," *Militär-Wochenblatt,* February 1891, 67–98.

65   Major Friedrich von Bernhardi, *Delbrück, Friedrich der Grosse und Clausewitz: Streiflichter auf die Lehren des Professors Dr. Delbrück über Strategie* (Berlin: E. S. Mittler, 1892); General Wilhelm von Scherf, *Delbrück und Bernhardi: Eine strategische Clausewitz-Studie für Gelehrte und Mititärs* (Berlin: Bath, 1892). The attack was carried against Delbrück also in various conservative newspapers. Cf. *Kreuz-Zeitung,* 26 January 1892; *Tägliche Rundschau,* 27 January 1892.

66   Cf. William R. Keylor, *Academy and Community: The Foundation of the French Historical Profession* (Cambridge: Harvard University Press, 1975). For the situation in Germany see Anthony O\bershall, *Empirical Social Research in Germany 1848–1914* (New York: Basic Books, 1965), especially pp. 12–15; Felix Kaufmann, *Methodenlehre der Sozialwissenschaften* (Wien: Julius Springer, 1934), pp. 193–234.

67   Iggers, *The German Conception of History,* pp. 9–11.

68   Ringer, *The Decline of the German Mandarins,* pp. 98–99.

69   Hans-Heinz Krill, *Die Rankerenaissance: Max Lenz und Erich Marcks: Ein Beitrag zum historisch-politischen Denken in Deutschland 1880–1935* (Berlin: Akademie Verlag, 1962); Heinrich Ritter von Srbik, *Geist und Geschichte vom Deutschen Humanismus bis zur Gegenwart,* 2 vols. (München: F. Bruckmann, 1951), 2:10–12.

70   Eckart Kehr, *Der Primat der Innenpolitik: Gesammelte Aufsätze zur preussisch-deutschen Sozialgeschichte im 19. und 20. Jahrhundert,* ed. Hans-Ulrich Wehler, 2nd ed. (Berlin: Walter de Gruyter, 1970), p. 259. Cf. Gordon A. Craig, editor, and Grete Heinz, translator, *Economic Interest, Militarism, and Foreign Policy: Essays on Germany History by Eckart Kehr* (Berkeley: University of California Press, 1977), p. 179.

71   Max Jähns, *Geschichte der Kriegswissenschaft,* 3 vols. (München: R. Oldenbourg, 1886–91).

72   Cf. Max Jähns, "Uber den Wandel der strategischen Anschauungen Friedrichs des Grossen," *Beilage zur Allgemeinen Zeitung,* München, 23 February 1892; Jähns letters to Delbrück of 8. 11. 1891, 27. 5. 1893, 6. 7. 1893, 9. 12. 1893, *Nachlass Delbrück,* DSB.

73   Jähns, *Geschichte der Kriegswissenschaft,* 3:2017–31. Cf. Gustav Roloff, "Die Strategie Friedrich des Grossen," *Beilage zur Allgemeinen Zeitung,* 20 February 1892.

74   Historische Vierteljahresschrift 4 (1902): 528–29.

75   Herman Oncken, review, *Deutsche Monatsschrift*, December 1907; and Richard Schmitte, review, *Göttingische Gelehrten Anzeigen* 22 (1892).

76   Franz Mehring, "Eine Geschichte der Kriegskunst," in *Die Neue Zeit* (Ergänzungheft Nr. 4), 16 October 1908, reprinted in Thomas Höhle, Hans Kock and Joseph Schliefstein, eds., *Franz Mehring Gesammelte Schriften*, vol. 8, *Zur Kriegsgeschichte und Militärfrage*, ed. Heinz Helmert (Berlin: Dietz, 1967), pp. 134–302. Another socialist who admired Delbrück's military writings—but after the World War—was Arthur Rosenberg. Cf. Francis L. Carsten, "Arthur Rosenberg: Ancient Historian into Leading Communist," *Journal of Contemporary History* 12 (January 1973): 72. For background on Mehring see Glen R. McDougall, "Franz Mehring: Politics and History in the Making of Radical German Social Democracy, 1869–1903," Ph. D. dissertation, Columbia University, 1977.

77   Gerhard Oestreich, "Die Fachhistorie und Die Anfänge der sozialgeschichtlichen Forschung in Deutschland," *Historische Zeitschrift* 208 (April 1969): 320–63; Iggers, *The German Conception of History*, p. 198ff; Ringer, *The Decline of the German Mandarins*, pp. 302ff. Dietrich Fischer, *Die deutsche Geschichtswissenschaft von J. G. Droysen bis O. Hintze in ihrem Verhältnis zur Soziologie* (Köln: Walter Kleikamp, 1966), pp. 70ff.

78   Max Lehmann, *Friedrich der Grosse und der Ursprung des Siebenjährigen Krieges* (Leipzig: Hirzel, 1894), forward, v.; Veit Valentin commented on the whole treatment of Frederick the Great in his essay, "Der Kampf um Friedrich den Grossen," reprinted in Will Schaber, ed., *Perspektiven und Profile: Aus Schriften Veit Valentins* (Frankfurt/m: Waldemar Kramer, 1965), pp. 179–95.

79   Review of Hans Delbrück, "Friedrich, Napoleon, Moltke," *Deutsche Heeres Zeitung*, 16 March 1892, front page.

80   *Lina Delbrück Memoirs*, Part 11, p. 274. Cf. Arnold Sachse, *Friedrich Althoff und sein Werk* (Berlin: E. S. Mittler, 1928); Bernhard vom Brocke, "Hochschul-und Wissenschaftspolitik in Preussen und im Deutschen Kaiserreich 1882–1907; das 'System Althoff,' " in Peter Baumgart, ed., *Bildungspolitik in Preussen zur Zeit des Kaiserreichs* (Stuttgart: Klett-Cotta, 1980), pp. 9–117.

81   Craig, "Delbrück, the Military Historian," 283.

82   According to his wife's memoirs, he was offered an ordinarius at Breslau in 1889, and could have moved either to Göttingen or Leipzig in 1893 at the same rank. *Lina Delbrück Memoirs*, Part 11, pp. 250, 273. For perceptive comment on the milieu in which all of this took place see Charles McClelland, *State, society and university in Germany, 1700–1914* (Cambridge: Cambridge University Press, 1980), pp. 239–331; Konrad Jarausch, *Students, Society, and Politics in Imperial Germany: The Rise of Academic Illiberalism* (Princeton: Princeton University Press, 1982), especially chapters 1, 2 & 3 and Konrad Jarausch ed., *The Transformation of Higher Learning, 1860–1930: Expansion, Diversification, Social Opening, and Professionalization in England, Germany, Russia and the United States* (Chicago: University of Chicago Press, 1983).

83   As Johannes Ziekursch suggests in his brief but perceptive essay, "Delbrück," *Deutsche Biographisches Jahrbuch*, 1929 volume, pp. 89–95.

84   Max Weber, Delbrück's contemporary, was *Ordinarius* (full professor) at Freiburg at the age of thirty; Adolf von Harnack, his neighbor and close friend, who had completed his doctoral dissertation in the same year as Delbrück (1873), was *Ordinarius* at Giessen in 1879; Lujo Brentano was a *Privatdozent* in Berlin in 1871, a full professor at Strassburg in 1882. Karl Helfferich, who habilitated at Berlin in 1899, was offered an *Ordinarius* at Bonn in 1904.

85   Franz Eulenberg, "Das Alter der deutschen Universitatsprofessoren," *Jahrbücher für die Nationalökonomie und Statistik* 80 (1903): 65–80.

86   Hans Werner, "Zu Hans Delbrück's 80. Geburtstag," *Berliner-Steglitzer Anzeiger*, 10 November 1928.

87   Hans Delbrück, "Aus meinem Leben," *Nachlass Delbrück*, DSB. Fasz. 95.

88   This meant the history of Western civilization.

89   Hans Delbrück, *Weltgeschichte*, 5 vols. (Berlin: George Stilke, 1925–29).

90   Gerhard Ritter, *Frederick the Great: An Historical Profile*, trans. Peter Paret (Berkeley: University of California Press, 1968), p. 130.

3 / THE GERMAN STRATEGIC DEBATE, 1891–1914

GENERAL CONSIDERATIONS

Beneath the facade of imperial power, doubt and dissension pervaded Prussian-German strategic thinking. The tensions of strategic decision related to a variety of factors: (1) the military organization and bureaucratic structure of Imperial Germany, (2) size increases in the German army, (3) the isolation of Germany within Europe, and (4) the dominant *Zeitgeist*. These matters have been well known for some time. The change in this interpretation comes in a new configuration: the pattern within which these factors are located, their relationship to military planning and to the German image of future war.

The lack of organizational unity within the Prussian-German bureaucracies seriously affected its dealing with questions of war. At least three major departments acted and competed in military decisions from the mid-1880s until 1914. The Great General Staff had charge of war planning and operations, including mobilization, training, and foreign intelligence. The office of the War Minister had responsibility for the technical backup of the army, including the nature and quantity of armaments. The Military Cabinet, the personal aides-de-camp of the kaiser, concentrated on higher personnel decisions. After 1889 creation of a fourth body, the kaiser's military headquarters, further complicated the situation. Each of the four agencies had access to Wilhelm II, and in several areas they were in direct competition; yet though they bickered and fought among themselves, all participants knew that responsibility for planning and execution, once war broke out, lay with the Chief of the Great General Staff. Even in peacetime this officer maintained a degree of power and authority over the others, a *primus inter pares*. Nevertheless, important disagreement broke out publicly over the choice of men for General Staff and army commands, the overall size of the army, and the introduction of new weapons.

The problem of army size was particularly difficult. The Great General Staff from 1891 on argued for a larger army. The Military Cabinet opposed the million-man army, fearing a dilution of the officers corps by "unsuitable elements," and the War Ministry wanted not a larger but a higher quality army. Schlieffen constantly fought with them for greater size, and Erich Ludendorff lost his General Staff job for advocating army expansion too strongly. In spite of these differences, the German army grew apace in the decade and a half prior to 1914.[1] This dominant aspect of the strategic puzzle was to trouble the officers for nearly a quarter century before the Great War. The quantitative aspect of war planning cannot be overemphasized: by 1914 army size represented a 400 percent increase over the armed forces of 1871. If the peacetime army was under a million men in July 1914, war mobilization so greatly expanded this that in the course of the World War thirteen million, three hundred thousand men matriculated through the German army at home and abroad.[2]

To put an army of such size into the field took very detailed plans, worked out in advance, and practiced, insofar as possible, during peacetime maneuvers. It required complex railroad and road timetables, long-range supply and logistical plans, and above all a minimum block of time, perhaps thirty days.[3] Since complete trial mobilization of all elements, active and reserve, was never carried out prior to August 1914, much of this remained a pure theorem on paper or became a fearful specter filling the dreams of the men responsible for its execution.

In addition to bureaucratic and mobilization problems, diplomatic isolation tended to blur and cloud strategic thinking during these years. After 1890 the Second Reich found itself gradually but inextricably estranged from France, Russia, England, and finally even Italy. This put additional psychological pressure on military planning, already burdened with the purely mechanical problems associated with a land war against two great powers on contraposed geographic frontiers. For the German people before 1914, this was the "hidden agenda" undergirding all political and military questions.

A fourth factor, the *Zeitgeist*, also encompassed strategic planning. Though difficult to pinpoint, one may hazard that the dominant ethos in this period was social Darwinism: a feeling that survival in an increasingly hostile, competitive world was a vital but by no means assured goal. Linked to this on a different level was the moral value of war. Many saw war as a positive good. It was in some inexact way unavoidable and an agent of "progress" in world affairs. A common thread of anxiety ran throughout German society, whether in the letters of the chief of the Great General Staff, the speeches of the kaiser, the novels and plays of Gustav Frenssen, Gerhard Hauptmann, and Theodor Fontane, or the paintings and graphics of August Macke, Emil Nolde, and Ernst Ludwig Kirchner. With increasing industrialization and urbanization, social and economic life became more complex and less understandable to its participants. A "systematic irrationalism" attributed to these years

Hans Delbrück
1890

complicated the search for unity of thought. Some considered war a proper antidote for an industrial urban society which they increasingly disliked and from which they sought escape.[4]

In 1913 Hans Delbrück noted with grave concern that idealistic nationalism was in danger of turning fanatical.[5] Gerhard Ritter later characterized this period as one in which a wave of national feeling, influenced by the second Moroccan Crisis and the Agadir Affair, led to a truly extraordinary escalation in popular military feeling.[6] Fritz Fischer has interpreted the years 1911–14 as the crucial underpinning for the policy of world power which erupted during the World War.[7] Fischer argues that the new ethnic nationalism arising around 1911 threatened to disrupt the old bureaucratic and authoritarian order.

Considering all the complexities of German war planning in the two decades preceding World War I, it is no surprise that the individual who put forth the solution to this enigma was depicted as an inscrutable genius, a man who worked silently within the General Staff as the brain worked within the skull. He was a Sphinx who enclosed the secret of victory.[8]

SCHLIEFFEN, THE GREAT GENERAL STAFF, AND HISTORY

All these conditions of turn-of-the-century Germany shaped Alfred von Schlieffen's war plan. He arrived at his final draft of 1905 with great difficulty. For more then ten years he puzzled, grappled with a variety of possibilities, put pieces in and took them out, readjusted relationships, until, beginning about 1901, he began to settle on a single solution. Even after retiring in 1905 he continued to work on his plan; those who knew him suggest it dominated his entire life. Symbolic of the great problem and its daring solution, his last clear words before death were supposedly, "Only make the right wing strong enough."

In 1891 Schlieffen had been a surprise choice for chief of the General Staff.[9] Few features in his career up to that time marked him for this critical role. Stemming from a military and *Junker* family, he was educated at the Hutterian (Christian Anabaptist) school at Niesky and the Joachimstal gymnasium, Berlin. He spent his more than fifty years in the officer corps as a *Garde-Ulan* (1853–58), staff officer (1866 and 1870–71), military attaché in Paris (1867–69), Potsdam Guards Commander (1876–84), and in the Great General Staff (from 1884 on). He was the protégé of Alfred von Waldersee from the time of their working on the same staff during 1870–71. In contrast to the ebullient court general Waldersee, Schlieffen, from his school days through a half century of military service, remained remote and taciturn to the point of apparent apathy—formally correct to superiors, often sarcastic or silent to subordinates, his reputation built on attention to detail and incessant work. From Hutterian training he learned self-denial, humility, and submissiveness. To the Brethren, education was viewed as self-surrender to Hutterite ideas, not self-development. Sermons, for example, were exact copies of seventeenth-century German texts and the unchallenged source of authority. Critical scholarship was unnecessary and suspect. Schlieffen's own life, his working habits, and personal relationships seem to accord well with Hutterian doctrine and life-style. This is especially true after the early death of his young wife in 1884.[10]

Chary of the facade of social life, Hutterian in belief and Spartan in character, from earliest school days history held a special place in Schlieffen's cognitive world. Schlieffen's participation in the patriotic reenactment of historic battles at Niesky School provided his first impression of the military past. It was further nurtured at the War Academy by the idealist images of Siegfried Hirsch. His own father characterized military history as "unusually refreshing." As the elder Schlieffen wrote to his son, aged sixteen:

> Military history provides us an insight into the splendid duty of the greatest profession which is invisible in the ordinary detail of daily life. History shows us the splendor and magnificence of an incomparable profession at times when the sun would scarcely seem to rise above the horizon without this historical image.[11]

For Schlieffen's gymnasium examination at Easter 1853, in answer to the question, "What attracts us so powerfully to history and historical study?" he wrote:

> Whatever greatness is achieved in the world is achieved mostly from the memory of how earlier achievements were brought about as these are recorded in the bronze tablets of history [ehernen Tafeln der Geschichte verzeichnet sind]. History is the fertile mother of new deeds, new heroes. . . .[12]

As for strategy, Schlieffen commented during his second year at the War Academy in 1859 that Garibaldi's Italian campaign

> cannot lay claim to our attention in terms of its military significance. An unbroken series of defeats without battle, of treason and capitulations, are not suitable material for the study of war—a subject whose first essentials are battle and resistance.[13]

In 1866, from what for many soldiers was the midst of death and human suffering, staff officer Schlieffen wrote to his fiancée from Gross Petrowitz, near the bloody battlefield Königgrätz. All the Schlieffen relatives had survived the fighting. The sun at evening illuminated the battlefield; amid many "hurrahs" the *Hohenfriedberg* march was played: everybody was full of joy and *Liebenswürdigkeit!*[14]

As an officer, Schlieffen was expected to be conversant with military history. In the 1880s as one of Waldersee's chief assistants, Schlieffen had charge of planning for the annual staff rides and maneuvers, and he worked on the General Staff military history series, begun in the late 1860s. This series aimed to combine the patriotic traditions of the "Prussian School" with painstaking military detail characteristic of "drum and trumpet" history.[15]

These goals were fully consistent with Schlieffen's own conception. As we have seen in chapter 1, volumes issued by the General Staff History Section, through the Berlin publisher E. S. Mittler, began with the Danish War of 1864, continued through the Austrian War of 1866 to the French War of 1870–71, the last volume completed in 1881. At that point Colonel von Taysen, at Moltke's suggestion, began a complete historical survey of Prussian wars, beginning with those of Frederick the Great.[16] These were the works that interpreted Frederick the Great as the strategic forerunner of Napoleon and Moltke, and which brought forth Delbrück's criticisms. According to its officer in charge, Freiherr von Freytag-Loringhoven, the series on Frederick's wars was produced at the express wish of Field Marshal von Moltke. Freytag tried to change the format. He wanted to publish a two-volume history of the Seven Years' War including everything that the modern soldier needed to know scientifically, and to leave the individual battle studies for later. He argued that a memorial for Prussia's greatest king would be valuable, but that a technical description of campaign operations would have only a few readers within the army and none outside it. Freytag's *"ketzerische"* (heretical) ideas were not approved and work went ahead on the individual battle studies.[17] As Eberhard Kessel remarked, Moltke's own historical writings took a patriotic and even self-emphasizing turn in the 1880s, far different from his earlier work. These later volumes probably influenced Schlieffen, for they were closely related to the purpose and use of military history within the General Staff during these years.

Military history was essential to the War Academy curriculum. It was included in the three-year course of study, three to four hours a week per course. By 1900 the first-year curriculum consisted of the campaigns of Frederick the Great and the wars of the French Revolution and Napoleon. The second year's course dealt with the campaigns of Napoleon and the Austro-Prussian war; the third year the Franco-Prussian War and the Russo-Japanese War. Each course included field trips to the major battle fields of the German past. As the final problem for each year the students wrote long essays based on particular questions, such as, "Marengo and Jena: accident or design?" How did the racial character of the Japanese bear up under the pressure of war against superior numbers? (to be done in connection with the tactics and strategy of the Russo-Japanese War)."[18]

Outside of writing and teaching military history, officers of the General Staff had opportunities to participate in several kinds of historically oriented exercises. General Staff trips, held once or twice each year, lasted from ten to fourteen days each, comprising twenty-five to thirty-five officers of different grades and branches. Tactical exercises were conducted indoors at a map or sand table at the close of the three-year War Academy course. Most well known were the fall maneuvers, known as *Kaisermanöver* after 1892 because of the oppressive presence of Kaiser Wilhelm II. Each of these activities had common features. They were based upon a specific historical situation, usually a recapitulation of a particular battle. Sides were chosen at the beginning of the exercise, and each was organized into a skeletal war command with a general staff, corps and army commanders, and so on. Each side had prescribed opening moves including specific geographic positions, and each was required to issue a series of orders in response to the tactical situation. At the close of the exercise the chief of the General Staff gave a final critique, known as the *Schlussbesprechung*, a general discussion and summary of what had been learned. The overall purpose was the same for all of these: to simulate a war situation and then ask officers to issue orders based upon it.

Two specific methods were used to join a particular point in the military past to the strategic exercise: the *"rückschauende"* or retrospective method and the *"applikatorische"* or application method. In the former, one looked briefly over the historical events of a battle to their conclusion, then traced them backwards to the origins of success or failure, with emphasis on what the commander could have done either to achieve a greater success or to avoid a defeat. An example of this method is the book by Julius Hoppenstedt, a teacher at the War Academy, *How Do We Study Military History?*[19] This work is constantly judgmental, comparing, for example, every command decision at Colenso-Magersfontein, in the December 1899 South African War, with Prussian Field Service Regulations. Hoppenstedt uses the perfect conditional tense of "could have" and "should have" and refers to what was "normal" and what kinds of variations were permitted. His examples were drawn from publications of the Historical Section of the Great General Staff. In the second or application method, one suspended action of an historical battle in the middle and sought to put the officers into the role of the commander at that point. On the basis of the knowledge available to the commander at that time, officers judged the tactical situation and issued specific orders for further action.[20]

The importance of history to the main mission of the General Staff, war planning, is indicated by all of this: the great effort exerted on historical study, the existence of the Military History Section directly subordinate to the chief, the publication of books, journals and newspapers, and the uniform method of approaching the military past. Even if one faults their approach as essentially unhistorical, these officers were linking the past and the future. They seem to have believed that, if they could in no way know the future, the next best method was to examine past military actions and to prepare for the future on that basis. Schlieffen emphasized this himself, when he said in a famous speech to the General Staff that they must obtain from history that knowledge which the present refused to yield. What did this mean? Was Schlieffen suggesting that armies were fundamentally created for future contingencies but that preparation for this future had to be based on an image of the past? Did Schlieffen believe that knowledge of the past was a proper substitute for war experience and therefore the only way to plan for the uncertain future? Schlieffen obviously referred to some relationship between military past and future—and history was the binding ligament in his strategic thinking.

Military history was clearly institutionalized within the Great General Staff, and its use went beyond that literary tradition associated with such Prussian officers as Frederick the Great, Clausewitz, or Moltke the elder. By the 1890s it had become a technical specialty, practiced to teach and inspire officers how to fight future wars. The question that remains is how historical images are translatable into strategic plans.

Schlieffen thought of himself as an intellectual at the head of an institution that he conceived of within an educational framework.[21] In spite of a great personal debt to Waldersee, Schlieffen was a disciple of Field Marshal von Moltke. To Schlieffen, Moltke was the intellectual in uniform, the man who came to his immortality from the writing table and the loneliness of the study. Moltke was not a commander, only the chief of the General Staff; not an order giver, only an advisor. Moltke had never wielded a sword in the field or held in his hand the staff of high command. He was a man of the map, the compass, and the pen.[22] As Schlieffen said in 1910:

> In front of everyone who wants to be a commander lies a book, titled, "Military History" that begins with Cain and Abel. . . . History is not always exciting

and one must work through a mass of less appetizing details, but behind this facade one finds the heartwarming reality, the knowledge of how everything has happened, how it must happen and how it will happen again. . . . Today, we must return to history for the practical experiences [Erfahrungen] which the present refuses to grant us.[23]

To Schlieffen this was the Moltke tradition: persistent searching of the past and the employment of learning in planning for the future. Schlieffen believed that fortune had cast him in an identical intellectual role.[24] Three years before his death he lamented that most members of his family had been either too young or too old to achieve positions of active command in war.[25] His own lack of war experience weighed heavily on him. He regretted not experiencing the victory evening at St. Privat, or seeing the white flags in the middle of the firefight at Sedan. As a staff officer he heard the "nun danket alle Gott" only on the heights of König-grätz and felt the relief of a great Prussian victory.[26] To compensate for his lack of experience, Schlieffen studied history.

This was natural considering the function and methods of the Great General Staff under Schlieffen. Its main purpose was planning for the future, and since this was unknowable, one had to speculate from images of the past.[27] Thus history became instrumentally important for Schlieffen. The "fertile mother of new deeds" now provided the basis for strategic planning. How did Schlieffen distinguish between military history, as he understood it, and operational plans for the future? We can only guess, but there are some clues in Schlieffen's mental workings beginning in 1891.

Gerhard Ritter has pointed out that Schlieffen's magnum opus, the war plan of 1905, was a "purely theoretical operational study," or as Schlieffen called it himself, "purely academic."[28] We have seen that Schlieffen's early life reveals a thoroughly idealistic and patriotic notion of military history. But the development of his historical thinking after 1891 is clearly reflected in an hitherto overlooked source.[29] It was an important part of Schlieffen's official duties to conclude and summarize the historically oriented staff exercises, maneuvers, and war games of the Great General Staff. Between 1891 and 1906, in over thirty of these summations, known as "final critiques," Schlieffen lectured to the younger subordinate officers. Here his thoughts on war, history, and the future are set down in a systematic and continuous pattern. The atmosphere of these lectures approximated a seminar, where the master teacher, as his students often called him,[30] concluded and summarized the discussion—in the process nurturing, transplanting, crossbreeding, and fertilizing the strategic ideas which Schlieffen hoped would be transmitted throughout the army.

Schlieffen crafted many planning models during the 1890s. Gradually he reached some conclusions which, although not yet fully reflected in his war plans, are clearly evident in the final critiques. His forces faced overwhelmingly superior numbers. The army could not count heavily on Austro-Hungary; it must plan its own war, virtually independent of positive help on the southern flank. Above all, Germany must seek to annihilate one opponent quickly, then turn against the second. To this end the German army had to take the initiative irrespective of conditions and circumstances; for Schlieffen this meant only one thing: to attack.

In the exercise for 1891, for example, a superior opponent (Russia) mobilizing several days before Germany, invaded East Prussia and Posen. In his final summation Schlieffen said that although the Prussian forces could complete their mission from the defensive, the First Army was in a position to turn the campaign against the invaders by immediately attacking the single enemy columns before they united. If one was destroyed, he said, the moral impact of this victory would be momentous.[31]

In 1893 the enemy attacked early in the morning on a front through Lothringen and Luxemburg, and the German Fifth Infantry Division was confronted by a twofold superiority of infantry and cavalry and a threefold superiority of artillery. At the close of the exercise Schlieffen chided the participants:

> I have the distinct impression that defensive ideas have a larger place in your minds than appears desirable. Even in the possession of the numerical superiority, in a favorable location, most gentlemen stand fast, waiting. The most daring hopes are lost, the victorious attack against the enemy is rejected. This is surprising since it is only twenty-two years since the time in which the idea of the offensive from first to last thrilled everybody. The weapons of the army have, surely, changed, but the fundamentals of strategy remain the same and these strategic laws [Gesetze] point to one thing: that one cannot be victorious over the enemy without attacking. I am thankful to those gentlemen who have preserved the idea that one must attack the enemy when one has the means to do so and that one must attack in such a way as to practically destroy him.[32]

The General Staff ride east in 1896 shows the beginning of a more systematic approach to mobilization: the days from declaration of war to initial enemy contact and beyond were for the first time specifically numbered. Thus, for example, on the twenty-fifth mobilization day the Germans fought a victory which forced the French out of their defensive positions, allowing a transfer of troops to the eastern front. This staff ride began with the Russian cavalry attacking Germany from two sides, followed by German counterattack against the Russian flanks.[33]

The problem for 1898 saw the invasion of East Prussia and Poland on

June 1. Russian forces streamed into the areas northeast of Tilsit, east of Wilkownszki and Suwalki, and north of Bialystok. The First German Army was threatened on three sides. What should the commander do? Schlieffen replied:

> The First Army could do nothing better than to attack the nearest enemy force, defeat it and then turn against the other two. The chosen battle must be decisive: if the fighting lingered on, keeping the German forces engaged, it would provide time for the other two Russian armies to attack in flank and rear. If the commander believes he cannot bring about a complete victory, he had better retreat behind the Weichsel River. . . . For a decisive victory over the next opponent the commander should concentrate all his forces on which ever Russian force moved east of Memel. . . . If the German force attacked quickly complete success could be expected.[34]

The 1899 exercise simulated an invasion of West and East Prussia by a Russian army twice as strong as the defending German army. Schlieffen stated that the smaller German army must attack the larger enemy. At the start of action, the First Army Corps should not await the Russian attack behind the Weichsel River but should attack the nearest Russian army before a second one arrived. To insure success, Schlieffen emphasized, it was necessary to concentrate power against a single enemy wing. The June 2 German offensive was risky and dangerous, Schlieffen concluded, but, as the exercise by June 3 showed, this action would "probably be accompanied by great success."[35]

The General Staff's ride east for 1899 assumed war against Russia and France, with Austro-Hungary "waiting," i.e., technically not counted on by the Germans for aid during the course of the operation. The German forces were outnumbered; at three-quarters strength of the Russian infantry, half the strength of the Russian cavalry, and four-fifths the strength of the Russian artillery. To meet this situation, Schlieffen invoked the examples of Napoleon in 1813 and of Moltke in 1870–71. Because of the numerical inferiority the Prussian army could not hold the front and attack one or two flanks at the same time, as at Sedan. Such action in a future war was no longer possible. He concluded:

> With our small army we must operate so that we not only attack the enemy flank with as much strength as possible but at the same time strike at the enemy lines of communication and transportation. Only in this way can a real decision and a quick end to the campaign be brought about. In the case of a war on two fronts this is an absolute necessity.[36]

In these rides and exercises of the 1890s, Schlieffen restlessly turned from east to west and back again, changing the nature of the attack from year to year, yet gradually becoming more certain of future German strategy. The practical fears undergirding these exercises are well expressed in a letter of 1892 to his sister:

> France has only 38 million inhabitants compared to Germany's 47 million, yet France has more soldiers. If war comes, we have an essentially larger . . . and younger army [to face] in France. It is well-known that on the other side stands a larger Russian army. . . . Thus against our enemies we will have a nearly double inferiority. . . . We must increase our army size. The most that we can do is to train all our men fit for service. By doing this we will not produce an army larger than France and Russia, but we will have done our best, our duty will have been discharged. . . . At the end of the last century it was given as the rule, that an army could not be larger than 40,000 men. Soon thereafter Napoleon showed a terrified Europe the opposite. Bismarck said that a 300,000 man army would be the largest possible. The German army in 1870 was more than double this number, and Bismarck said we did not have enough men in front of Paris. The idea of such maximum limits is worthless. Some place value on a small but very high quality army. The first condition we have fulfilled: our army is, in relation to others, small. But is it so much better than other armies, that it can be considered by its quality equal to large enemy numerical superiority? How can [the potential] of this high quality army be estimated in an age when weapons, equipment and training of all armies is about the same? It is our hope that our army is better than the French and Russian. But that it is so much better, as, for example, the European armies in contrast to the Indian and African armies, that our quality will make a difference against superior quantity, this has not yet been proven.[37]

The staff exercises of the 1890s related only indirectly to the actual German war plans of this period, that is, to the plans which would have been implemented had Imperial Germany become involved in a European war. Rather, the exercises were just that: attempts to examine hypothetical plans—to try to see "what would happen if"—by juxtaposing two staffs of officers and allowing them to work through a situation against each other.

Questions to be resolved concerned the essential details: whether to turn East or West first, what forces to send out, and above all, in what manner to carry out the attack. Schlieffen began to resolve these questions about 1900. Gerhard Ritter, noting the decisive difference between Schlieffen's plans of 1897–99 and that of 1905, says that the period after 1899 marks a "sudden and radical change" which "is the central problem in the historical understanding of the Schlieffen Plan."[38]

We know that Schlieffen had read Hans Delbrück's account of the Battle of Cannae (216 B.C.) sometime before 1901; by then he had ordered the Military History Section to embark on a series of studies proving that the Cannae-type battle was prototypical in all of the major epochs of Western military history.[39] Cannae pitted a Carthaginian professional army of approximately 40,000 infantry and 10,000 cavalry commanded by Hannibal against a Roman citizen army of approximately 86,000 men, including 6,000 cavalry. For Delbrück it was one type of classic battle in that (1) it resulted in the virtual annihilation of the Romans, (2) a small Carthaginian force defeated a much larger opponent, and (3) the moral strength and esprit de corps of the Carthaginians undergirded their triumph. Hannibal's army was backed up against a shallow fordable river. His opponents the Romans faced him from deep columns, unusually compressed together in tight formation. In addition, their infantry was only thinly protected by cavalry. But they were confident because of an almost two-to-one superiority in numbers, and the Roman Consul Varro wanted to fight a decisive battle. The key to Carthaginian victory lay in their plan to render impotent the Romans' greater strength. As the two forces approached each other, Hannibal allowed his center to recede. Taking advantage of what seemed to be their enemy's weakness, the Roman infantry advanced into the Carthaginian center. This allowed the Carthaginians to move simultaneously around the flanks and across the rear of the Roman infantry. In this way the Carthaginians separated the Roman infantry from its protective riders, dispersed the Roman horsemen, and encircled the Roman foot soldiers. The Roman army became a compressed, terrified mass: the soldiers on the inside were powerless to help their compatriots on the exterior, who were being cut to pieces. The Romans were virtually annihilated.[40]

Obviously this strategy appealed to Schlieffen, the center or core of whose strategic conundrum was numbers. How could a smaller force defeat a larger one? Surely this is why the Seven Years' War appealed so much to him and other officers. Frederick the Great had been faced with the same, perhaps even a worse strategic situation in a "world war for Prussia's survival," as the officers often described it. Increasingly after 1900, Schlieffen referred to the "Cannae type" strategy.

Schlieffen's lecures at the conclusion of General Staff exercises again provide an hitherto little used source to examine the development of his thinking. In July 1900 at the final critique of the General Staff exercise in East Prussia, Schlieffen noted that a defensive, seeking only to turn the enemy forces without a counteroffensive, would not carry out the duty of the Second Army. By attacking the enemy flank the Second Army could bring a decision.[41] Although he stated in a speech in November of that year that Moltke's teaching was that no one method, no one body of strategic rules was by itself adequate, when he returned to his lonely workroom the practical dilemmas of the future still confronted him.[42]

Increasingly, he sought a simpler, more drastic solution. In his next speech, Schlieffen asked what had happened on July 3, 1866 (the Battle

of Königgrätz), so that school children in the smallest German villages
spelled out Moltke's name? A battle had been fought, a victory won. But
this had not been an ordinary conquest. This triumph in one blow cut
the Gordian knot that for a hundred years had entangled Germany. For
such deeds, history had placed Moltke in the ranks of the few great heroes
of all time.[43]

In the June 1901 strategic critique, Schlieffen for the first time confided
the secret of victory. In war games and General Staff trips, he said, con-
venient means were at hand to eliminate unpleasant or doubtful situations, but in reality these means would not always be available. Army
corps were not chess figures to be moved here and there, but human
beings with feelings and sentiments. An army of 800,000 men which
crossed a border with patriotic speeches and cheers to destroy the enemy
could not return after two days having annihilated an enemy patrol!
Large armies could not receive new march directions every other day.
Reports and orders had to go a long way. Some believed that the modern
million-man army, aided by the telegraph, could be as easily directed as
an earlier corps of 15,000 or 20,000 men. At home this might be possible;
in enemy provinces the field telegraph was as much denied to one as it
was during maneuvers. Bicycles were not possible in bad weather or on
poor roads, and automobiles were prone to accidents. Progress in these
areas, Schlieffen hoped, would someday make command easier. Now,
however, the large army was a cumbersome and intractable mass. In
spite of these obstacles, he went on, this battle could end with a Russian
defeat.

Schlieffen noted that many officers believed that a frontal attack might
accomplish this. At one time a campaign began with a battle against the
enemy lines of communication and with a completely inverted front. By
1800 completely different views were set forth and have continued to the
present: the essence of this has been the concentration of power to seek
the enemy front. But Schlieffen wondered how, under the devastating
impact of modern weapons, one could attack. Thirty years previously
superiority of numbers had allowed the German army to march frontally
against the enemy. Today, this could not be, for Germany had only a
smaller force.

How then to employ this force, Schlieffen asked? When too weak to
attack the whole, then one attacked a part. This had many variations.
The most sensitive part of an enemy army was its flank. Schlieffen regarded a flank attack with a company, a battalion, or a detachment as
very difficult. The difficulty increased with a stronger enemy, with
longer, stretched-out lines which took more time to envelop. How could
the enemy flank be attacked? Not with one or two corps, but with one or

more armies! A large part of this attack must penetrate the rear retreat lines as was done at Ulm in 1805, in the winter campaign of 1807, and at Sedan in 1870. This kind of attack led immediately to cutting off the enemy retreat, to chaos and bewilderment, and gave the opportunity for a battle of annihilation.[44]

These same sentiments, but in more extreme language and looking farther into the future, reappear at the final critique of the General Staff ride east in 1901. The first blow, Schlieffen said, must be made with full power so as to be absolutely decisive: a Solferino was of no use; it must be a Sedan or a Königgrätz. If the army held fast to the ground rule that it must attack the retreat line of the opponent, then it might expect a complete victory in a war on two fronts.[45]

As 1905 approached, Schlieffen repeated this single theme over and over, buttressed by more and more examples from his image of military history. Increasingly, a single concept dominated his language, discussions, and writings. For a battle of annihilation it was necessary to attack the rear lines of communication and transportation. Germany must not aim for a simple moderate success to push back the enemy, but for a victory of annihilation.

In the 1903 General Staff ride east the French and Russians had invaded Germany simultaneously on the eighteenth day of mobilization. Germany sent most of its army against France, but by the thirty-fifth mobilization day she anticipated transferring some strength east. Why? Schlieffen explained that a war on two fronts was not ended by forcing back one or the other opponent, but by annihilating first one enemy and then the other. The means for such an annihilation, he said, were known from military history. Frederick the Great had tried for it repeatedly, Napoleon had successfully used the idea, and Moltke had employed it in 1870. All of one's power, or the largest part, must concentrate against the rear flank of the enemy; if successful on two sides, as at Leipzig, Gravelotte, and Sedan, it led to a surrounding of the enemy. Following the example of earlier times, Schlieffen said, this was the way not only to resist enemies but also to annihilate them![46]

Modeling the exercises of 1903 around Moltke's operations in 1870, Schlieffen emphasized that the same rules applied in strategy and in tactics. Whoever wanted to surround, must plant his force quickly in front, thus hindering the enemy from movement and making possible the surrounding wing attack.[47] In 1903 the General Staff Historical Section book commissioned by Schlieffen several years earlier appeared, *Success in Battle: How is it Achieved?*[48] It reviewed the actions of a number of great historical commanders and concluded that each one's greatest victories came by the flank attack.

The 1904 tactical-strategic exercise presumed that most of the German army was deployed in the western campaign area and that a smaller part faced a two-pronged invasion in the east. The exercise was based upon the battle of Liegnitz, "that memorable Prussian victory of 150 years ago," as Schlieffen described it. Since then all military relationships had changed so that a true copy of this battle was impossible. But its essential underlying idea, attacking one army while defending against another, was feasible, and the classic terrain of three famous battles could be used again.[49]

At the close of the 1905 exercise in East Prussia and Posen, Schlieffen criticized the assembled officers:

> The principle of annihilation, which distinguished all the battles of Frederick the Great, which prevailed in all the operations of Napoleon and on whose basis Field Marshal Moltke achieved his exemplary successes, appears gradually to have become lost. In recent staff exercises, I have only twice seen the goal expressed: I will destroy the enemy! . . . All great commanders have done essentially the same thing. When Frederick the Great on a foggy December morning marched around the flank of the Austrians, when Napoleon in October 1806 moved down the Saale, and when Field Marshal Moltke in the August days of 1870 went over the Mosel, their actions appeared very different, but fundamentally all . . . were based on a single idea: The enemy shall be attacked on one flank and defeated.[50]

The dominant theme in these exercises unsurprisingly reappears in the 1905 Schlieffen plan, with its "sudden and radical changes" from his plans of the 1890s. This plan concentrated seven-eighths force on the right flank and one-eighth on the left flank in a gigantic envelopment which included the Dutch border, the whole of Belgium, half of Luxemburg, and a third of France. This attack, as eventually formulated, was spearheaded by five army corps, reinforced by two additional corps, and backed up by six reserve divisions for a total of 1,733,000 men. The front was 200 miles wide and 250 miles deep at its furthest penetration, encompassing a land area of about 40,000 square miles in a huge triangle. To oppose this thrust, the French had to mobilize almost four million men, transporting them into battle on 7,000 trains, at times one every eight minutes day and night for sixteen days! The successes of this enormous operation was predicated, as Gerhard Ritter points out, upon a vast enlargement of the German army. Yet the size requirements were so great that the unprecedented army increases in the three years before the war were still inadequate. The plan of December 1905–January 1906 differs in one other significant respect from previous Prussian-German plans. It was not just an *Aufmarschplan*, that is, a deployment plan for

Alfred von Schlieffen

the first few days of fighting; it was a technical-mechanical plan for an entire campaign to the end of the war, an advance through Belgium and across France planned like a field drill exercise, down to the concluding gunshot.[51]

After Schlieffen's retirement in 1905, virtually to his death in 1913, he worked on the plan. In 1904, he had created a vehicle to propagate these ideas: the *Quarterly Journal for Troop Leadership and War Science.*[52] If Schlieffen saw himself as an intellectual while on active duty, he followed this model even more faithfully in retirement. He became one of the main contributors to the *Quarterly Journal,* and the General Staff later collected his contributions and published them in a single volume known as the "Cannae series."[53] In all of these essays, as in the rest of Schlieffen's historical thinking, there is a willingness to do violence to the ascertainable facts, to rearrange them in conformance with a preordained image to serve didactic purposes.[54] As in some Hutterian and much Wilhelmian thought, his writing often had an almost mystical quality. For example, Schlieffen's parting words to the officers of the Great General Staff as he retired on 30 December 1905 were:

No foreign power would risk action against the Prussian General Staff because it stands under the aegis of a great name. Our enemies know that the General Staff is safe in the legacy of the man from Sedan. They know we are in sure possession of the secret of victory.[55]

This was the formal benediction to his professional colleagues of an officer who a few years later in correspondence with Hans Delbrück signed his name "Dr. Graf Schlieffen."[56]

By appealing to history in what appeared to his contemporaries as a daring stroke of genius, Schlieffen had put forth a solution to a most baffling strategic enigma. By an extraordinary stroke he apparently resolved the problem of deploying the million-man army. From a cloudy and obscure situation he seemed to have broken through into clear sunlight. His colleagues were surprised and overwhelmed with a solution which, in addition to its military-technical features, fit so nicely into the intellectual and psychological trends of those years. Schlieffen somehow combined in one plan a rational construct lacking any relationship with reality. If he interpreted the contemporary armaments competition as a knightly struggle for victory unrelated to political or economic structures, he did so in terms of intellectual not practical, total not halfway, ideal not real solutions. The relation between end and means was out of balance. In place of a mere battle he postulated a total campaign which combined the Frederician multiple-front attack, the Napoleonic war of

annihilation, and the Moltkean concentration for encirclement: a sylla-
bus of Schlieffen's image of military history.[57]

SCHLIEFFEN'S CRITICS

Already in the 1890s, criticism of the "Schlieffen School" came from
retired army officers. A leader in this was Sigismund von Schlichting
(1828–1909) who saw combat while leading a company in 1866 and a
battalion in 1870–71, before serving eight years as commanding general
of the fourteenth Army Corps in Karlsruhe.[59] Schlichting was forced out
of active duty in 1896 as a "sacrifice to the mechanical brains of the
army."[60] In his first essay after retirement, he cautioned that what had
been correct for the Frederician era and overwhelmed the opponent at
that time could be a fatal mistake today. In 1907 he scathingly censured
the published Schlieffen essays.[61] Schlieffen's comments on the Battle of
Leuthen, Schlichting wrote, were clear only insofar as they related to a
reenactment of this battle carried out on the parade field of Berlin Kreuz-
berg! Frederick's operations at Leuthen were a first-class stroke of genius
for his time, for Napoleon's actions at Eylau they appear highly problematic, and in the present they would lead to catastrophe.[62] He concluded: "Schlieffen believed that the battle of encirclement was the philosopher's stone, which in all times and for all great commanders was
the truth."[63]

In 1899 the Great General Staff itself published *Frederick the Great's
Views on War in Their Development from 1745 to 1756*[64] against the
fears of some that "Delbrück will think he has won"; for this official
publication agreed that Frederick's strategy had been much more limited than Napoleon's. If Frederick, the work began, preferred wars of
attack, he aimed at reasonable bounds and achievable goals.[65] A comparison of the "refined restraint" of Frederick with the "reckless employment" of Napoleon showed clearly that the correct way in war did not lie
in magnificent plans but in the adjustment of plans to reality. Beyond a
certain size, it was impossible for tiny Prussia to enlarge its army, and
from this came Frederick's teaching of economy of forces.[66] Frederick
wanted to attack and destroy his opponents, but he understood that this
might cost enormous casualties without achieving the desired goal.[67] He
kept within the bounds of the possible. His war theory harmonized with
his circumstances.

General Friedrich von Bernhardi, retired from the army in 1909, very
possibly for his outspoken criticism of the "Schlieffen School" of
strategy,[68] published *On Today's War*[69] in 1912. This work is usually
interpreted as an imperialistic bombast. The political and historical

sections were lifted out and published under a separate title, *Germany and the Next War*, from whence numerous translations were made. It became a best seller and a political disaster, the first comprehensive expression of the militarist orientation.[70]

Something different, however, appears in the original German edition. Although bombastic and aggressive in its political statements, it also contains criticism of Schlieffen's ideas, in the purview of future war, which reflect the uncertainties of General Staff thinking in the decade before the war. According to Bernhardi, neither Frederician nor Napoleonic strategy, each created in a particular historical period, had been used unchanged in the campaigns of 1870. He considered it improbable that the experiences of these last wars could be applied without further modification in the future.[71] Bernhardi himself suggested the possibility of a return to the conditions of eighteenth-century warfare, dependence on magazines, and long lines of communication and supply.[72] Above all he feared the onset of technical bureaucratic control at the expense of personal leadership. The cavalry officer contrasted mechanistic operations, directed by telephone and telegraph from a rear-based headquarters, with the necessity for the commander himself to be at the decisive point of battle.[73] (Schlieffen envisioned the modern commander behind the lines in a comfortable chair surrounded by maps, telegraph, and telephone, sending inspired words forward.) Bernhardi did not think the General Staff had the correct operational or philosophical approach to warfare.

In an essay of 1912, General von Freytag-Loringhoven, chief quartermaster in the Great General Staff, revealed his own fears.[74] He admitted that even Frederick the Great had failed to carry out a strategy of annihilation. The weak armies of the period, filled mostly with mercenaries, were not sufficient for a far-ranging offensive. A strategy of annihilation had to await the larger national armies which came with Napoleon. The expansion of forces, the development of modern technology, and modern forms of credit created new means of strategy during the nineteenth century. But if the offensive power of the army had increased in contrast to earlier times, the expectation of fully annihilating an enemy state had been greatly reduced. Freytag thought it not entirely unlikely that a limited offensive might again be necessary.

Between 1904 and 1914, War Academy teacher Reinhold Koser delineated his position toward strategy in a multivolume *History of Frederick the Great*,[75] and in a series of articles.[76] On many points Koser concurred with Delbrück, although he, like his colleague Max Jähns, steadfastly refused to admit this publicly. Frederick, he wrote, understood he had insufficient strength for a total annihilation of Austria or Russia, but he remained strongly inclined to destroy an Austrian or a Russian army in the field: renunciation of a war of annihilation did not mean renunciation of battles of annihilation. Delbrück, Koser admitted, correctly placed eighteenth-century strategy within the framework of its political and military relationships.[77]

Delbrück was pleased to read Koser's views. Academically, the great controversy appeared over. But Delbrück wondered whether the officers understood this view. Had the voluminous work of the Historical Section of the Great General Staff correctly interpreted the wars of Frederick the Great? Delbrück answered no. A century after Frederick the Great, the Prussian General Staff no longer knew what kind of strategy Frederick had used.[78]

DELBRÜCK AS DEFENSE ANALYST

We have suggested that Delbrück served a dual role in German society as both historian of war and editor of the leading journal of political commentary. Although criticizing the officers for their image of the past, he did not attempt to do the same for future war planning. It did not occur to Delbrück to become a direct, public critic of current defense policy. The most basic reason for this lies in Delbrück's philosophy. His intellectual methods were above all historical, and he was well aware that they yielded relative value only when applied to past events. On more than one occasion he called the future an area of prophesy or fantasy. Although as historian he tried to bridge the gap between officer and professor, as a journalist he accepted a distinction between military historian and practitioner of war.[79]

Delbrück was well aware of the formal as well as the unwritten censorship laws of Imperial Germany. It is no accident that the most outspoken criticism of Schlieffen's ideas came from retired, inactive officers and that the most vehement criticism came only after 1905, when Schlieffen had left office. As noted by several officers from the relative sanctuary of the Weimar Republic, there was a formal system through which officers submitted work to the General Staff censor prior to publication. The army viewed itself as a closed family corporation whose intimate questions and internal disputes did not belong before the public.[80] In addition to a concern for a uniform, practical war doctrine, the General Staff desired to maintain a favorable public image of past wars. Finally, there was the touchy matter of subordinates criticizing superiors. Criticism of the ideas of the chief of the General Staff was by implication criticism of the kaiser.

Some if not all of these strictures extended to civilian society. We have seen that criticism of the General Staff image of Frederick the Great evoked suspicions of disloyalty to the Prussian State. Public criticism of the active army was unheard of in Imperial Germany. Delbrück, as a member of the bureaucratic elite, well knew the penalties for lèse majesté, for approaching too close to the allowable limits in public debate. Three times during the 1890s he had been threatened with legal action for statements in the *PJ*. The third time he was fined and reprimanded, after being threatened with removal from the university. These actions came in response to his criticism of Prussian "Germanization" policies in Posen and Schleswig.[81] To oppose the government directly on strategic matters, a much more sensitive area, would have courted disaster.

In any event, it is highly unlikely that Delbrück would have attempted this. For one thing he knew nothing of the actual German war plans. He had no access to such classified matters, and as we have indicated, he was both intellectually and socially inclined to leave future planning to the legitimate specialist. Delbrück had no inkling until after 1914 that the historical images of the General Staff might have any relationship to operational war planning. He did not take note of Schlieffen's published essays, recognizing they were unhistorical and considering them, in any event, only the reminiscences of a retired officer. Schlieffen's war images appeared to have little impact on the affairs of the nation. Few beyond the inner circle of the General Staff realized the tremendous impact of Schlieffen's "legacy." In short, Delbrück did draw a line between himself and the officers. As a professional historian he regarded the military past as his specialty; war in the future he relinquished to the officers.

But if Delbrück tended to separate his roles as historian and political commentator, nevertheless his own fears for the future were carefully expressed on a few occasions. In 1897, for example, Delbrück warned that it was thoughtless to imagine that the next war would be as short as Germany's last wars: a future war against France and Russia would be lengthy.[82] Only once prior to 1908 did he examine discussions which sustained such arguments. That occasion was his 1899 review of Ivan S. Bloch's *The Future of War in Its Technical, Economic and Political Relations.*[83] This celebrated work by a Polish-Jewish banker was translated from the Russian into German, English, and French and was widely circulated at the turn of the century. "Why has not humanity freed itself from the terrible evil of war?" Delbrück began. "Is it possible that our generation in the coming century will finally bring about this emancipation?"

Delbrück described Bloch's thesis: Modern weapons technology and mass conscription will result in a war so terrible that the misery resulting will be all out of proportion to the anticipated goal. Battles were no longer feasible because the fire of modern guns and cannons destroys everything within its range. If the old needle gun was deadly at eight hundred meters, today's rifles killed at two thousand meters. Rapid-fire smokeless cartridges and lighter weapons and cartridges produced much more severe wounds. The grenade of 1870 burst into about thirty pieces; modern schrapnel exploded into three hundred forty splinters. Cannons of 1891 were said to cause five times more casualties than those of 1870. Bloch asked who would win in this kind of war. His answer: no one.

Delbrück analyzed Bloch's discussion of demography, economics, and warfare. Until recently armies had fought with relatively small numbers. Prussia had about 3 percent of its population in the army in 1866 and 1870; at Königgrätz and Gravelotte 200,000 men fought. In the future, however, armies would not be counted in the hundred thousands but in the millions. In 1896 one reckoned that the war power of England, France, and Russia was 5,135,000 men, Germany-Austria 5,354,000 men. What would happen to modern economic life when all the leading personalities, all the businessmen, technicians, and factory directors were taken away and sent to the field? How would the families of these men be taken care of? Sea war destroys the trade on which economic life depends. Credit and banking will break down together. Not only England, but Germany needed large imports of food to live. If war cut this off, terrible hunger would result.

To what extent Bloch's view accorded with reality could not be known, Delbrück stated, but Bloch erred if he thought that the progress of technology had for the first time brought humanity into difficulties. The invention of the crossbow appeared so horrible that the Lateran Council of 1139 prohibited it. In the sixteenth century, French Marshal Tavannes complained that the newly perfected handguns had made battle murderous: earlier knights had fought for half a day without losing more than ten of five hundred men; now the same losses occurred in less than an hour.

Bloch's view of war in the future reminded Delbrück of eighteenth-century war. Frederick the Great tried a few times to overcome this fate, to pounce upon his enemies with enormous energy and destroy them, but it did him no good. Frederick remarked resignedly in the introduction to his *History of the Seven Years' War* that a victorious battle which sacrificed fifteen to twenty thousand men left a great breach in the army. Recruits could make up for the lost quantity but not for the quality of soldiers. Training was lengthy and the countryside was depopulated in rebuilding the army. In a long war, one found oneself finally at the head of poorly drilled, poorly disciplined peasants, with whom one scarcely dared to face the enemy.

Later, Frederick wrote in his *Military Testament* that the commander could attack strong positions only as a last resort, because the defense had the advantage. Frederick's victorious battles—such as Mollwitz and Leuthen—freed him temporarily from danger, but did not by themselves achieve victory. Casualties were enormous, almost a third of his entire army at Zorndorff, at Kunersdorf 35 percent, at Torgau 27 percent. Yet despite such sacrifices there was no decisive victory. Delbrück asked if these pictures out of the past were not similar to Bloch's image of the future.

If all these perceptions of Bloch's were correct, Delbrück admitted, the future world power would belong to the agricultural lands. Germany could not endure a long war of attrition. If it was true that great decisive battles were no longer possible—and there was no contemporary empirical evidence to support this—then the disruption of the opponent's economic life could destroy him. In the eighteenth century not so much the last man as the last thaler had made the difference. The only real reason to avoid battle in the future was the understanding that nothing could be gained.[84]

But similarity was not sameness, Delbrück carefully concluded. Historical analogies were instructive but could lead easily into error. It was not certain that contemporary strategy was forced necessarily into this eighteenth-century mold. Better weaponry had reduced tactics to the point where theoreticians were quite divided as to how a future battle should be fought. Delbrück admitted that even the German military could put forth no clear picture of future war. Many opposing theories were taught in the War Academy. But few had concluded that armies could no longer fight battles and had to defeat the enemy through limited war. Such questions were decided only with difficulty by theory; mainly they were decided by experience. If Bloch was correct about the impossibility or the purposelessness of great battles, his theories were in no way the same as evidence from current war experiences.

By comparing Bloch's arguments on the future with his own interpretation of the eighteenth century, Delbrück further supported his original thesis on Frederician strategy. But at the same time he carefully maintained that there was an important disjunction between past and future; the past was an imperfect guide for the future. History contained ambivalent evidence for peering ahead. Delbrück could not know how prophetic Bloch's description of war and economic life would be for World War I. In 1899 Delbrück's realistic imagination was unable to picture a war fought with heavy industrial weapons and million-man armies.

In the aftermath of the Bosnian crisis of 1908, Delbrück again considered current defense policy. He believed it was highly unlikely that there would be a war only between France and Germany; more probably England and Russia would support France. Therefore, population and army-size relationships became crucial in determining a realistic German foreign policy, and, if all else failed, military strategy as well. Clearly the military strength of France, England, and Russia was superior, and Delbrück did not believe that his country could count on significant Austrian support: in all probability the German Empire faced a two-front war alone. He wondered if Germany might anticipate a quick victory over France as had been the case in 1871. His conclusion was negative. Massive French fortifications, new technology, and difficult logistics associated with the million-man army would make any victory over France difficult and slow, especially with the necessity of sending part of the German army to the eastern front. He admitted there was a slim chance for a rapid victory against a portion of the Russian armies, before they had entirely mobilized, but this possibility had to be weighed against the continuing threat in the west. If the war went as the Seven Years' War had gone, both sides would become exhausted, international borders would remain unchanged, and the continent would be in ruins.[85]

During the Agadir Crisis of 1911, Delbrück strongly criticized those chauvinists who stirred up popular passions. He cautioned that a future European war would bring untold suffering with very little certainty of a favorable outcome for Germany. It would bring down upon Europe a deluge unparalleled in all of history, and would unleash the most terrible weapons of death ever invented. The Russo-Japanese conflict was only a limited colonial skirmish when compared to this potential devastation.[86]

Amid the rising tide of extreme nationalism in 1913, Delbrück cautioned that the greatest threat to the future of Germany was an unnecessary or accidental war. In a celebrated essay which evoked conservative wrath, Delbrück dismissed the possibility of leftist revolution. The greatest danger was not domestic revolution but Pan-German pressure for an extreme, thoughtless, and militant foreign policy. France, he reminded his readers, had been plunged into the catastrophe of 1870 by chauvinistic flood currents which had not been sensibly restrained. The greatest

threat to Germany's future was the spectre of a European war undertaken by accident or without sufficient cause. Unless conditions of absolute necessity arose, in which the existence of the nation was at stake,
Germany must keep the peace.[87]

Whether in politics or in military theory, Delbrück clearly was a voice
crying in the wilderness. If some of his ideas were known and accepted
within the military establishment, they had little or no impact on strategic philosophy or operational planning.

STRATEGIC IDEAS AND ACTIONS, 1904-14

Although the factors making for German strategic entry into World
War I coalesced only in the summer of 1914, many can be seen in the first
war of Wilhelmian Germany, in German South-West Africa against the
Herero, the Nama, and other African peoples in 1904-1907. The only
war experience of Imperial Germany in the forty-three years between
1871 and 1914, it confirmed not only the military images of the Schlieffen
School but also the political hopes of aggressive Pan-German foreign
policy.

In response to the killing of a hundred German colonists, the General
Staff launched a war of annihilation which resulted in the actual extir-
pation of several hundred thousand Africans. Although the Herero War
was initially accompanied by disagreements between the War Ministry,
General Staff, and Reich Chancellor over the German response, nonetheless it was Schlieffen who ordered a war of annihilation. General
Trotha stated that within the German boundaries every Herero, with or
without animals, with or without weapons, would be shot. Women and
children not fleeing outside German territory were to be killed along
with the rest. Schlieffen wrote to Reich Chancellor von Bülow that the
entire population had to be annihilated or at least removed from the
country. Investing 585 million marks and more than fourteen thousand
troops in a three-year war, the Germans attempted to surround and destroy these African peoples. Although not completely successful, the
Germans nevertheless destroyed more than 60 percent of the popula-
tions.[88] Schlieffen, who often stayed up all night to work on the plans,
issued the operations orders himself from Berlin. Officers who appeared
before him to give situation reports prepared as if for an examination.[89]

When General von Deimling negotiated a peace in 1907, ending the
Herero War, the Conservatives and Pan-Germans attacked him viru-
lently. "What you have done, Herr General, is un-Prussian. It is Prussian to destroy the enemy, not to make peace with him."[90]

Despite doubts, Schlieffen's ideas remained, except for minor changes, the basis for the war plan of Imperial Germany. There are some indications that Schlieffen's successor after January 1906, General von Moltke the younger, did not completely believe in them. Moltke was uncertain if the Belgian railway network, considered essential for troop transportation in the Schlieffen plan, would fall into German hands intact at the start of the war.[91] Clearly aware of the political problems which might be created by an invasion of Belgium, Moltke kept to the Schlieffen Plan, but without enthusiasm. For Moltke it was a last resort, a desperate act in a serious strategic dilemma. As for army strength, Moltke had no strong opinion prior to 1911, when a conflict developed within the military bureaucracy similar to that of the 1890s. Colonel Erich Ludendorff, chief of the deployment section of the Great General Staff and a Schlieffen disciple, transformed the latter's vague hope for eight new army corps into a high-priority, specific buildup. Under Ludendorff's promptings, General von Moltke in 1912 requested size increases of 300,000 men in two years, or an approximate 40 percent increase in peacetime effective strength. The War Ministry and Military Cabinet opposed this, and Ludendorff was removed from his post and given a regimental command to keep the peace between General Staff, War Ministry, and Military Cabinet.[92]

Nevertheless, the army bills of 1912 and 1913 enlarged the peacetime army by nearly 10 percent.[93] Moltke gave no indications of any original or new ideas for employing this enormous mass. Intelligent and sensitive, he may have recognized the truth in General von Haeseler's statement that the armed forces of a major power could not be carried off like putting a cat in a bag.[94] However, Moltke's attitude toward the Schlieffen Plan and to the general lines of the Schlieffen approach to war was symbolized in his advice to his son, Adam von Moltke. In preparation for Adam's entrance into the War Academy, in February 1914, his father sent him a copy of the "great Schlieffen standard work, *Cannae* and told him to study it energetically."[95]

NOTES

1 Ritter, *Sword and Scepter* 2:123ff.; Gordon Craig, *The Politics of the Prussian Army* (New York: Oxford University Press, 1955), pp. 251ff; Walter Goerlitz, *The History of the German General Staff*, trans. Brian Battershaw (New York: Praeger, 1957), pp. 116ff; Martin Kitchen, *The German Officer Corps, 1890–1914* (Oxford: Clarendon Press, 1968), pp. 1–23; Bernd F. Schulte, *Die deutsche Armee, 1900–1914: Zwischen Beharren und Verändern* (Düsseldorf: Droste Verlag, 1977), pp. 54–93.

2   Craig, *The Politics of the Prussian Army*, p. 235. Walter Elze, *Tannenberg* (Breslau: Ferdinand Hirt, 1928), pp. 5–6. Ritter, *The Sword and the Scepter* 2:202ff, 303.

3   A clear depiction of the complicated railroad timetables and planning is provided in the discussion of Groener's ten years as chief of the railroad section of the Great General Staff in Helmut Haeussler, "William Groener: General of the Imperial German Army," unpublished University of Wisconsin dissertation, 1953; J. W. Wheeler-Bennett, "Men of Tragic Destiny: Ludendorff and Groener," in R. Pares and A. J. P. Taylor, eds., *Essays Presented to Sir Lewis Namier* (London: St. Martins, 1956), pp. 475ff. Writing about the problem of understanding the July 1914 crisis and European war mobilization, Stephen Kern notes that "An accurate reconstruction of events up to July 25 requires a temporal precision accurate to the day; after that the hour, sometimes even the minute, becomes crucial." Stephen Kern, *The Culture of Time and Space, 1880–1918* (Cambridge: Harvard University Press, 1983), p. 264.

4   H. Stuart Hughes, *Consciousness and Society* (New York: Vintage, 1958), chs. 4 and 9; cf. George Mosse, *The Crisis of German Ideology* (New York: Grosset & Dunlap, 1964); Jacques Barzun, *Darwin, Marx, Wagner* (Garden City, New York: Doubleday Anchor, 1941); Gertrude Himmelfarb, *Darwin and the Darwinian Revolution* (New York: W. W. Norton, 1962), pp. 412ff.; Robert Wohl, *The Generation of 1914* (Cambridge, Mass.: Harvard University Press, 1979); Eric J. Leed, *No Man's Land: Combat & Identity in World War I* (London: Cambridge University Press, 1979); Roland N. Stromberg, *Redemption by War: The Intellectuals and 1914* (Lawrence, Kansas: The Regents Press of Kansas, 1982). How all of this reflected and often amplified in the Kaiser's retinue is nicely detailed in Isabel V. Hull, *The Entourage of Kaiser Wilhelm II, 1888–1918* (Cambridge: Cambridge University Press, 1982), chap. 9 and passim.

5   Hans Delbrück, "Die Alldeutschen," *PJ* 154 (December 1913): 577.

6   Ritter, *The Sword and the Scepter* 2:222ff. Cf. Fritz Klein, ed., *Deutschland im Ersten Weltkrieg*, 3 vols. (Berlin: Akademie-Verlag, 1971), 1:60–139.

7   Fischer, *War of Illusions*.

8   Walter Elze, *Graf Schlieffen* (Breslau: Ferdinand Hirt, 1928), p. 7.

9   Schlieffen recognized his own surprising move from obscurity to prominent appointment in the speech at his retirement dinner, 25 January 1906. Grosser Generalstab, ed., *Generalfeldmarschall Graf Alfred v. Schlieffen Gesammelte Schriften*, 2 vols. (Berlin: E. S. Mittler, 1913), 2:457.

10 General von Stein, *Erlebnisse und Betrachtungen aus der Zeit des Weltkrieges* (Leipzig: R. F. Koehler, 1919), pp. 28–30; Ernst von Eisenhart-Rothe, *Im Banne der Persönlichkeit* (Berlin: Oskar Franz Hubner, 1931), pp. 28–32; *Mackensen: Briefe und Aufzeichnungen*, ed. Wolfgang Eberster (Leipzig: Bibliographisches Institut, 1938), pp. 20–21; Helmut Kittle, *Alfred Graf Schlieffen: Jugend und Glaube* (Berlin: Verlag des Evangelischen Bundes, 1939), pp. 16ff.; John Hostetler, *Hutterite Society* (Baltimore: Johns Hopkins University Press, 1974), pp. 148ff.

11 Letter from his father of 13 April 1857, in Eberhard Kessel, *Alfred Schlieffens Briefe* (Göttingen: Vandenhoeck & Rupprecht, 1958), pp. 97–98.

12 Friedrich von Boetticher, *Schlieffen* (Göttingen: Musterschmidt, 1957), p. 21.

13 Quoted in Hugo Rochs, *Schlieffen* (Berlin: Vossische Buchhandlung, 1921), p. 15.

14 Quoted in Friedrich von Boetticher, "Der Lehrmeister des neuzeitlichen Krieges," in F. E. von Cochenhausen, *Von Scharnhorst zu Schlieffen* (Berlin: E. S. Mittler, 1933), p. 253.

15 Eberhard Kessel, "Die Tätigkeit des Grafen Waldersee als General Quartiermeister und Chef des Generalstabes der Armee," *Welt als Geschichte* 14 (1954): 181ff; Eberhard Kessel, "Moltke und die Kriegsgeschichte," *Militär-Wissenschaftliche Rundschau* 2 (1941): 96ff.

16 Kessel, "Moltke und die Kriegsgeschichte," 99.

17 Leszcznski was also chief of the War Archives and librarian of the General Staff. Hugo von Freytag-Loringhoven, *Menschen und Dinge wie ich sie in meinem Leben sah* (Berlin: E. S. Mittler, 1923), pp. 90−91.

18 From the memoirs of a student there before 1914, Heinrich Aschenbrandt, *Kriegsgeschichtsschreibung und Kriegsgeschichtsstudium im deutschem Heere* (Koenigstein: Historical Division, Foreign Military Studies Branch U.S. Army Europe, 1952), pp. 44ff. See Bernard Poten, *Geschichte des Militär-Erziehungs-und Bildungswesen*, 6 vols. (Berlin: A. Hoffmann, 1896), 4:253−91. Scharfenort, *Die Königliche Preussische Kriegsakademie.*

19 *Wie studiert man Kriegsgeschichte?* (Berlin: E. S. Mittler, 1904).

20 C. Hierl, "Ziele und Wege für das Studium der Kriegsgeschichte," *Militär-Wochenblatt*, 1910, 419. A well-known practitioner of this method was General Verdy du Vernois; cf. his *Studien über den Krieg*, 6 vols. (Berlin: E. S. Mittler, 1902−07), especially 1:1−29.

21 Friedrich von Bernhardi, a cavalry officer like Schlieffen, emphasized that aside from preparation of war plans and intelligence, the most important task of the Great General Staff was the education of the officer corps. *Denkwürdigkeiten aus meinem Leben*, p. 223.

22 Schlieffen speech at the unveiling of the Moltke statue on the Königsplatz, Berlin, 24 October 1905; Schlieffen, *Gesammelte Schriften* 2:442ff. It is interesting to compare Schlieffen's interpretation of Moltke with Delbrück's: in Schlieffen's mind Moltke appears as an intellectual, whereas in Delbrück's image Moltke's superior quality was his binding together of theory and practice.

23 Schlieffen's speech at the hundred-year anniversary celebration of the War Academy, 15 October 1910, ibid., 2:447. His definition of history reminds us of the Hutterian view of the past and of Schlieffen's reminiscences of the Battle of Königgrätz, where he sang the hymn, "Now Thank We All Our God." The final stanza of the hymn goes, "For thus it was, is now and shall be ever more."

24 Freytag-Loringhoven, Schlieffen's close associate from the 1890s on, wrote that Schlieffen looked back to Moltke's generation of officers, that generation which had been so influential in the era of Kaiser Wilhelm I, because they had studied so hard. The same could not be said of the present generation, Schlieffen lamented. Freytag-Loringhoven, *Menschen und Dinge*, p. 98. Erich Ludendorff, who worked with Schlieffen's operations plans from 1904, remarked that Schlieffen was too much a theoretician of pure strategy and not enough a practitioner of the military craft. Ludendorff, *Mein militärischer Werdegang* (Berlin: E. S. Mittler, 1923), pp. 88, 101. Eberhard Kessel downplayed Schlieffen's role as intellectual and his attachment to history. Kessel, however, failed to consider several kinds of evidence: (1) Schlieffen's final critiques from the staff exercises and maneuvers in the period 1891−1905 which, as we have seen, are based on historical references; (2) the impression which Schlieffen made as an intellectual upon contemporaries, one so strong that virtually the entire next generation referred to Schlieffen as the "master teacher" and "genius"; (3) Schlieffen's Hutterian background; and (4) the institutional framework in which Schlieffen was educated and lived throughout most of his life. In our interpretation we return to an older view orginally presented in Walter Elze's *Antrittsvorlesung* at Berlin in 1928.

Elze, one of Delbrück's last students, characterized Schlieffen as virtually a "fanatic of thought," which suggests that Schlieffen might be best understood from a psychological viewpoint. Elze, *Graf Schlieffen*, p. 8. Kessel, *Alfred Schlieffens Briefe*, p. 11. I am indebted to Professor Kessel for his comments on an earlier draft of an essay on Schlieffen. My indebtedness is all the more important as my own research has led me to conclusions which are often in direct contrast to his own. Generalleutnant a. D. Von Zoellner, "Schlieffens Vermächtnis," *Militär-wissenschaftliche Rundschau*, 4 January 1938, 54; Wilhelm Groener, *Das Testament des Grafen Schlieffen* (Berlin: E. S. Mittler, 1927), pp. 217, 244; Wilhelm Groener, *Der Feldherr wider Willen: Operative Studien über die Welt-Kriege*, 2nd ed. (Berlin: E. S. Mittler, 1931), p.xii; Ludwig Beck, *Studien* (Stuttgart: C. H. Beck's sche, 1955), pp. 83–87; Graf Hutten-Czapski, *Sechzig Jahre Politik und Gesellschaft*, quoted in Ritter, *The Sword and the Scepter* 2:205. Hajo Holborn in an important sense continued Walter Elze's interpretation in Holborn's "Moltke and Schlieffen: The Prussian-German School," in Earle, ed., *Makers of Modern Strategy*, pp. 172–205, especially p. 190.

25   Schlieffen, *Gesammelte Schriften* 2:488.

26   Ibid., 2:451.

27   Rudt von Collenberg, "Graf Schlieffen und die Kriegsformation der deutschen Armee," *Wissen und Wehr* 8 (1927): 606.

28   Gerhard Ritter, *The Schlieffen Plan: Critique of a Myth* (London: Oswald Wolff, 1958), p. 46.

29   Ritter traced the evolution of the plan of 1905, following Schlieffen's successive revisions from 1891 on as recorded in many very incomplete fragments, but he did not examine the development of Schlieffen's ideas beyond or outside these plans except in the comments by his chief aides. Eberhard Kessel edited his letters, few of which touch upon strategy or history in any orderly and comprehensive way. Kessel noted that Schlieffen had a definite attachment for history from his earliest days. Wilhelm Groener, one of Schlieffen's assistants in the Great General Staff, asked if Schlieffen was an historian and a scholar, and concluded that he was a genius. Walter Elze called Schlieffen a "fanatic of thought" and quoted the famous "War of the Present" essay of 1909, in which Schlieffen wrote that what was imaginable was attainable. Ritter, *The Schlieffen Plan*, passim; Kessel, *Alfred Schlieffens Briefe*, p. 11; Wilhelm Groener, *Das Testament des Grafen Schlieffen* (Berlin: E. S. Mittler, 1927), p. 237ff. Elze, *Graf Schlieffen*, pp. 8–9.

30   One of his biographers entitled his work, "Der Lehrmeister des neuzeitlichen Krieges," Friedrich von Boetticher, in Generalleutnant von Cochenhausen, *Von Scharnhorst zu Schlieffen* (Berlin: E. S. Mittler, 1933). Cf. Generalleutnant von Zoellner, "Schlieffens Vermächtnis," in *Militär-wissenschaftliche Rundschau*, 4 January 1938; Ernst von Eisenhart-Rothe, *Im Banne der Persönlichkeit* (Berlin: Verlag Oskar Franz Hubner, 1931), p. 8.

31   See Generalstab des Heeres, Kriegswissenschaftliche Abteilung, ed., *Dienstschriften des Chefs des Generalstabe der Armee Generalfeldmarshalls Graf von Schlieffen*, vol.1, *Die taktische strategischen Aufgaben aus dem Jahren 1891–1905* (Berlin: E. S. Mittler, 1937), pp. 3ff. (Hereinafter Schlieffen, *Dienstschriften 1*).

32   Ibid., p. 22.

33   Generalstab des Heeres, Kriegswissenschaftliche Abteilung, ed., *Dienstschriften des Chefs des Generalstabes der Armee Generalfeldmarschalls Graf von Schlieffen*, vol. 2, *Die Grossen Generalstabsreisen-Ost aus den Jahren 1891–1905* (Berlin: E. S. Mittler, 1937), pp. 53–101. (Hereinafter Schlieffen, *Dienstschriften 2*).

34   Schlieffen *Dienstschriften* 1: 51–52.

35   Ibid., pp. 61–66.

36   Ibid., 2: 171.

37   Kessel, *Alfred Schlieffens Briefe*, p. 296. Many of Schlieffen's contemporaries felt these same fears, as demonstrated in Jonathan Steinberg, "The Copenhagen Complex," pp. 21–44 of Walter Laqueur and George L. Mosse, eds., *1914: The Coming of the First World War* (New York: Harper Torchbook, 1966). Interestingly enough, such fears also gripped the French General Staff during these years. Cf. Paul-Marie de la Gorce, *The French Army*, trans. Kenneth Douglas (New York: George Braziller, 1963), pp. 55, 85.

38   Ritter, *Schlieffen Plan*, p. 43.

39   Freytag-Loringhoven, *Menschen und Dinge*, pp. 96–99.

40   Delbrück, *Geschichte der Kriegskunst* 1: 326ff.

41   Schlieffen, *Dienstschriften* 1:68–69.

42   Speech at the General Staff celebration of the one-hundredth anniversary of Moltke's birth, 25 November 1900. Schlieffen, *Gesammelte Schriften* 2: 439.

43   Schlieffen speech at the dedication of the Moltke memorial, 26 October 1905. Ibid., 2: 442.

44   Schlieffen, *Dienstschriften* 1:85–87.

45   Ibid., 2:222, 230.

46   Ibid., 2:301–09.

47   Ibid., 1:102–17.

48   Grosser Generalstab, ed., *Der Schlachterfolge, mit welchen Mitteln wurde sie erstrebt?* (Berlin: E. S. Mittler, 1903).

49   Schlieffen, *Dienstschriften* 1:123.

50   Ibid., 1:138–39. In reaching these conclusions, Schlieffen falls squarely within the mainstream of European military thought at this time. As the commandant of the French War School, Jean L. A. Colin, wrote in 1912: "It would be absurd to think that one could fight without attacking. The attack is the normal mode of action in war. . . . No one should be allowed to command armies who is not disposed by nature to take the offensive. Far from fearing a struggle, a general should desire it, he should be eager to fight." Jean Colin, *The Transformations of War*, translation of *Les Transformations de la guerre* (Paris, 1912), by L. H. R. Pope-Hennessy (London: Hugh Rees, 1912), p. 335.

51   Gerhard Ritter's conclusions, *Schlieffen Plan*, p. 50; Ritter, *Sword and Scepter* 2:224; Fischer, *War of Illusions*, p. 119. Stephen Kern calls the Schlieffen Plan "the most ambitious project ever undertaken for controlling the immediate future of so many people." *The Culture of Time and Space*, p. 285.

52   *Vierteljahreshefte für Truppenführung und Heereskunde*, Freytag-Loringhoven, *Menschen und Dinge*, p. 100. Freytag-Loringhoven not only edited this, with the help of Hermann von Kuhl, but made the original contact with the publisher, E. S. Mittler, the General Staff publishing house.

53   See the *Vierteljahreshefte* issues for 1906–12, reprinted in Schlieffen, *Gesammelte Schriften* 1:23ff. Less than a year before his death, Schlieffen wrote to Freytag-

Loringhoven that the flank attack was the essence of all military history. Kessel, *Alfred Schlieffens Briefe*, p. 317.

54 Hajo Holborn, "Moltke and Schlieffen: The Prussian-German School," in E. M. Earle, ed., *Makers of Modern Strategy*, p. 190; Jehuda Wallach, *Das Dogma der Vernichtungsschlacht* (Frankfurt a/M.: Bernard & Graefe, 1967), pp. 68–69. General von Freytag remarked in the introduction to the 1925 edition of Schlieffen's essays that Schlieffen often attributed his own ideas to military leaders of the past, that he was not always just to the actors of war history, and that Schlieffen always aspired to illustrate the ideal in his writings in order to establish clear guidelines for the officer corps. General-Fieldmarshall Graf Schlieffen, *Cannae* (Berlin: E. S. Mittler, 1925), pp. vii–ix; General von Schlichting had already written before the World War that Schlieffen's historical writings mixed together local outflanking, attack around a forward battle line, and attack across two operational fronts because Schlieffen wanted to create a uniform teaching in regard to the battle of encirclement. Freiherr von Gayl, *General von Schlichting*, p. 350.

55 Schlieffen, *Gesammelte Schriften* 2:456.

56 In a letter of 7 November 1910 to Hans Delbrück, *Nachlass Delbrück*, DSB.

57 Eckart Kehr, *Battleship Building and Party Politics*, pp. 363–65; Walter Elze, *Tannenberg* (Breslau: Ferdinand Hirt, 1923), p. 30ff.; Hans-Ulrich Wehler, *Krisenherde des Kaiserreichs 1871–1918* (Göttingen: Vandenhoeck & Ruprecht, 1970), pp. 92–96. Ideas for battles of annihilation also dominated naval strategic planning at this time. Carl-Axel Gemzell, *Organization, Conflict, and Innovation: A Study of German Naval Strategic Planning, 1888–1940* (Lund: Esselte, 1973), pp. 50ff.; L. C. F. Turner, "The Significance of the Schlieffen Plan," in Paul M. Kennedy, ed., *The War Plans of the Great Powers, 1880–1914* (London: George Allen & Unwin, 1979), pp. 199–221.

58 Egon Freiherr von Gayl, *General von Schlichting und sein Lebenswerk* (Berlin: George Stilke, 1913), p. 261.

59 Ibid.

60 Goerlitz, *History of the German General Staff*, p. 136.

61 Gayl, *General von Schlicting*, pp. 342ff. Cf. letters from Schlichting to Delbrück from the period 1900–1907, *Nachlass Delbrück*, DSB, in which this criticism is repeated. Schlichting had written a favorable review of the first volume of *Geschichte der Kriegskunst* in the official *Reichs-Anzeiger*, which Delbrück was apparently very much concerned about. Letter of 13.7.1901. Most of their correspondence, however, related to various perspectives on the Prussian and Austrian generals of the years 1866–71 and after, whom Schlichting knew personally or by anecdote.

62 Gayl, *General von Schlichting*, p. 345.

63 Ibid., pp. 346–50.

64 Grosser Generalstab, Abteilung für Kriegsgeschichte II, ed., *Friedrich des Grossen Anschauungen vom Kriege in ihrer Entwicklung von 1745 bis 1756* (Berlin: E. S. Mittler, 1899).

65 Ibid., p. 346.

66 Ibid., p. 349.

67 Ibid., p. 346.

68 Goerlitz, *History of the German General Staff*, p. 136; Ritter, *Sword and Scepter* 2:112.

69 *Vom Heutigen Krieg*, 2 vols. (Berlin: E. S. Mittler, 1912).

70   Ritter, *Sword and Scepter* 2:113.

71   Bernhardi, *Vom heutigen Krieg* 1:41.

72   Ibid., 1:45.

73   Ibid., 1:57–64; 2:157–90. Bernhardi, a cavalry officer, was undoubtedly reacting to Schlieffen's image of the commander of the future, which the latter had described in one of his essays in the *Quarterly Journal for Troop Leadership and Army Science*. The modern commander, Schlieffen posited, remained far to the rear in a house with roomy offices, where telegraph and wireless, telephone, and signalling instruments were at hand, while a fleet of automobiles and motorcycles waited for orders. Sitting in a comfortable chair before a large table, the modern Alexander overlooked the whole battlefield on a map, sent inspiring words by telephone and received reports from his army and corps commanders. Quoted in Hajo Holborn, "Moltke and Schlieffen: The Prussian-German School," in Earle, ed. *Makers of Modern Strategy*, p. 194.

74   "Die Offensive mit beschränktem Ziel," *Vierteljahreshefte für Truppenführung und Heereskunden* 1 (1911):250–57. Two years before this, Freytag emphasized that the officer corps needed practically trained officers, not those with scholarly education. Cf. his "Theorie und Praxis bei König Friedrich, Napoleon und Motlke," *Vierteljahreshefte für Truppenführung und Heereskunden* 1(1909):31.

75   Geschichte Friedrichs des Grossen, 4 vols., 5th ed. (Berlin: Cotta, 1914).

76   For example, "Die prussische Kriegführung im 7-jährigen Kriege," *HZ* 132(1904): 238–73; essay by the same title, *HZ* 133(1905):71–76; cf. correspondence between Delbrück and Koser, *Nachlass Delbrück*, Deutsche Staatsbibliothek, Fas. 125.

77   Koser, "Die preussische Kriegführung im Siebenjahrigen Kriege," *HZ* 132(1904):258.

78   Hans Delbrück, "Ein Nachwort zu Kosers Aufsätzen über Friedrichs des Grossen Kriegführung," *HZ* 133(1905):66–70. Delbrück had had a long letter exchange with Herrn Toeche-Mittler of E. S. Mittler, publisher of the General Staff *History of the Wars of Frederick the Great* in 1890 and 1891. Toeche-Mittler tried to mediate between Delbrück and the officers. Delbrück sought to convince Toeche-Mittler that his position on Frederician strategy was the correct one. As with most of Delbrück's controversies, the exchange left both parties unchanged. Cf. Toeche-Mittler letters from February 1890 through May 1891 and Delbrück's replies, *Nachlass Delbrück*, DSB.

79   Delbrück considered historical depth valuable for the military practitioner, but also potentially dangerous because many things may appear relatively the same, whereas the practitioner must seek an absolute rule; he must strive to attain absolute certainty of a single view as a basis for action. Hans Delbrück, "Review of von Caemmerer, Die Entwicklung," *PJ* 115:347–51.

80   Generalleutnant z. D. Otto von Moser, *Ernsthafte Plaudereien über den Weltkrieg* (Stuttgart: Chr. Belser, 1925), p. 34; Generalmajor z. D. von Gleich, *Die alte Armee und ihre Verirrungen* (Leipzig: R. F. Koehler, 1919), p. 88. It is worth noting that these works, critical of the imperial army, were not published by the "official" General Staff publisher, E. S. Mittler of Berlin. Cf. Wilhelm Deist, "Die Armee in Staat und Gesellschaft 1890–1918," 321; cf. David Schoenbaum, *Zabern 1913: Consensus Politics in Imperial Germany* (London: George Allen & Unwin, 1982).

81   Thimme, *Hans Delbrück als Kritiker der Wilhelminischen Epoche*, pp. 77–100; cf. Jörn-Peter Leppien, "Theodor Brix—ein Kritiker der preussischen Nordschleswig-Politik (1888–1905)," in *Zeitschrift der Gesellschaft für Schleswig-Holsteinische Geschichte* 95 (1970): 159–94.

82   Hans Delbrück, *PJ* (October 1897), 176.

83   Delbrück used the German edition: Johann von Bloch, *Der Krieg,* Übersetzung des russischen Werkes des Autors: *Der Zukünftige Krieg in seiner technischen, volkswirtschaftlichen und politischen Bedeutung* (Berlin: Puttkammer und Muhlbrecht, 1899). See "Zunkunftskrieg und Zukunftsfriede," *PJ* 96 (May 1899), reprinted in Delbrück, *Erinnerungen, Aufsätze und Reden,* pp. 498-525.

84   Delbrück, "Zukunftskriege und Zukunftsfriede," pp. 520-25. For Delbrück's analysis of Bloch from a different perspective, see Roger Chichering, *Imperial Germany and a World Without War: The Peace Movement and German Society, 1892-1914* (Princeton: Princeton University Press, 1975), pp. 403-06. Cf. T. H. E. Travers, "Technology, Tactics, and Morale: Jean de Bloch, the Boer War and British Military Theory, 1900-1914," *Journal of Modern History,* vol. 51, no. 2 (June 1979), 264-86.

85   Hans Delbrück, "Kriegsgefahr," *PJ* (23 December 1908), reprinted in Delbrück, *Vor und nach dem Weltkrieg* (Berlin: Otto Stollberg, 1926), pp. 259-75.

86   Hans Delbrück, "Der Abschluss des Morokko-Kongo-Handels und die Reichstagswahlen. Verstärkte Rüstungen: Flotte oder Armee?" *PJ* (December 1911), reprinted in Delbrück, *Vor und nach dem Weltkriege,* pp. 352-61.

87   Hans Delbrück, "Die Alldeutschen," *PJ* (December 1913), reprinted in Delbrück, *Vor und nach dem Weltkrieg,* pp. 397-403. Delbrück's fears were well-founded as Roger Chickering has so well pointed out in *We Men Who Feel Most German: A Cultural Study of the Pan-German League, 1866-1914* (Boston: George Allen & Unwin, 1984), especially chapters 4, 10 & 11; for the political pressure groups of Wilhelmian Germany see Geoff Eley, *Reshaping the German Right: Radical Nationalism and Political Change after Bismarck* (New Haven: Yale University Press, 1980).

88   See Helmut Bley, *Kolonialherrschaft und Sozialstruktur in Deutsch-Südwestafrika* (Hamburg: Leibniz Verlag, 1968), pp. 189-208; Hans-Ulrich Wehler, *Krisenherde des Kaiserreichs* (Göttingen: Vandenhoeck & Ruprecht, 1970), ch. 3.

89   General von Freytag-Loringhoven, *Graf Schlieffen* (Leipzig: Historia Verlag, 1920), p. 40.

90   Letter of General von Deimling to Reichsminister Matthias Erzberger, front page, *Vorwärts: Berliner Volksblatt,* 8 August 1919. "Do You remember me, Herr Erzberger?" Deimling asked. "As I was attacked in 1907 you were the only one who defended me in the Reichstag. During the war I was in favor of a peace of agreement; it was clear we could not win against the whole world. May you come safely out of this heavy bombardment and please accept this small comfort from an old soldier in this difficult battle."

91   Wallach, *Dogma der Vernichtungsschlacht,* pp. 129-32. Cf. Martin van Crefeld, *Supplying War: Logistics from Wallenstein to Patton* (Cambridge: Cambridge University Press, 1977) pp. 109-41.

92   Ritter, *Sword and Scepter* 2: 218-26. Elze, *Tannenberg,* pp. 36ff.

93   Ritter, *Sword and Scepter* 2: 220ff., 306.

94   Quoted in Wallach, *Dogma der Vernichtungsschlacht,* p. 145.

95   Ibid., p. 133. Bernd Schulte's thesis is that an "objective weakening of the German army took place between 1900 and 1914. This was caused by tension between the army's domestic function—employment in a possible civil war—and demands for large-scale expansion and the introduction of massive technological change and new weapons. Thus it was caught and held between demands for continuity and those for change. *Die deutsche Armee,* pp. 548-50 and passim.

4 / THE WORLD WAR

"War images" as we have been using the term, a confrontation between two theories of strategy, attrition and annihilation, and two kinds of thought, historical and operational, had reached an inconclusive deadlock by 1914. Some of Delbrück's original opponents were dead or had retired; others, like General Friedrich von Bernhardi, played important roles in the World War. The writing of military history ceased during hostilities. Officers were preoccupied with fighting the war, while professors supported these efforts with speeches, writings, and service in governmental or patriotic organizations. Students in the university dwindled to a very few by 1917. War Academy classes were given accelerated courses to speed them to active duty. Apparently the controversy had died. Just at this point, however, it was given new life. As Delbrück had so clearly pointed out in his assessment of Bloch's *The Future of War,* strategic questions were not ultimately decided by theory. The "proof" of a strategic idea was found only in experience.

World War I profoundly altered the conflict, for here the images of prewar history and theory joined with the realities of the first industrial mass war. Delbrück's historical concept of attrition received complete and terrible expression while the war proved Schlieffen's strategic ideal of annihilation incorrect under these unique circumstances.

Although many military leaders were uncertain and apprehensive, Imperial Germany entered World War I committed to the Schlieffen Plan: a lightning war of annihilation to destroy France, followed by a rapid deployment of troops east for an attack against Russian forces. Victory in a two-front war, as Schlieffen had often preached, was attainable by following religiously the timetable of the plans. But war has its own dynamics. The preplanned victory in the west failed to materialize. By September 1914 Erich von Falkenhayn had replaced the German commander in chief, Helmuth von Moltke the younger, and a second period of war began whose dominant motif was attrition and stalemate in the west, gradual success in the east. For an officer corps, a monarchy, and a bureaucracy educated in the tradition of a single legitimate form— attack and annihilate—the strain of attrition was too great and its successes too unclear. Few could appreciate a moderate policy with modest results until they had to compare it with an extreme policy whose failures became disastrous. The strategy of attrition was not continued to successful political conclusion of the war. Germany's third strategic period began in August 1916 with Falkenhayn's replacement by Erich Ludendorff and a return to the annihilative strategy of the Schlieffen School. Temporary victory in the east against Russia was followed by final defeat in the west at the hands of Britain, France, and the United States. The German attempt to win by a strategy of annihilation— unrestricted submarine warfare in 1917, and the spring offensive in 1918—was halted and overwhelmed by Allied superiority and German deficiency in men and material.

As editor of the most important political monthly in Prussian-Germany, Hans Delbrück was finally compelled to apply his historical expertise to current military affairs, which, with a few exceptions, he had carefully avoided prior to 1914. In doing so, he faced great obstacles. The dictum that fifty years should pass before an historical assessment could be valid was virtually a rule in German scholarship. The historian needed adequate sources and a dimension of time from the events in order to write with scientific objectivity: defense analysis appeared to violate proper intellectual procedure. War, moreover, meant the cessation of party politics *(Burgfrieden)*, tight censorship, and an incomplete flow of information.[1] Reichstag members, government officials, and the German chancellor had difficulty at times in discovering truth about the war. A civilian professor, even with many political contacts, had little chance to obtain sufficient trustworthy information. Finally, Delbrück was a patriot. He had fought in 1870, taught within the royal family, served in politics under Bismarck and in the military under Moltke. He believed in Prussian-Germany.

Despite the great obstacles of methodology, incomplete information, and his own strong patriotism, Delbrück tried his best to convey to readers and friends what was happening during the fifty months of World War I. His general understanding of armies and society, his perception not only of the large-scale battlefield action but of its interworkings with politics and economic life, allowed him to understand as few of his contemporaries did. Delbrück's historical methods informed his wartime perceptions, and the experience of war deepened his historical insights. By 1918 his writing fully evoked the material realities which had overwhelmed his country. He declared that large doses of idealism could not ultimately overcome a misunderstanding of technology and insufficient economic means to wage war.

This understanding, though incomplete, caused him great pain. As he wrote in December 1918, persons with moderate views during war faced a dilemma. It was easy to sound clarion calls to annihilate the enemy. Those who advised Germany to destroy the enemy completely, he said, led to its downfall. But whoever said that Germany should not do this was in danger of weakening confidence in victory and the will to fight. Until 1914 Delbrück separated his two lives, as professor dealing with the military past and as publicist concerned with the political present. His striving for historical reality did not openly conflict with his sense of political legitimacy. After 1914 this became increasingly difficult and finally impossible.

Delbrück's analysis of the war and his changing position regarding the military leadership fall into four distinct periods: (A) 1914, (B) 1915–August 1916, (C) August 1916–1917, and (D) 1918.[2]

THE FIRST WAR YEAR

The first official German war aims proclaimed on August 4, 1914, in speeches to the German Reichstag by Kaiser Wilhelm and Chancellor Bethmann Hollweg, were defensive and emphasized that Germany would by necessity defend its place in the European political system but was animated by no will to conquest.[3] These declarations sharply contrasted with the General Staff war plans and strategic doctrine of the previous quarter century. The initial German victories, the emotional release of a great war after decades of peace, the underlying desire for a larger share of world power which for years inspired German rhetoric, and the great outflow of German blood in the first few weeks soon resulted in an entirely different spirit. A ground swell of popular enthusiasm soon was in step with the first great military actions. For many Germans the war psychosis, known as "the ideas of 1914," invested the fighting with an ideological cloak of necessity to conquer.[4]

From the outset Delbrück's patriotism was different. He did not become caught up in the flurry of war-born psychological emotions. In the *Preussische Jahrbücher* for August 23, 1914, he urged moderation.[5] Imperial Germany should aim to restore the European balance of power on land and at sea. By declaring war, England had forfeited her position as guarantor of this equilibrium. To a colleague he suggested that in order to break English sea power it might be necessary to make peace with France or Russia or with both.[6] Delbrück cautioned against the economic dangers of a long war. He noted that the fighting had begun at a fortunate time for Germany. Because of a good harvest, food would last for at least a year. However, raw materials for German industry could no longer be easily obtained. Germany needed enormous imports to keep her factories in operation. He suggested the possibility of widespread unemployment resulting from a long-lasting English sea blockade. Voicing deep concern over the march through Belgium, he said that while this gave the chance for a decisive battle, without it Germany might have gained British neutrality and more active assistance from Italy. The same restrained optimism was reflected in public lectures of August and September, warning against chauvinism and unlimited war aims.[7]

By October 1914 Delbrück already perceived that the World War differed from nineteenth-century European wars and from the expectations based upon them. He cautioned that information on current military actions was fragmentary and impossible to understand completely; however, certain fundamentals were clear. Most important, the enormously increased impact of new, more powerful weapons had brought dramatic changes. The attacking lines were organized into threadlike formations. Columns had virtually disappeared. With a front 400,000 meters long, German troops were concentrated in some places and spread out at others. Breakthrough by a massed force, which commanders of earlier periods had advocated, was no longer possible. The defensive power of modern weapons was so great that even the thinnest line resisted frontal attack. Because the wide-planted flanks of the defense could circumvent their attackers, an initial advance could be thrown back and turned into a rout.

As a muted corollary to this military analysis, Delbrück broached the idea of peace. As long as each side hoped to defeat the other there was no prospect of peace; neutrals, however, were already discussing it. Complete security would come only by subjugating an enemy who was thus forcibly prevented from renewing the war. The Romans used this as the basis for their world empire. Fortunately this was no longer possible. A second method was to create great provincial dependencies, to build occupation fortresses and squeeze the enemy economically. Napoleon I did this in Prussia after 1807: material oppression served only to awaken German moral power. God protect the German Reich from embarking on Napoleonic conquests after its expected victory. An unending series of wars would result. Conditions for peace will only be created by a combination of power and forbearance: political moderation to disarm the mistrust aroused by armed force. "We must avoid the mistake Napoleon made," he cautioned, "in simultaneously trying to defeat England and to achieve continental hegemony. In attempting both, Napoleon lost everything."[8]

Belgium, he emphasized in private correspondence, must be returned as an independent state upon successful conclusion of hostilities. This was absolutely essential to effect a stable peace and not just an armistice.

Although Germany might hope for additional colonies abroad if the war ended soon and successfully, Belgium should not be used as a bargaining pawn in these negotiations.

A few days before Christmas, 1914, Delbrück reinforced these views with a direct analogy to eighteenth-century warfare.[9] He noted that since September both armies had faced each other from virtually unattackable positions. Although the German assault might have been decisive after Antwerp fell, the enormous Allied forces were too great. Actions by both sides had caused tremendous damage but had not altered the military situation. Since the days of Frederick the Great a strategic situation such as this had been unknown. As in the eighteenth century, increased firepower and changed technology made attack treacherous. Frederick the Great, however, faced many unattackable positions by employing a "double-poled" strategy. He tried both to destroy his enemy in battle and to exhaust him by limited warfare—by maneuver, by seizing provinces, and by waging economic warfare. Delbrück reassured his readers that both similarities and differences existed between contemporary war and war in the eighteenth century. For one thing, it was yet unclear if the pause in fighting in the west was only temporary and might end with a breakthrough and the complete annihilation of the French. For another, the victories of Hindenburg over the Russians were much greater than Frederick's victory at Zorndorf. By 1758 Frederick had lost significant portions of his land, in addition to the battles of Kolin, Kunersdorf, Hochkirch, and Maxen. The German Empire, by contrast, had not lost a single battle.

Delbrück's moderation evoked intense criticism. The German crown prince called publicly for his removal from the university, and the conservative press attacked his statements.[10] The deputy commander in the Mark Brandenburg, General von Kessel, forbade Delbrück to discuss specific war aims in public. After failing to convince the general of the necessity for limited war aims, Delbrück argued that his writings were sanctioned by the chancellor of the German Reich prior to publication. So much the worse for the chancellor, Kessel remarked: the prohibition stood.[11] Delbrück's stand evoked limited support even from leftist groups. The Socialist *Vorwärts* compared his views to the kaiser's defensive proclamation at the beginning of the war.[12]

In response to German military successes, to public clamor for conquest, and to attacks by political opponents, Delbrück further defined his position. As compensation for giving up political expansion in the war-conquered western theatre, he proposed limited German expansion in the east: the creation of a buffer state out of part of Tsarist Poland. He was to build on this idea of eastern expansion as the war progressed,

changing it as his perception of German strategic possibilities and problems developed.[13]

Because of his broad view of armies and society, Delbrück saw the
World War in a far different light than most of his contemporaries. At
the height of emotional patriotism he urged limited strategic aims. Sixty
days into the fighting he mentioned the possibility of peace. Before the
first war Christmas, Delbrück evoked the example of Frederick the Great
and placed the World War into the context of his familiar dialectic of the
history of war in Western civilization. As in the prewar period, few in
positions of political or military influence could understand his analysis
or support his conclusions.

THE WAR OF ATTRITION, 1915–AUGUST 1916

During the next eighteen months, Delbrück tried a variety of means to
turn his country away from a strategy which he feared would lead to its
destruction. Two statements of early 1915 reiterated his limited war aims
and underlined what he considered the proper role of civilian government in military planning. In comparing the German army with that of
France, England, and Russia, Delbrück asserted that it was superior, but
only for defensive operations.[14] The German army—which he said was
15 percent professional, 85 percent reserve—fought only to defend the
existence and honor of the Reich against foreign attack. Somewhat
naively he argued that it was not an effective instrument for an expansionist foreign policy because the German people desired no war of
conquest.

In his book *Bismarck's Heritage*, Delbrück suggested that Germany
should carry forward Bismarckian traditions in four aspects of national
life.[15] First was the sharing of responsibility within the government.
Each of the three major Reich positions had its own sphere of action.
The chancellor was a politician but not a strategist. The chief of the
General Staff was a strategist but not a politician. The kaiser stood between and above both, ready to accept counsel, to mediate, but having
the final say in all matters. It was important for the kaiser to follow the
best available advice.[16] Second was the significance of the Reichstag as an
important arm of government. Bismarck did not retire, Delbrück reasoned, because of personal difficulties with the kaiser but because he
could no longer work with the parliamentary majority. General von
Caprivi accomplished things which Bismarck could not because he was
free from the specific obligations and relationships which had hindered
the Iron Chancellor.[17] The power of the Reichstag had to be respected.
As for foreign policy, Delbrück mentioned that although Bismarck had

opposed colonization in Poland and East Africa, circumstances had changed since the 1880s; Germany could now aspire to expansion, but this should be in Africa or Asia, not in Europe.[18] He hoped that proper compensation for Germany in a future peace would include enlarged colonial possessions—a "German India" large enough to support its own troops, with coaling stations, harbors, munitions and weapons factories.[19] Finally, Delbrück noted Bismarcks's overriding concern for peace and the balance of power. Bismarck in the 1890s, like Delbrück in 1915, hoped that no German kaiser would look at the European map with longings of Napoleonic conquest.[20]

As was his custom before the war,[21] Delbrück communicated his views regularly to various Reich officials. Rudolf von Valentini, chief of the kaiser's Civil Cabinet, and very sensitive to the balance of power between kaiser, chancellor and generals, read *Bismarcks Erbe* with interest and pleasure. "Many of these viewpoints are new to me," he wrote Delbrück, "but the general line of argument, in relation to our present situation, is thoroughly sympathetic."[22] The kaiser read his book,[23] as did the chief of the General Staff, Erich von Falkenhayn, who wrote to Delbrück, "I have read your book with the liveliest interest, and cannot suppress one question: What did Bismarck and what do you understand by a 'preventive war'?" Delbrück replied that one could differentiate between several kinds of preventive war: (1) conscious and desired offensive warfare, the great *moteur* of world history; (2) purely defensive war; and (3) a preventive war undertaken because an opponent had offensive action clearly in mind and therefore war was unavoidable. Delbrück emphasized that the boundary between forms (2) and (3) was uncertain and changeable, but that the main distinction between them was very important. Germany could conceivably have gained certain strategic advantages by starting a war in 1909 or 1911. In that case, however, the government would have lacked one essential advantage: broad public support for the government's policy of defensive war.[24] The difference between a preventive and a defensive war, Delbrück maintained, was a certain sense of reality that would not overlook political factors so crucial in military decisions.[25]

By the summer of 1915, domestic war aims groups had coalesced around positions which became more sharply defined as the war progressed. The larger group, the "annexationists," headed by Dietrich Schäfer and Georg von Below, carried forward aggressive Pan-German political aims. With over thirteen hundred professors, officials, officers, and businessmen, they published the "Petition of the Intellectuals" of June 1915, which called for exactly what Delbrück warned against: German political expansion in Belgium and eastern France. On July 7, during a meeting of the smaller moderate group, Delbrück spoke at length urging a counterpetition, and his committee drafted a resolution which drew fewer than two hundred signatures—including Max Planck's, Albert Einstein's, and Max Weber's—opposing the annexation of politically independent peoples.[26]

With the western front stabilized during most of 1915 and German victories on the eastern front, Delbrück's commentary turned to the economic undergirdings of war. Although unable to perceive its full impact clearly, Delbrück discerned that both the possibilities and the problems of long-term war depended on economics and technology.

In reviewing the fighting at Ypres, he noted that each side had equally strong positions and that even when they overwhelmed the first position, the attackers were halted by a second and a third. In the east, however, the Germans had achieved the "impossible" breakthrough. One reason was that the eastern front was twice as long as the western, and therefore more thinly defended. Another reason was that the Central Powers could bring up reserves by rail, whereas the Russians had far fewer rail lines.[27] Even though both sides lost huge amounts of weapons and supplies, Germany retained the advantage.[28] Delbrück reasoned that Russian industry was incapable of equipping its newly raised armies. Even with imports from Japan and America, Russian war requirements were met by extracting raw materials and economic goods from the civilian sector. Delbrück predicted that this kind of robbery would eventually bankrupt the civilian economy.[29]

In spite of German successes in the autumn of 1915, Delbrück cautioned that this new kind of war imposed hitherto unknown pressures. By quoting foreign newspapers and masking his arguments in patriotic rhetoric acceptable to the censor, he attempted to present arguments not normally allowed in print. For example, in October 1915, to restate his fears regarding Germany's material vulnerability, Delbrück quoted neutral observers. They believed that Germany's inability to replenish her losses would ultimately bring defeat, whereas England and France had free access to the world market. This may be true, Delbrück carefully observed; however, the moral power to act and the will to resist were the decisive elements in war. In Russia, tension between government and people was so great that a revolution might be expected. In England, public opinion was badly divided over general conscription. In France, the government experienced difficulty financing the war. He concluded patriotically that belief was half of victory. This was beginning to wane in France and Russia. It may still exist in England, but it continued strong in Germany.[30]

As both a concession to German military successes and an attempt to turn the powerful annexationist war aims movement away from western Europe, Delbrück gave his assent to the "freeing" of Kurland and Livland from the Tsarist yoke. Beyond this, however, he separated himself sharply from those Pan-Germans who demanded "Germanization" of the newly conquered areas.[31]

As 1915 closed, Delbrück realized that few of Germany's leaders understood the war of attrition. In October and December he repeatedly warned that the fighting on the eastern front had reached a deadlock similar to that which had prevailed on the western front for more than a year. In lecturing to business and social groups around Berlin and to faculty gatherings within the university, Delbrück admitted the difficulties of treating scientifically the yet incomplete present. However, the contrast between the ideas the military strategists had postulated before 1914 and the reality of the war was apparent. Technological developments such as the machine gun and rapid-fire, high-velocity artillery had progressed so quickly after 1890 that even military experts were unable to estimate their impact in battle. After nearly two years of war, it was clear that the new technology had strengthened the defensive powers at the expense of the offensive. Strategic planners were unprepared for such a development.[32]

Late in 1915, Delbrück appealed directly to Chancellor Bethman Hollweg and to Generals Ludendorff and von Falkenhayn, the three who seemed to him most influential in strategic planning. To Ludendorff he wrote:

> During the war my commentary has reiterated that Germany should seek additional lands not in the west but in the east. Belgium must remain neutral, although perhaps without an army or any fortresses after the war. . . . If we treat her correctly Poland is a natural ally against Russia. . . . Some are now arguing that in order to insure German expansion in the east we must fight a war of annihilation in the west. But both aims together are not feasible and will ultimately result in uniting all of Europe against us as it was once united against Napoleon. . . . A very able politician from a neutral state recently visited me. He believed that the western powers are ready for peace negotiations on the basis of the integrity of France and Belgium, a German central Africa and war indemnities.[33]

Military power was the only thing to rely on, Ludendorff replied. Diplomacy would not work: Russian hatred and English fear of Germany would only increase. France and Spain will die. Poland must be partitioned, and such economically valuable parts of Belgium as Bray and Belfort taken. German annexation of Belgium would open the way to Holland—with its harbors—the basis for a sea war against England. If

Germany could gain all this by making peace, she would do so now. Agreements meant nothing. Ludendorff concluded that only power counted, that everything else was a delusion.[34]

In a long memorandum to Chancellor Bethmann Hollweg, Delbrück argued against the dominant conservative view that the annexation of Belgium was a military necessity. Belgium, he wrote, had to be considered within a political context. In his letter to General Staff Chief von Falkenhayn, Delbrück requested a personal meeting for exchange of ideas.[35] During the third week of January, when Falkenhayn was heavily involved in planning for the Verdun campaign, this discussion took place.[36] Sources for the meeting do not exist; however, the context indicates that Delbrück discussed with Falkenhayn the necessity for a strategy of attrition. Delbrück did not realize that Falkenhayn needed little convincing, for he had already reached the same conclusion.

A former military advisor in China in the 1890s, and troop commander at home thereafter, Erich von Falkenhayn became German war minister in 1913 and General Staff chief in 1914 as the kaiser's favorite. No adherent of the Schlieffen School of strategy, some believed that his greatest weakness was the lack of sufficiently clear and well-defined strategic views. Inclined toward prudence and caution, Falkenhayn was opposed by Ludendorff and Hindenburg, men of strong ideas and impressive public reputations.

By the end of 1915 Falkenhayn's views on the war closely approximated those of Hans Delbrück. His pessimism is clear in a long memorandum to the kaiser of December 1915.[37] Aware of shortages in officers and men caused by the disastrously attritious combat, and of munition scarcities caused by consumption which exceeded peacetime estimates many times over, cognizant that the enemy was increasingly able to build up its resources more quickly than Germany, and aware that weapons technology limited battlefield accomplishments,[38] Falkenhayn was convinced that Germany could not win by a strategy of annihilation. Instead he advocated a strategy of attrition.[39] In doing so, he faced a twofold problem. First, he knew only inexactly how to define and carry out such a strategy. Far more important, very few of his subordinate commanders could recognize this strategy as valid.

When Falkenhayn announced plans for Verdun in February 1916, he repeatedly emphasized its limited goals. The main purpose, Falkenhayn wrote, was not to seize the fort but to engage and mutilate large numbers of French troops. From the German crown prince and his military aides this produced no response. They did not grasp a strategy aimed at bleeding but not wiping out the enemy; it was not a part of their military vocabulary. Consequently they misunderstood Falkenhayn's instruc-

Erich von Falkenhayn

tions. Their operations orders specified—in the traditional Prussian-German way—that the attack aimed to capture the fortress of Verdun by a battle of annihilation. Chief of Staff General von Knobelsdorf admitted afterward that if he had understood Falkenhayn's intentions he would never have supported them.[40]

Bearing in mind the strategic traditions that dominated General Staff thinking up to 1914, we can understand why the battle of Verdun, planned by Falkenhayn as a limited offensive with the goal of forcing France to sue for peace, miscarried so badly. It became instead a terrible bloodbath for German and French armies—596,000 killed from February to December—an important cause of Falkenhayn's dismissal, and the beginning of the third, or Ludendorff, period of war leadership. Although the military outcome was a catastrophe, the political result was more or less what Falkenhayn had aimed for: the summer of 1916 marked the beginning of the entente powers' desire to end the war by negotiation.[41] Nevertheless, in August Falkenhayn was replaced as chief of the General Staff. Unable to understand the novel conditions of industrial mass war and the necessity for new approaches, representatives of the Schlieffen School moved to dominate strategic planning.

THE WAR OF ANNIHILATION

Delbrück's response to the war changed during 1916, reflecting two major concerns: an increasing certainty that Germany should seek peace and a growing anxiety over the submarine question and German-American relations. Germany, he felt, could only with enormous efforts dictate terms to the enemy. Much had already been won; the resources to achieve more were lacking. In spite of huge losses suffered by the Russian Brusilov offensive and by the English-French on the Somme, the Allies had achieved only small tactical gains. The French were calling it a war of attrition with analogies to the wars of Louis XIV, Prince Eugene, and Frederick the Great, when statesmen and commanders fought only if something could be achieved; otherwise they made peace. If the Russians were unable to advance and the Somme offensive failed, the psychological moment would be ripe for negotiations.[42]

Delbrück's prediction for the war front came true; his hopes for negotiations did not. Did the military situation promise everything that Germany truly needed? Delbrück answered yes. Continuation of military action would only with great difficulty bring the chance to dictate a more favorable political settlement. Politics, he emphasized, must be the ruling and dominant partner: strategy was only the means to the political ends, and strategy was shaped by economics and technology.[43] Napo-

leon and Moltke had concentrated forces in decisive battles. Field fortifications, heavy artillery, and machine guns now meant that decisions
were won on side battlefields but not in the main theatre. All of this was
reminiscent of the wars of Frederick the Great, who avoided great battles
which rarely accomplished anything. Few have recognized these resem-
blances, Delbrück remonstrated. "We must take note of them," he
pleaded.[44]

A major new concern of 1916 was submarine warfare. An accident of
technological development, Delbrück had written in February, created a
new problem in the international law of the sea. Historically, warships
had been able to approach quite close to commercial vessels for examination without danger. Under the old law, commercial vessels could not
be armed; today, however, they were built specifically to attack submarines. Although the submarine had a fearful offensive weapon in the
torpedo, it was vulnerable defensively. Even a lightly armed commercial
vessel could inflict heavy damage. Thus the submarine could not approach for inspection without risk of destruction.

This technical naval problem was tied to German-American relations. Delbrück cautioned that the possibility of war with America as a
result of unrestricted submarine warfare could not be dismissed lightly.
Would a ruthless submarine campaign force England out of the war
without bringing America into it? Could England be persuaded, by neutral protests—especially from America—to lift her illegal blockade
against Germany? Whichever way, Germany faced an alien interest
whose decision and power could not be fully calculated beforehand. Although it appeared that America's best interests were to trade freely with
Germany, unfortunate accidents, such as the loss of American lives at
sea, could suddenly provoke popular feelings and plunge America into
the maelstrom. The essential point in question, he asserted, was timing.
How long would it take to convince the Americans to exert pressure
against the British to open the blockade? Conversely, could Germany
end the war in the west by unrestricted submarine warfare against England before American animosity increased to the point of war? How long
would it take to force England to her knees, if indeed Germany could
accomplish this? Delbrück warned that the general public did not grasp
the complexities of the situation. It failed to distinguish between moderate and weak policies. When confronted with such a dilemma, statesmen
sought to avoid the extremes by compromise.[45]

As feared, during midsummer 1916 public clamor for unrestricted
submarine warfare increased, not only from annexationists and Pan-
Germans, but also from Reichstag members and responsible govern-

ment leaders. Countering this, Delbrück urged caution and restraint. He feared the extraordinary danger of an American declaration of war on Germany.[46] Naval officers and hot-blooded patriots argued that Germany's sufficiently numerous submarines could force England to an early peace. The crucial question, Delbrück recognized, concerned numbers. Did Germany clearly have enough submarines to attain this goal before the entry of America? This question was primarily economic and political, not military. Graf Reventlow, noted Pan-German agitator, responded that the professional judgment of the high naval officers should decide. The political leadership, Reventlow wrote, must subordinate itself to expert military opinion. Such an extension of professional competence was erroneous and dangerous, Delbrück replied. The number of submarines may in the future become sufficient to achieve the desired result quickly. If so, the conditions of the sea war would then be changed, and the technical naval situation would become significant to the political leadership. Presently, Delbrück insisted, political judgment, not military specialist opinion, should settle the matter.

Delbrück's suggestion that Germany had insufficient submarines for effective total war at sea resulted in a stiff reprimand from the censor's office. He was ordered thereafter to submit everything to the censor before galley proofs had been set for the *Preussische Jahrbücher*.[47] Delbrück had had trouble with this office on many occasions during the war. In September 1914 the censors criticized his mention of limited war aims; in November 1915 they objected to his discussion of peace. Many times they had forced deletion of details, such as specific mention of German commanders and armies, of Russian successes, of possible preparation for new offensives, of Austrian army movements.[48] On each occasion Delbrück had acquiesced. In August 1916, however, he protested strongly.[49] If the government, Delbrück wrote to State Secretary Arthur Zimmermann, officially suggested or implied that Germany had enough submarines to force England out of the war quickly, then it would be difficult for the people to believe or understand why this should not be done immediately. Public opinion would be whipped to a frenzy against a government that did not utilize available means to end the war.[50]

By the summer of 1916 Delbrück had become a major impetus behind the moderate war aims movement. However, as the two critical decisions of midwar approached, the replacement of Falkenhayn with Hindenburg and Ludendorff (August 1916) and the beginning of unrestricted submarine warfare (February 1917), Delbrück found himself unable to influence military or political decisions. Few shared his view that a strategy of attrition could win the war. Delbrück's interpretations of strategy—within a political and economic context—were alien to Germany's leaders. Strategy was seen as a technical competence under the specialized aegis of the General Staff.

Scarely anyone in Germany appreciated the significance of the change of military commanders in August 1916. In retrospect, Falkenhayn's operations within the framework of a strategy of attrition had been politically successful, but they appeared a military failure. Following the Verdun campaign, Rumania declared war and Falkenhayn was replaced. Delbrück's response was mixed. Falkenhayn had not gotten along easily with Bethmann Hollweg. Delbrück feared that Hindenburg and Ludendorff would cause as many difficulties for the chancellor's policies as had Falkenhayn. But strategically he did not see how a new commander could improve upon Falkenhayn's actions.[51] Delbrück did not realize until 1918 what a momentous change this was for Imperial Germany. As in the August 1917 removal of Bethmann, Delbrück, like most Germans, was unable to appreciate a moderate policy whose successes were unclear until he was able to compare it with an extreme policy whose failures became a disaster.

With the change in military command of August 1916, conditions for total submarine warfare began to crystallize. In the succeeding five months military and naval leaders agreed that this "ultimate weapon" had to be used; the high naval officers had favored it for more than a year.[52] In the face of unanimous technical-specialist advice and his own lack of confidence in proposing anything better, Chancellor Bethmann Hollweg's opposition to the submarines gradually weakened.[53] This same lack of confidence when confronted by the military "technical" specialists characterized other Reich officials, such as Karl Helfferich, and certainly helped to form Kaiser Wilhelm's views.[54] This attitude is typified in Bethmann Hollweg's remarks at the crown council of August 31, 1916. After seconding Helfferich's conclusion that unrestricted submarine warfare would probably lead to catastrophe, the chancellor concluded that the final decision rested, nevertheless, with the generals.[55] The annexationists fostered exactly this attitude toward all major wartime decisions. Graf Reventlow had declared that the question of future German-Belgian relations belonged strictly to the General Staff.[56] Pan-German Professor Eduard Meyer found laymen incompetent to judge questions of naval warfare. Germany had to put its complete faith in the authority of the military specialist.[57] Delbrück resisted this approach to war. Unrestricted submarine warfare, like the military disposition of Belgium, had political implications which had to be considered.

As these questions were being decided, Delbrück's views went unheeded. This was due partly to his temporary exhaustion and remoteness from events in the autumn and winter of 1916—17. His eldest son was to die fighting in Macedonia in the spring. He had given up his university lectures and retired to a sanitarium for several months' stay. His student Emil Daniels had taken over much of the routine editing for the *Preussische Jahrbücher*.[58] Precisely during these months both public sentiment and official opinion moved to favor unrestricted submarine warfare. Accordingly, plans for concluding the war stressed great, decisive strokes: a strategy for annihilation on land and sea carried out irrespective of political and economic considerations.

On February 1, 1917, Germany declared total war at sea. Delbrück understood immediately that Germany had crossed a fateful turning point. Some persons consider this the beginning of the end, Delbrück wrote privately to friends. Others see the possibility of victory. The decisive point was America. Many factors indicated danger: the United States might declare war against Germany, which would greatly stimulate morale among Germany's enemies, improve their finances, and lead to the landing of American troops in Europe. The chancellor believed that America would sever diplomatic relations. "As for myself," Delbrück declared, "whether the submarine decision is to be denigrated depends on whether one believes that without it President Wilson might have arranged a negotiated peace—a view toward which I am very much inclined—and whether one believes that the submarine war will now cut off these negotiations or set them forward in earnest."[59] Soon thereafter Delbrück's worst forebodings came true: the United States broke off diplomatic relations on February 3 and declared war on April 17. By midsummer the technical experts were proved wrong: England had not been forced out of the war, and the first American troops landed in Europe.

Soon after this, the German command began planning for a final great land offensive. Precisely how Ludendorff constructed this is uncertain. However, his main scheme of thought seems clear. By July 1917 he had lost hope that submarine warfare would succeed, and had turned to the land war. He seemed convinced that increased war production would support Schlieffen's strategy: defend one front and attack on the second, then reverse this and end the war. Surely military victory seemed close in the east by the autumn of 1917.[60] The American declaration of war meant that decisive victory had to be won *before* large-scale American reinforcements arrived on the continent. But Ludendorff never accurately assimilated the differences between the eastern and the western fronts in terms of human and economic requirements. Having succeeded on the eastern front by December 1917, he expected to transfer these same strategic methods to the west.

His ideas were those of Schlieffen, under whom he had worked be-

Erich Ludendorff

tween 1904 and 1906. From the start of the war Ludendorff had sent plans and requests for battles of annihilation to Berlin. In 1915 he had advocated an attack at Lodz to encircle the main Russian armies at the bend of the Vistula. In 1916 he called for a large-scale assault in the east at the time of the Verdun action. In 1917 he agreed to unrestricted submarine warfare. All of these assumed the power of German moral supremacy and misunderstood the impact of the new techonology. He scoffed at the tank as a "walking pantry." In response to the English success at Cambrai in December 1917, he stated that German troops were suffering under "tank panic," a psychological condition. His idealism allowed him to ignore the material superiority of this new invention against which German troops had no defense.[61] Like his teacher Schlieffen, Ludendorff believed in the paramountcy of discipline, courage, and morale. Ludendorff's education and training in the General Staff and his experiences on the eastern front tended to confirm each other. If the Supreme Command could assemble a large enough force, a decision would be achieved.[62] The spring offensive of 1918, like the Schlieffen Plan, was not just another operation. It was a mighty stroke to cut the Gordian knot, releasing Germany from the strategic shackles which had bound her for four years. An opening would be made, it would be enlarged, and through it the German army would pass to victory.[63] Ludendorff aimed to end the war.[64] General von Kuhl, who helped plan it, later wrote that everyone, including the enemy, expected and understood that an attack was destined. Despite insufficient resources of men and material, there was no other legitimate strategic choice.[65]

As these plans took form, Ludendorff's major strategic critic was having very different thoughts. More important than Delbrück's fears for the battlefield were his apprehensions regarding the political context. He was certain that if the enemy could not break through the German lines, and if the freedom of the seas had been achieved, then Germany should open peace negotiations.[66] To convince England of Germany's readiness for discussions, the government should declare Belgium independent and simultaneously oppose the chauvinism of the Pan-Germans—those fanatics who championed "Napoleonic" politics and demanded Belgium, the French coast, and fortifications from Verdun to Belfort. The Pan-Germans were leading the nation to destruction. Delbrück urged patriotic Germans to fight against them.[67]

Although his public position on German war aims changed only slightly in 1917, privately he had given up hope of expansion by June 1917. To Valentini he wrote that colonial expansion was no longer achievable, but it was necessary to give the popular imagination something tempting to divert its attention away from Belgium.[68]

The war situation, his son's death together with the Reichstag peace resolution of July, and Bethmann Hollweg's dismissal in August, depressed Delbrück greatly by autumn 1917. Although he was apparently unaware of all the behind-the-scenes maneuverings, especially preceding the removal of Bethmann Hollweg, he nonetheless sensed that Germany faced a profound political crisis.[69] The monarchy was in grave jeopardy.[70] The Reichstag, without strong leadership, was ambivalent, going this way and that. A fourth war winter could scarcely be avoided.[71] He wrote to State Secretary Wilhelm Solf suggesting that if a new Reich chancellor were under consideration, a liberal-minded one such as Prince Max von Baden would have a demoralizing effect on the Western powers.[72] The prince was acceptable to the political left, and Germany's enemies would recognize the symbol of a humanitarian, nonexpansionist policy.

Writing to the head of the kaiser's Civil Cabinet, Delbrück repeated that a frank declaration of Belgian independence would overturn Lloyd George and bring a favorable peace for Germany in 1917. The unclear and confused politics of Chancellor Michaelis, however, prevented this. Delbrück feared that if the Reich chancellor was unable to overcome the opposition of Ludendorff, under whose power he seemed to be, or if he was unsure of what to do, the Reichstag would soon force the issue. If that happened, it would put Germany in an unfavorable light abroad, give her a poor negotiating position, and ruin the monarchy. This new crisis must be resolved from above. A policy against the Reichstag majority was possible, but a sound national policy could be carried out in cooperation with the Reichstag. The kaiser and chancellor must take the intitiative. The Reichstag was strong in the press but not with the people. "Our military position now enables us to begin negotiations, but this position will be weakened if the Kaiser relinquishes the initiative and the Reichstag takes it up."[73]

If Delbrück feared the rising power of the Reichstag, symbolized by its resolution of July 19, 1917, asking for peace without forced annexations, he realized that this resolution had been won using arguments similar to his own. In his speech of July 6, 1917, which led directly to the resolution of July 19, Reichstag delegate Matthias Erzberger asked whether it was reasonable to expect that Germany might hope for a better peace next year? His answer, like Delbrück's, was no. Erzberger concluded that a negotiated end to the war was Germany's sole remaining hope.[74]

As for domestic political reform, here too Delbrück was forced to change by his hopeless view of Germany's military circumstances. On July 1, 1917, Delbrück and ten others called publicly for general, direct, equal, and secret elections in Prussia. Had Delbrück suddenly become a democrat? Far from it. The submarine war had failed. America was becoming increasingly dangerous. The political collapse of Russia seemed doubtful. The only way, Delbrück wrote privately, to prevent political collapse was by a large concession to democracy.[75] Political liberalization was a necessary resort in extremely bad military circumstances.

1918

In January 1918, amid rising conservative expectations, the High Command moved to resume offensive warfare. Delbrück held urgent discussions with Rudolf von Valentini. Valentini, the closest political advisor to the kaiser, was as worried as Delbrück by the boundless pursuit of "peace by victory" and the Fatherland Party's incitement of popular enthusiasm to this end.[76] A week later Hindenburg and Ludendorff forced Valentini to resign.[77] Too late, Delbrück fully understood the realities of civil-military relations:

> Was the Supreme Command now coming out from behind the Kaiser to lead the politics of the Reich? . . . Intrigues caused the resignation of the Chief of the Civil Cabinet and now the Pan-Germans press was demanding removal from the Kaiser's circle of all men of such views as Herr von Valentini's. Was Germany moving so far from monarchical ideals that the Kaiser could no longer choose his ministers or his personal advisors? A proletarian revolution in Germany was always a phantom: was the monarchy now in danger from the right?[78]

Delbrück pleaded for negotiations.[79] "Once before in German history," he wrote, "a war, which stands before our eyes in great glory, was successfully ended without conquest and without any general political changes—the Seven Years' War." Professor Dietrich Schäfer responded that although Prussia survived the Hubertusburg peace, the German Reich was lost if it ended the World War without increased power. Pan-Germanist Georg von Below, another member, with Schäfer, of the newly created ultraconservative Fatherland Party, attacked Delbrück, demanding a "Hindenburg Peace"—a peace of annihilation.[80]

All great idealistic movements in history contained the risk of fanaticism, Delbrück replied. This potential had always accompanied German nationalism, but it was now growing dangerously. Fanaticism was blind to truth; it desired not to understand its opponents but only to destroy them. The Pan-Germans knew only friends and supporters; everyone else was a defeatist, pacifist, or traitor. He pleaded with his countrymen to work against the Pan-German poisoning of political life.[81]

In this way, during the closing months of the war Delbrück sharply conflicted with the conservatives while moving in close correlation with the political left, with Philip Scheidemann and other Socialist politicians. Opposition to Delbrück's political position and also to his academic work became hostile and virulent.[82]

In April 1918, in the wake of a sixty-kilometer breakthrough by German troops on the western front, Pan-Germans and military conservatives demanded that the Reichstag recant its peace resolution, called for large-scale changes in Polish boundaries that doubled the land area of Prussian Poland, claimed parts of France and Belgium, and supported the violent peace of victory.

These new demands were based upon a serious misunderstanding of the relationship between politics and war, Delbrück remonstrated. Large-scale changes in the Polish boundaries based on military cosiderations would only create greater political problems. This fourth partition would provoke Polish nationalism against Germany. Enlarged Polish representation in the Reichstag would further splinter German political life. A better way to buttress Germany's eastern boundary was to foster a pro-German movement within Poland and encourage a Polish alliance. Delbrück admitted that his country needed a peace which would insure its future, but Germany had to consider the political necessities of other European nations. He asked why political dangers had to be created to protect military positions.[83]

Privately Delbrück was much more pessimistic. Aware of Ludendorff's attacks on State Secretary Kühlmann, he feared the renewed clamor for extreme war aims and was gravely doubtful about the ultimate success of the western offensive.[84] When Kuhlmann was forced to resign in early July 1918[85]—as a result of his admission in the Reichstag that purely military means could no longer win the war—the situation became intolerable. Delbrück lashed out at the generals: No policy could be carried out with the Supreme Command informing the press of their dissatisfaction with the German Foreign Office. The Supreme Command had to understand that Germany could not be governed without the ministers and the Reichstag.[86] "It is tragic," he wrote privately, "that Ludendorff, whose strategy once saved us, now by his politics is taking us on the road to catastrophe."[87]

In both July and August 1918 the censors bothered Delbrück. In July they refused him permission to state that the German offensive had been halted and forced partially backwards. In August they forced deletion of statements concerning German submarine numbers,[88] and denied permission to reprint material from the London *Times* listing the number of American troops safely landed in Europe.

At mid-August, unaware of the desperate situation at the front, Delbrück again censured Pan-Germanism. The German people, he wrote, entered World War I to fight an honorable and correct defensive war. Yet United States senators argue that the Allies must win the war to save the world from German conquest. Delbrück asked where this erroneous image of German war aims had originated. It had started before the war, among the Pan-Germans, with the false naval policies of Tirpitz and the dreams of world hegemony. In 1914 and 1915 they said Germany must take over Belgium, France, Poland, and other lands. In 1917 they promised that unrestricted submarine warfare would force England to sue for peace in six months. America, they said, would not enter the war; she was only bluffing. When Bethmann Hollweg did not go along with them, they attacked him. Public opinion in Germany would not have been won over, Delbrück reiterated, except in the belief that unlimited submarine warfare would bring peace. Instead it brought another enemy. The men who said that this could not happen, the false prophets Reventlow and Tirpitz, were responsible. Unfortunately the German people must suffer the consequences for their mistakes, but the world had a right to demand that Germany renounce Pan-Germanism—the spirit of arrogance and paganism.[89]

By September 1918, Delbrück sensed the approach of a decisive blow, but publicly he voiced optimism. Strategic reverses, he wrote, had placed German forces again on the Siegfried line. Things, however, were not so bad. The situation for Germany was simple: what cannot be negotiated, must be fought over. Two things seemed beyond doubt: that Germany was unbeatable on the defensive, and that diplomatic efforts could bring a negotiated peace. When the enemy realized that they could not beat Germany militarily, negotiations would begin.[90] Delbrück, along with most others in Germany, did not realize the seriousness of the German military situation. Lacking accurate information, he remained publicly optimistic about British willingness to negotiate.

October 1918 was chaotic; although expecting that the military front could hold out through Christmas, nonetheless, Delbrück sensed that momentous political events were working toward a conclusion. He had telephone calls at strange hours and was called to various Berlin government offices for urgent discussions. This was the month of Max von Baden's government during which, according to his wife, Delbrück's Wednesday discussion group, the *Mittwochabend*, served as a kind of shadow cabinet.[91] A feeling of uncertainty before a vague but impending doom is reflected in his writings of this period.[92]

Since September, he wrote, the most terrible fate had befallen Germany. The Balkan front had broken completely open. In Syria the English had destroyed the Turkish army and taken Damascus. In Constantinople the German-oriented government had fallen. Austria-Hungary was in full retreat. On the western front the enemy offensive had passed through the Siegfried line; under heavy losses of men and material the German army retreated steadily. When one remembered the German success from March through June, such abrupt changes were scarcely believable.

Delbrück admitted that before 1914 Germans had thought their system of government better than Western parliamentarianism. The deficiency in this system was in the selection and education of political leaders. During the war it became clear that there was a fissure in German political education between bureaucrats and the officer corps on the one hand and popular speakers, journalists, and parliamentarians on the other. Germany had only specialists *(Fachmenschen):* men skilled in narrow, highly defined areas such as finance, taxation, and law, but no one trained for general political leadership. Every time a high position became vacant, a serious dilemma occurred, and under wartime pressures this dilemma led to catastrophe.

Delbrück found the origin of Germany's military fate in its constitutional system. In his mind, total submarine warfare, a one-sided military decision, had carried Germany to her destiny. He reasoned that if the chancellor had been legally superior to the Supreme Command this might have been prevented. A far-ranging reform was unavoidable. This reform had to strengthen the power of the parties, limit that of the bureaucracy, and above all, subordinate military authority to civilian. If the current German system was militaristic, as the enemy said, then such militarism must be ended.

Regarding the dismissal of General Ludendorff, Delbrück admitted that his name would have a place in the history of the World War, but not one of greatness. A strong organizer, a splendid tactician, a man of strong will and ideas, Ludendorff lacked what every commander needed above all, a unity of strategic and political vision. Lundendorff's policies for Poland, the Baltic and Russia, Belgium and America were based upon purely mechanical concepts of power. Politically ignorant, his chicanery ultimately proved disastrous.

To compare Ludendorff as a strategist with Falkenhayn was not yet possible, Delbrück cautioned, as the documents for objective analysis were lacking. The main point at issue was whether the expanded total attack that Clausewitz taught was the only possibility or, because of technical problems and material limitations, a new strategy should have been used. A real commander must have both the determination to proceed and the courage to retreat. In foreign eyes, Ludendorff was not a strategist but a characteristic symbol of the German military system. Such was Delbrück's final statement published prior to the German "revolution" of November 1918.

World War I posed a serious problem for Hans Delbrück: to what extent could an historian of the military past become a critic of current war policy? Despite insights which were consistently clearer than most of his contemporaries, by November 1918 Delbrück had achieved only very limited success in his new role. This is true for a variety of reasons. The sources available to him were poor both in quality and in quantity. Government censorship and official propaganda worsened the situation. To try to overcome this, Delbrück regularly quoted from English, French, and American publications, comparing them with German, Austrian, and Swiss sources. Although this improved his comprehension of the war considerably, it aroused the antagonism of both censor and conservative. In their minds, Delbrück associated himself with the foreign enemies. Not only were his sources inadequate, but Delbrück was forced to disregard the important historical quotient of distance: in the eyes of many, he described the war primarily as a publicist, not as an historian. Finally, Delbrück, like Ludendorff, underestimated the full impact of technology. He was unable to back up his correct overall estimate that material realities had overwhelmed Germany with complete, specific details of weapons, logistics, or casualties. All of these factors tended to reduce his credibility in the eyes of friend and foe alike.

In the preceding chapter we discussed the reasons that Delbrück had not criticized Reich defense policy prior to 1914. If there was no forum for public opposition to military policy during peacetime, war conditions made such discussion dangerous and illegal. Prior to 1914 Delbrück himself had resisted the application of his historical theories to operational planning. When several officers, such as Friedrich von Bernhardi, had tried to define this relationship, Delbrück was uncomfortable. He was an historian, not a defense analyst. In spite of the iconoclastic nature of his work in military history, Delbrück's political ideas kept him firmly within the Imperial elite. Not until after 1914 did he separate himself from the conservative majority, and even then he chose not to become a radical critic. His wartime statements were for the most part carefully executed to stay within the bounds of what was allowable. Above all, he did not lose faith in the military leadership until late 1918, and in the Prussian-German monarchy until after that. Although a materialist and realist in his historical assessments and wartime analysis, Delbrück retained his idealistic expectations for the German political system and his faith in the royal house. This, combined with a lack of access to the royal and military entourage, led him to misunderstand the character and relationships of the leading decision makers until late in the war.

Delbrück's wartime position related his overall political and social views to his historical methods. Although after 1918 his conservative opponents repeatedly accused him of attacking the monarchy that had so richly rewarded him, Delbrück remained a patriot. Radical political opposition, which might have been called for had Delbrück pressed his resistance to the government's strategy to the uttermost limit, was as alien to him personally as it was illegal during the war. More important perhaps than his political philosophy were his historical methods. Delbrück was primarily an historian and only secondarily a political commentator. His political views were derived from his historical understanding. As historian, he was never so convinced of the correctness of his interpretation to be moved to drastic political action. Delbrück remained skeptical. He never forgot the relative and tentative nature of historical images. His purpose and methods separated him from the officers. Here the central difference between historian and military officer became decisive. Officers were trained to act in the future following a single operational idea, responding to real world conditions and extreme, often life-threatening circumstances. Historians were schooled to consider the past using many different perspectives, creating a verisimilar image based upon the best available evidence and informed opinion. Although his assessments were more realistic than those of most German commentators, they remained sufficiently flawed so that his friends could doubt them, his enemies could attack them, and he himself was restrained from complete acceptance and the political actions which might have resulted from such a position.

The outcome of the war proved Delbrück "right" in the abstract sense that his overall strategic views were very nearly correct. Yet in the real political world he failed. Few influential figures in the government or the military could agree with him, and most could in no way understand his point of view. Germany's defeat, the Treaty of Versailles, and the economic and political woes of the 1920s made this understanding much more difficult.

NOTES

1   Cf. Fritz Epstein's remarks on the World War writings of Otto Hoetzsch and Delbrück in his essay "Otto Hoetzsch as Commentator on Foreign Policy during the First World War," in *Germany and The East*, selected essays of Fritz T. Epstein edited by Robert F. Byrnes (Bloomington: Indiana University Press, 1973), pp. 102–04.

2   Hans Delbrück's activities during World War I are known only in general outline. Thus Hans Gatzke accurately assesses Delbrück's moderate position within the war aims movements; Fritz Ringer calls Delbrück the most rigorous and consistent opponent of annexationist foreign policy, and Klaus Schwabe correctly describes Delbrück as the leader of the movement for a negotiated peace during the war. For World War I, more than before it, Delbrück fits into generalizations regarding the German professoriate as a whole only with great difficulty and some distortion. He was in various ways, both methodologically and politically, a kind of *rara avis*. Above all, no writer adequately relates Delbrück's analysis of the war to his main contributions to historical knowledge, his work in military history. Hans Gatzke, *Germany's Drive to the West* (Baltimore: Johns Hopkins University Press, 1950), passim. Ringer, *The Decline of the German Mandarins*, p. 196. Klaus Schwabe, *Wissenschaft und Kriegsmoral* (Göttingen: Musterschmidt, 1969), passim.

3   Fischer, *Germany's Aims*, p. 95; Gatzke, *Germany's Drive to the West*, p. 8; Konrad Jarausch, *The Enigmatic Chancellor* (New Haven: Yale University Press, 1973), pp. 178ff.

4   Schwabe, *Wissenschaft und Kriegsmoral*, chapter 2; Fischer, *Germany's Aims*, pp. 155ff.; Gatzke, *Germany's Drive to the West*, p.7ff.; Ringer, *The Decline of the German Mandarins*, pp. 180ff.; Roland Stromberg; *Redemption by War*, op. cit., pp. 39ff.; David Lipton, *Ernst Cassirer: The dilemma of a liberal intellectual in Germany, 1914–33* (Toronto: University of Toronto Press, 1978), pp. 36–39.

5   Hans Delbrück, "Die Ursachen des Krieges. Die Chancen. Das Ziel," *PJ* dated August 1914, reprinted in Delbrück, *Krieg und Politik*, 3 vols. (Berlin: Georg Stilke, 1918–19), 1:28ff.

6   Delbrück to Max Lenz, 24 August 1914, *Nachlass Delbrück*, DSB.

7   In Frankfurt am Main and Wiesbaden in August, and at the Concordia Hall in Berlin in September, *Lina Delbrück Memoirs*, Part 11, pp. 65–66.

8   Hans Delbrück, "Die Kriegsereignisse von Ende August bis gegen Ende September, 1914. Der zukünftige Friede," *PJ* dated September 1914, reprinted in Delbrück, *Krieg und Politik* 1:48–60. This analogy between Imperial Germany and Napoleon I was used later in the war by a wide range of opponents to German wartime politics. Cf. Harry F. Young,*Prince Lichnowsky and the Great War* (Athens, Georgia: University of Georgia Press, 1977), pp. 144–45.

9   Hans Delbrück, "Das Zahlenübergewicht unserer Gegner und die Politik Belgiens. Die strategische Lage Ende Dezember 1914," *PJ* dated January 1915, reprinted, Delbrück, *Krieg und Politik* 1:70–73.

10 Gatzke, *Germany's Drive to the West*, pp. 57ff.; *Lina Delbrück Memoirs*, Part II, pp. 58ff.; Wilhelm Deist, *Militär und Innenpolitik im Weltkrieg*, 2 vols. (Düsseldorf: Droste, 1970), 1:208.

11 *Lina Delbrück Memoirs*, Part 11, ibid.; the censored essays, together with notes from Delbrück's meeting with the censorship officials, are contained in the *Nachlass Delbrück*, Part 20, BAK.Cf. Gatzke, *Germany's Drive*, p. 58; Schwabe, *Wissenschaft und Kriegsmoral*, p. 236. For an evaluation of Delbrück's political impact during the World War, his relationship to Bethmann-Hollweg is an important one. If one accepts Delbrück's statement, one might conclude that he held regular meetings with the Reich chancellor throughout the war. If this is so, there is little evidence to support it. It is true that Bethmann held similar views to Delbrück at various times during the war on particular issues; for example, on unrestricted submarine warfare and, to a lesser extent, on war aims. However, the most recent, exhaustive, and objective examination of Bethmann, Konrad Jarausch's *Enigmatic Chancellor*, treats Delbrück as an extremely marginal figure in Bethmann's life and decisions as chancellor. Although

there are suggestions here and there in various primary accounts from this period of a more substantial relationship between the two, hard evidence for this is lacking. In the Delbrück Nachlass, BAK, for example, which contains the most extensive materials for examining this question, there are only a few direct indications reflecting on this relationship. Cf. the six page typescript, "Bericht über meine Unterredung mit dem Reichskanzler am 16 November 1915," the only one of its kind. Perhaps Delbrück did not want or could not keep records of such conversations. For example, there is very little correspondence between the two in either the Delbrück or Bethmann papers, and none which evidences a substantial and consistent influence from one to the other. For a discussion of Delbrück's political life, then, this is an interesting question to be pursued. Cf. Jarausch, *Enigmatic Chancellor*, pp. 205, 263, 343, 387–88; Schwabe, *Wissenschaft und Kriegsmoral*, pp. 114ff.; testimony of General Hans von Haeften before the second subcommittee of the Reichstag Committee to Investigate World War I, in Wolfgang Steglich, ed., *Die Verhandlungen des 2. Unterausschusses des Parlamentarischen Untersuchungsausschusses über die päpstliche Friedensaktion von 1917* (Wiesbaden: Franz Steiner, 1974), pp. 219, 269; Hans Peter Hanssen, *Diary of a Dying Empire*, trans. Oscar O. Winther, edited by Ralph H. Lutz, Mary Schofield, and O. O. Winther (Bloomington, Indiana: Indiana University Press, 1955), p. 103, 337; Erich Matthias and Susanne Miller, eds., *Das Kriegstagebuch des Reichstagsabgeordneten Eduard David 1914 bis 1918* (Düsseldorf: Droste, 1966), pp. 46, 72, 256, 275, 282.

12   Gatzke, *Germany's Drive*, p. 58. F. L. Carsten, *War Against War: British and German Radical Movements in the First World War* (Berkeley: University of California Press, 1982), pp. 19–24 and passim.

13   Hans Delbrück, "Das englische Weltreich," *PJ*, October 1914, reprinted in Delbrück, *Kreig und Politik* 1:61–62; Delbrück, "Denkschrift über die Zukunft Polens," December 1914, *Nachlass Delbrück*, BAK. Folders 40, 42 contain material amplifying Delbrück's political position with regard to Poland in the years 1914–1916.

14   Hans Delbrück, "Das deutsche militärische System, Vergleichen mit dem französischen, englischen und russischen," in Otto Hintze, et al., ed., *Deutschland und der Weltkrieg* (Berlin: B. G. Teubner, 1915), pp. 171–85.

15   Hans Delbrück, *Bismarcks Erbe* (Berlin: Ullstein, 1915), was originally commissioned as a "popular" biography to commemorate the one hundredth birthday of Bismarck (April 1, 1915). It was not a popular work at all. As Delbrück's daughter said, he could speak so that everyone could understand him easily, but he could not write in this way. As Delbrück explained in the opening pages, he wrote the book to counteract the steady erosion of Bismarck's reputation and to help restore the good image of the founder of the Reich. Conversation with Frau Helene Hobe, Berlin-Dahlem, 29 May, 1974; Hans Delbrück, "Selbstanzeige über Bismarcks Erbe," *PJ* (July 1915).

16   Delbrück, *Bismarck's Erbe*, p. 71.

17   Ibid., p. 162.

18   Ibid., pp. 177–82, 203.

19   Ibid., p. 202.

20   Ibid., p. 213.

21   Delbrück had sent his first published essays in the 1870s to Leopold von Ranke; later he sent various essays and books to officers and officials such as Field Marshall von der Goltz, Graf von Schlieffen, and Chancellor Bethmann Hollweg. "Thank you" letters, few with significant content, are contained in the *Nachlass Delbrück*, DSB.

22   Valentini to Delbrück, 13 June and 5 June 1915, *Nachlass Delbrück*, DSB.

23 Delbrück to Max Lenz, 7 August 1915, Briefkonzeptbücher, ibid.

24 *Lina Delbrück Memoirs*, Part 11, pp. 165–71.

25 Hans Delbrück, "Der Krieg im Juni 1915," *PJ*, dated July 1915, reprinted in Delbrück, *Krieg und Politik* 1:114–15.

26 Klaus Schwabe, *Wissenschaft und Kriegsmoral*, pp. 81ff.; Hans Gatzke, *Germany's Drive*, pp. 8ff.; Fritz Frischer, *Germany's Aims*, pp. 155ff.; Wolfgang J. Mommsen *Max Weber und die deutsche Politik 1890-1920* (Tübingen, 1959), p. 213; Gotthart Schwarz, *Theodor Wolff und das Berlinger Tageblatt* (Tübingen: J. C. B. Mohr, 1968), pp. 43ff.; Wilfried Eisenbeiss, *Die bürgerliche Friedensbewegung in Deutschland während des Ersten Weltkrieges: Organisation, Selbstverständnis und politische Praxis 1913–1919* (Frankfurt/M: Peter Lang, 1980), pp. 244ff.

27 Hans Delbrück, "Die Kriegsereignisse im April-Mai 1915," *PJ* dated June 1915, reprinted in Delbrück, *Krieg und Politik* 1:105–14.

28 Throughout the war, Delbrück's estimates of German losses were usually wide of the mark. He did not have access to correct figures, and the government figures were usually very much weighted in Germany's favor. For example, for Verdun, 1916 official figures indicated that Germany had lost 100,000 in the fighting, whereas real losses were more than three times this many. Cf. C. R. M. F. Cruttwell, *A History of the Great War* (Oxford: Clarendon Press, 1934), p. 252; Alistair Horne, *The Price of Glory: Verdun 1916* (New York: Harper, 1967), pp. 327ff.; Cyril Falls, *The Great War* (New York: Capricorn Books, 1961), p. 192; cf. John Keegan, *The Face of Battle* (New York: Viking Press, 1976), p. 280.

29 Hans Delbrück, "Die Kriegsereignisse Mai bis July 1915," *PJ* dated August 1915, reprinted Delbrück, *Krieg und Politik* 1:118–25; Delbrück, "Die Kriegsereignisse im August," *PJ* dated September 1915, reprinted Delbrück, *Krieg und Politik* 1:124–29; "Die Kriegsereignisse im September 1915," *PJ* dated October 1915, reprinted in Delbrück, *Krieg und Politik* 1:145–49.

30 Hans Delbrück, "Die Kriegsereignisse im Oktober 1915," *PJ* dated November 1915, reprinted in Delbrück, *Krieg und Politik* 1:160; "Die Kriegsereignisse im November 1915," *PJ* dated December 1915, reprinted in Delbrück, *Krieg und Politik* 1:180.

31 Hans Delbrück, "Politische Korrespondenz" *PJ* 116 (29 August 1915): 560; cf. Bernhard Mann, *Die baltischen Länder in der deutschen Kriegszielpublizistik* (Tübingen: J. C. B. Mohr, 1965), pp. 20ff.

32 Hans Delbrück, "From Moltke to Falkenhayn: The Development of Modern Strategy," a lecture presented 14 December 1915 in Posen and widely reported in the newspapers, *Nachlass Delbrück*, Part 88, DSB. Hans Delbrück, "The Development of Modern Strategy from Gustav Adolphus to the Present," Berlin University lecture series, January 1916, *Lina Delbrück Memoirs*, Part 11, p. 3.

33 Delbrück to Ludendorff, *Lina Delbrück Memoirs*, Part 11, p. 6.

34 Ludendorff to Delbrück, 29 December 1915, in Egmont Zechlin, "Ludendorff im Jahre 1915, Unveröffentlichte Briefe," *Historische Zeitschrift*, no. 2 (October 1970), 351–53.

35 *Lina Delbrück Memoirs*, Part 10, p. 2.

36 Ibid., Part 10, p. 3; Delbrück to Buchfinck, March 14, 1916, Briefkonzeptbücher *Nachlass Delbrück*, DSB.

37 Ritter, *The Sword and the Scepter* 3:158.

38   General Erich von Falkenhayn, *General Headquarters and Its Critical Decisions* (London: Hutchinson & Co., 1919), pp. 11, 33, 43, 44, 174, 210. Cf. Karl-Heinz Janssen, *Der Kanzler und der General: Die Führungskrise um Bethmann Hollweg und Falkenhayn 1914–1916* (Göttingen: Musterschmidt, 1967), pp. 14–27, 181ff. Karl H. Jannsen, "Der Wechsel in der obersten Heeresleitung 1916," *Vierteljahresheft für Zeitgeschichte*, 11 (October 1959): 334ff., argues that it was political factors, not strategic ones, which accounted for his downfall. While not discounting these, we will emphasize Falkenhayn's strategic views and their incomprehensibility to both officers and politicians. Beyond this there were personal antagonisms involved. Both Bethmann Hollweg and Ludendorff resented Falkenhayn's influence on the kaiser, not to mention the political ambitions of Falkenhayn. Cf. Feldman, *Army, Industry Labor*, pp. 138ff.

39   Falkenhayn had spent considerable time as a "front" or line commander and as an advisor in China until 1911, when he became a guards commander and later War Minister; thus he was not a part of the Schlieffen-Moltke General Staff during his formative military years. Cf. General von Zwehl, *Erich von Falkenhayn* (Berlin: E. S. Mittler, 1926); Major von Wienskowski, *Falkenhayn* (Berlin: E. S. Mittler, 1937); Heinz Kraft, "Das Problem Falkenhayn: Eine Würdigung der Kriegführung des Generalstabschefs," *Welt als Geschichte* 21 (1962): 49–78.

40   Horne, *The Price of Glory*, pp. 39–40; Ernest Kabisch, *Verdun: Wende des Weltkrieges* (Berlin: Otto Schlegel, 1935); Ritter, *Sword and Scepter* 3:182ff.; Janssen, *Der Kanzler und der General*, pp. 181–89.

41   Cf. Kent Forster, *The Failure of Peace* (Philadelphia: University of Pennsylvania, 1941), pp. 30–59, 76–90, 145–48. Another study argues that Falkenhayn's political ambitions were most important in explaining his actions. His strategic theories remain weakly defined and vague. Wolfgang Mommsen, "The Debate on German War Aims," in Walter Laqueur and George Mosse, eds., *1914: The Coming of the First World War* (New York: Harper Torch Book, 1966), pp. 66–67. For French domestic politics and pressure see David Stevenson, *French War Aims Against Germany, 1914–1919* (Oxford: Clarendon Press, 1982), pp. 36ff.

42   Hans Delbrück, "Der Krieg im August 1916," *PJ* dated 23 August 1916, reprinted in Delbrück, *Krieg und Politik* 2: 29–33.

43   Hans Delbrück, "Das deutsche Friedensangebot. Die amerikanische Vermittlung," *PJ* dated 29 December 1916, reprinted in Delbrück, *Krieg und Politik* 2:94–104.

44   Hans Delbrück, "Heutige Strategie und friderizianische Strategie," speech given in the Berlin Rathaus before a meeting of the Society for the History of Berlin, which was widely reported in the newspapers. *Neue Preussische Kreuz-Zeitung*, 11 December 1916; *Germania*, 12 December 1916; *Berliner Börsen Zeitung*, 10 December 1916; *Berliner Volkszeitung*, 10 December 1916; *Berliner Lokalanzeiger*, 11 December 1916; *Berliner Börsen Courier*, 10 December 1916; *Der Reichbote*, 11 December 1916.

45   Hans Delbrück, "Amerika zwischen Deutschland und England", *PJ* dated 26 February 1916, reprinted in Delbrück, *Krieg und Politik* 1:202–16.

46   Hans Delbrück, "Der Konflikt mit Amerika," *PJ* dated April 1916, reprinted in Delbrück, *Krieg und Politik* 1:252; *Lina Delbrück Memoirs*, Part 13, p. 43.

47   Letter from Ober-Kommando in der Marken, 8 August 1916, *Nachlass Delbrück*, section 20, BAK. Contained here are the galley proofs and typescripts of Delbrück's articles, with the censor's lining-out and stamp permitting publication for more than a dozen articles, 1914–18. On German press politics during the war, see Kurt Koszyk, *Deutsche Pressepolitik im Ersten Weltkrieg* (Düsseldorf: Droste, 1968).

48   In November 1915 he had a hearing at the Berlin police headquarters in regard to his discussion of a possible peace. Letter of 13 November 1915, from the Police-Praesidium, Berlin, *Nachlass Delbrück*, BAK.

49   Hans Delbrück, "Unnötige Sorge," *Tag*, 13 July 1916, and "Divide," *Tag*, 21 July 1916. Cf., Delbrück to Königliches Ober-Kommando in der Marken, 18 August 1916, Briefkonzeptbücher, *Nachlass Delbrück*, DSB.

50   Delbrück to Zimmerman, 10 August 1916, ibid.

51   Delbrück to his wife, from Obersdorf, 20 August 1916, *Lina Delbrück Memoirs*, Part 13, p. 52.

52   Holger Herwig, *The German Naval Officers Corps* (New York: Oxford University Press, 1973), pp. 186ff.; *'Luxury' Fleet: The Imperial German Navy, 1888–1918* (London: George Allen & Unwin, 1980), pp. 194ff. Williamson, *Karl Helfferich*, pp. 162ff.; Klaus Epstein, *Matthias Erzberger* (Princeton: Princeton University Press, 1959), pp. 154ff.; Ritter, *Sword and Scepter* 3:265ff.; Carl-Axel Gemzell, *Organization, Conflict, and Innovation: German Naval Strategic Planning, 1888–1940* (Stockholm: Lund, 1973), pp. 140ff.; Arthur Rosenberg, *Imperial Germany* (New York: Oxford University Press, 1970), pp. 131–33; Gerald Feldman, *Army Industry and Labor* (Princeton: Princeton University Press, 1966), pp. 140ff.; Martin Kitchen, *The Silent Dictatorship: The Politics of the German High Command under Hindenburg and Ludendorff, 1916–1918* (London: Croom Helm, 1976).

53   Ritter, *Sword and Scepter* 3: 300ff.; Feldman, *Army, Industry, and Labor*, pp. 40ff.; Jarausch, *Enigmatic Chancellor*, pp. 280ff.

54   Williamson, *Karl Helfferich*, pp. 162–96; Bernhard Schwertfeger, *Kaiser und Kabinettschef* (Oldenburg: Gerhard Stalling, 1931), p. 145; Ritter, *Sword and Scepter* 3: 308–15.

55   Williamson, *Karl Helfferich*, p. 163; Jarausch, *Enigmatic Chancellor*, p. 300.

56   Hans Delbrück, "Der diplomatische Winterfeldzug-Die Wilsonische-Friedens-Rede," PJ dated 28 January 1917, reprinted in Delbrück, *Krieg und Politik* 2:116; cf., Erich Ludendorff, *Ludendorff's Own Story*, 2 vols. (New York: Harper & Brothers, 1919), 1: 369ff.

57   Quoted in Schwabe, *Wissenschaft und Kriegsmoral*, p. 236.

58   *Lina Delbrück Memoirs*, Part 14, pp. 86–95.

59   Ibid., pp. 161–64. Cf. Forster, *The Failure of Peace*, pp. 42ff.

60   Fischer, *Germany's Aims*, pp. 505ff.; Ritter, *Sword and Scepter* 4:83–117; Feldman, *Army, Industry and Labor*, passim; Craig, *Politics*, pp. 320ff.

61   Tschuppik, *Ludendorff*, p. 135.

62   Erich Ludendorff, *Kriegführung und Politik* (Berlin: E. S. Mittler, 1932), p. 212.

63   Jehuda Wallach, *Das Dogma der Vernichtungsschlacht* (Frankfurt/M: Bernard & Graefe, 1967), p. 279. Ludendorff became even more dogmatic after the war. See Hans Speier, "Ludendorff," in Earle, *Makers of Modern Strategy*, pp. 306ff.; Jehuda Wallach, *Kriegstheorien* (Frankfurt/M: Bernard & Graefe, 1972), pp. 184–93.

64   Ritter, *Sword and Scepter* 4:229–33.

65   Reichstag, 12 Ausschuss, *Beilage zu den stenographischen Berichten über die öffentlichen Verhandlungen des Untersuchungsausschusses (4. Unterauschuss): Gutachten*

des Obersten A. D. Schwertfeger, des Generals der Infanterie A. D. von Kuhl und des Geheimrats Professor Hans Delbrück (Berlin: Reimar Hobbing, 1923), p. 217.

66 Hans Delbrück, "Kriegs-und Friedensparteien in der Welt, Reichskanzler und Reichstag, -Die Papstnote," *PJ* dated 25 August 1917, reprinted in Delbrück, *Krieg und Politik* 2:282.

67 Hans Delbrück, "Die auswärtige Politik und die Alldeutschen," *PJ* dated 21 April 1917, reprinted in Delbrück, *Krieg und Politik* 2:186−94.

68 *Lina Delbrück Memoirs*, Part 10, p. 19. Letter of 6.6.1917, quoted in Schwabe, *Wissenschaft und Kriegsmoral*, p. 260.

69 See Ritter, *Sword and Scepter* 3:457; Williamson, *Karl Helfferich*, p. 197ff.; Feldman, *Army, Industry and Labor*, pp. 349ff.; Craig, *Politics*, pp. 323ff.; Jarausch, *Enigmatic Chancellor*, pp. 364ff. Delbrück's eldest son, Waldemar, had died fighting in the German army in Macedonia in May 1917. He was buried in a mass grave with many of his comrades near Monastir. *Lina Delbrück Memoirs*, Part 12, p. 181.

70 Hans Delbrück, "Der Kanzlerwechsel—Die Friedensresolution. Lloyd Georges Antwort," *PJ* dated 28 July 1917, reprinted in Delbrück, *Krieg und Politik* 2:253−74.

71 Letter of 14 September 1917 to his wife, from Warnemünde, quoted in *Lina Delbrück Memoirs*, Part 13, p. 31.

72 Letter of 28 October 1917, Briefkonzeptbücher, *Nachlass Delbrück*, DSB.

73 Delbrück to Valentini, 5 September 1917, ibid.

74 Epstein, *Matthias Erzberger and the Dilemma of German Democracy*, pp. 153−54; Hans Peter Hanssen, *Diary of a Dying Empire*, pp. 201−04.

75 Delbrück to Valentini of 1 July 1917, quoted in Schwabe, *Wissenschaft und Kriegsmoral*, p. 258. Those who signed the resolution printed in the *PJ* 119 (July-September 1917): 194, were Mayor Alexander Dominicus, Paul Rohrback, Friedrich Thimme, Walter Nernst, Emil Fischer, Friedrich Meinecke, Adolf von Harnack, and Ernst Troeltsch. K. Mendelssohn, *The World of Walther Nernst: The Rise and Fall of German Science 1864−1941* (Pittsburgh: University of Pittsburgh Press, 1973), pp. 92−93.

76 Letter of 10 January 1918, Valentini to Delbrück; Delbrück's response, 11 January 1918; Briefkonzeptbücher, *Nachlass Delbrück*, DSB.

77 Ritter, *Sword and Scepter* 4:97−102; Tschuppik, *Ludendorff*, p. 156; Gatzke, *Germany's Drive*, p. 250.

78 Hans Delbrück, "Die preussische Wahlreform—Die Bedrohung der Monarchie," *PJ* dated January 1918, reprinted in Delbrück, *Krieg und Politik* 3:10. For a week in January and early February 1918, Delbrück was in The Hague, Holland, an invited speaker by Professor Brinkman. Accompanied by Kurt Hahn, Delbrück spoke to a number of German diplomatic personnel stationed there, gave several formal speeches and a number of press interviews in which he emphasized his views as we have been describing them. Later, this seems to have led to more discussions between Hahn, Colonel von Haeften, and American representatives; but it came to nothing, first, because of the German position over Belgium, and secondly, because of the weakening of the German offensive. See Ritter, *Sword and Scepter* 4:439−40; Delbrück's letters to his wife, January 30−February 8, 1918, quoted in *Lina Delbrück Memoirs*, Part 13, pp. 40−45. Letters, memorandas, and reports in *Nachlass, Delbrück* BAK, folder 39, support this. An attempt was made to build an informal network to start negotiations, but it met with very limited success.

79   Hans Delbrück, "Der Hubertusburg-Frieden," *Deutsche Korrespondenz*, 17 January 1918.

80   George von Below, *Das gute Recht der Vaterlandspartei* (Berlin, 1917); see Gatzke, *Germany's Drive*, pp. 206–09. Folder 44, Delbrück Nachlass, BAK, contains letters, newspaper clippings, and memoranda on the conservative political attacks and Delbrück's response.

81   Hans Delbrück, "Professor von Below als Vorkämpfer der Vaterlandspartei," *PJ* dated March 1918, reprinted in Delbrück, *Krieg und Politik* 3:45.

82   Thimme, *Hans Delbrück als Kritiker*, p. 144.

83   Hans Delbrück, "Die erneute Kriegszielerörterung," *PJ* dated 26 April 1918, reprinted in Delbrück, *Krieg und Politik* 3:64–73.

84   Delbrück to his wife, letters of February 16, 17, 19, 1918; quoted in *Lina Delbrück Memoirs*, Part 13, p. 61. Letter exchange with Max Lenz, March 22 and 26, 1918, *Nachlass Delbrück*, DSB.

85   Cf. Williamson, *Karl Helfferich*, pp. 266–72; Ritter, *Sword and Scepter* 4:311ff.; Fischer, *Germany's Aims*, pp. 619ff.

86   Hans Delbrück, "Die Aufgaben Deutschlands im Osten und Westen-Mitteleuropa-Staatssekretär von Kuhlmann," *PJ* dated 29 June 1918, reprinted in Delbrück, *Krieg und Politik* 3:103–23.

87   Delbrück to wife, 3 March 1918, *Lina Delbrück Memoirs*, Part 13, p. 75.

88   *Lina Delbrück Memoirs*, Part 13.

89   Hans Delbrück, "Ehrlicher Friedenswille. Der Tauchbootkrieg und Amerika," *PJ* dated 18 August 1918, reprinted in Delbrück, *Krieg und Politik* 3:137–53.

90   Hans Delbrück, "Die Buriansche Note. Die Verhandlungen des Hauptausschusses. Die Krisis," *PJ* dated 29 September 1918, reprinted in Delbrück, *Krieg und Politik* 3:167–79.

91   *Lina Delbrück Memoirs*, Part 13. The importance of the Wednesday evening discussion group *(Mittwochabend)* to all of this is a question we have avoided. The reason for this is that it does not seem as central to War Images as it would be, for example, to a discussion focusing on Delbrück's political views during this period. But, more important, the sources with which to answer the question are insufficient and they are not always in agreement. We know that the *Mittwochabend* was founded in August 1914 by Reichstag member Eugen Schiffer and Hans Delbrück and met through 1929. Averaging approximately twenty per evening, the group gathered first in a Berlin restaurant, later in a bank, and finally in a Prussian government office. The discussions were informal—with no written agenda or record of discussions. Delbrück usually proposed the topic and asked many of the questions himself. One of the younger participants later described it as resembling a seminar. Those who participated included Reichstag members, professors, bureaucrats, nobles, editors, businessmen, and a few officers. A wide variety of men took part: throughout the war, Delbrück's Berlin colleagues Friedrich Meinecke, Adolf von Harnack, and Ernst Troeltsch; during the early days of the war, Hermann Fürst von Hatzfeld-Trachenberg, Bogdan Graf von Hutton-Czapski, Karl Helfferich, and Paul von Schwabach; during the later war years, Prince Max von Baden, Paul Rohrbach, and Kurt Hahn; and after the war, Wilhelm Solf, Otto Hammann, Kurt Riezler, Friedrich von Siemens, Walter Simons, Theodore Wolf, Heinrich Scheuch, and Wilhelm Groener. Delbrück's wife suggested that the *Mittwochabend* was an influential body, writing, for example, that during Prince Max's chancellorship it acted as a kind of shadow cabinet. This may have been

so; however, there is not sufficient evidence to support such a position. Prince Max's memoirs and their most recent editors do not give Delbrück or the *Mittwochabend* much credit. According to them, Prince Max was much more under the influence of Kurt Hahn and Paul Rohrbach. Prince Max, they argue, inherited a political and military situation in which the boundaries of action were very circumscribed. At the same time, Prince Max attended the *Mittwochabend* from time to time, he called Delbrück the "father of the peace of agreement," and Delbrück's influence is certainly visible in Prince Max's life in the period 1917–18. *Prince Max von Baden: Erinnerungen und Dokumente*, ed. Golo Mann and Andreas Burckhardt (Stuttgart: Ernst Klett, 1968) pp. 19, 25, 125, 162, 183, 310. Cf. Ernst Jackh, *Der Goldene Pflug: Lebensernte eines Weltbürgers* (Stuttgart: Deutsche Verlags Anstalt 1954), pp. 188, 434, 441. Cf. Dieter Fricke, et al., *Die bürgerlichen Parteien in Deutschland*, 2 vols. (East Berlin: das europaische Büch, 1970), 2:330–34.

In 1919 Delbrück joined a group known as the *Heidelberger Vereinigung für eine Politik des Rechts*, whose purpose was to try to promote international understanding of World War I. Some of its members had participated in the *Mittwochabend*: Max and Alfred Weber, Hermann Oncken, Lujo Brentano, Walter Schucking, Konrad Haussmann, Graf Max Montgelas, Albrecht Mendelssohn-Bartholdy, and Prince Max. Cf. Eisenbeiss, *Die bürgerliche Friedensbewegung in Deutschland während des Ersten Weltkrieges*, pp. 244ff.; Leo Haupts, *Deutsche Friedenspolitik, 1918–1919: Eine Alternative zur Machtpolitik des Ersten Weltkrieges* (Düsseldorf: Droste, 1976), pp. 104ff. and passim.

Another potential offshoot of the *Mittwochabend* related to politics was the group which signed the declaration asking for Prussian electoral reform in the July 1917 *PJ*. This included Delbrück, Meinecke, Harnack, Troeltsch, Rohrbach, Alexander Dominicus, major of Berlin-Schoenberg, Professor Friedrich Thimme, and Walter Nernst. *Prince Max von Baden: Erinnerungen und Dokumente*, p. 151. Several months earlier, in approximately February 1917, Nobel Prize winning physicist Walter Nernst had requested an audience with Kaiser Wilhelm at military headquarters. Nernst, like Harnack, had been a frequent visitor to the palace and was considered a friend of the kaiser. The audience was granted and, with Hindenburg and Ludendorff present, Nernst put forth a position very similar to that of Delbrück. The American entry into the war would give the enemy powers a limitless potential, he said, and he went on to compare this with the shrinking resources of Germany. A negotiated peace would soon become inevitable, he concluded. Ludendorff brushed aside his arguments, saying that they were only the incompetent nonsense of a civilian. Karl Mendelssohn, *The World of Walter Nernst: The Rise and Fall of German Science 1864–1941* (Pittsburgh: University of Pittsburgh, 1973), p. 92. This statement, like so many of Delbrück's, was made known to the kaiser and his entourage in a variety of ways.

Another institution related to Delbrück, his military and political position, and to his colleagues and students—in particular Martin Hobohm—was the Zentralstelle für Auslandsdienst, apparently created as an offshoot of the Foreign Ministry in Berlin around May 1915. Founded to collect and publish material against the Pan-Germans (Alldeutsch), to work against annexations, German chauvinism, and, by 1917, conservative anti-Semitism, by November 1916 the office had a leader, three secretaries, and received substantial financial support from such business leaders as Bankhaus Delbrück, Schickler; Bleichröder; and Robert Bosch. Hans Schleier, *Die bürgerliche deutsche Geschichtesschreibung der Weimarer Republik* (East Berlin: Adademie Verlag, 1975), pp. 540–46.

My original hypothesis that the *Mittwochabend* was a powerful wartime group by means of which Delbrück influenced political and military affairs proved untenable. The most that can be said is that though well-funded, its influence was limited and the views expressed, at least Delbrück's, went unheeded. Sources which seemed promising at first did not prove to be so. Thus, Paul Rühlmann's brief essay, "Delbrück's Mittwochabend," pp. 75–81 in Emil Daniels and Paul Rühlmann, eds., *Am*

Webstuhl der Zeit: Eine Erinnerungsgabe Hans Delbrück dem Achtzigjährigen von Freunden und Schülern dargebracht (Berlin: Reimar Hobbing, 1928), is essentially a list of some of those who participated and a general description of the nature of the discussions. The Delbrück papers do not contain anything more than this. Cf. *Nachlass Delbrück*, DSB, Fasz. 23; *Nachlass Delbrück*, Bundesarchiv folders 38, 43, 48. Cf. Werner Schiefel, *Bernhard Dernburg: Kolonialpolitiker und Bankier im wilhelminischen Deutschland* (Zurich: Atlantis, 1974), pp. 155ff.; Dieter Fricke et al., *Die Burgerlichen Parteien in Deutschland*, 2 vols. (East Berlin: das europaische Buch, 1970), 2:330–34.

92 Hans Delbrück, "Der militärische Umschlag—Prinz Max Reichskanzler—Die Verfassungskrise—Die Verantwortung für den Krieg mit Amerika—Diplomatische Aussichten—General Ludendorff," *PJ* dated 26 October 1918, reprinted in Delbrück, *Kreig und Politik* 3:181ff.

Hans Delbrück
1917

5 / EMPIRE TO REPUBLIC, 1918–1920

If the victories of 1866 and 1871, instrumental in the creation of the second German Empire, were disturbing, defeat in the World War and the dissolution of the imperial government was disastrous. The impact encompassed the whole society, particularly the General Staff and the professoriate, which had spurred on the officers' most extreme aims of military annihilation and political expansion.

Some saw the formal ending of the World War (armistice of November 1918 and Versailles Treaty of June 1919) as a dictated peace. Germany was not allowed to participate in the peace conference. She was presented with a finished treaty and finally, after balking at signing it, given the choice of acceptance or an immediate resumption of the war. Terms included forfeiture of colonies, territorial losses, reduction of the army to 100,000 men, abolition of offensive weapons, outlawing of the General Staff, and unlimited monetary and material reparations. All of this was predicated on Clause 231, which implied that Germany accepted responsibility for causing the war and for the loss and damage which followed. It is no wonder that German military and civilian leaders tried to escape responsibility for such a treaty, and newspapers printed with black borders announced its acceptance.

In spite of these terms, the fact that the treaty was not a peace settlement negotiated between military equals, but a surrender document extracted from the vanquished by the victors was never widely understood in Germany. The reasons for this are complicated and most of this chapter tries to shed light on them. Briefly stated, wartime propaganda and censorship, reinforced by successes on the battlefield and at the conference table (Treaties of Brest-Litovsk and Bucharest) had prepared Germans for victory. The suddenness of defeat was impossible to understand. Although at war's end German troops stood in every theatre on foreign soil, the military commanders requested the armistice and assented to the treaty because the army could no longer fight on, circumstances never clear to many Germans. The economic and social woes of the Weimar period made clarity in these questions difficult if not impossible, and gave all strategic questions a strongly political cast. In the relatively free postwar press, the Germans contested the domestic war guilt issue: who or what had caused the German defeat?

Every interpretation of the World War supported or denied the over-turning of the monarchy and the validity of the new republic. Put another way, the legitimacy of republican Germany depended on accep-tance of a particular war image. If the imperial regime, dominated by the military, had engendered its own demise through inept and weak leader-ship, then the "revolution" of 1918, the transformation in governmental forms, could be justified, however difficult to accept. If, on the other hand, domestic but internationally inspired forces, such as the Social Democrats, Socialists, and Communists, had caused the collapse by stabbing the imperial regime in the back, the *"Dolchstoss,"* then the legitimacy of the revolution and of these parties to head the new gov-ernment was considerably weakened, and, much more serious, they be-came vulnerable to the charge of treason during wartime.[1]

Hans Delbrück was seventy years old on November 11, 1918. Before the dust of battle had settled, he was engaged in a bitter confrontation before German public opinion. In a series of publications and in testi-mony before the German Reichstag committee and Munich *Dolchstoss* trial, Delbrück opposed the validity of the "stab in the back" legend and became involved in a controversy with the World War officers, led by Erich Ludendorff. Conservative associations, rightist politicians, offi-cers, and journalists attacked him. For a time even members of the Del-brück family disowned him.[2]

While this was going on, the long-standing disagreement over meth-ods and philosophy of history with the university professors and the General Staff officers reached conclusion. Delbrück failed to create a chair for military history at Berlin and was unable to influence the offi-cial history of World War I. Professors and officers rejected his historical thinking. The pioneer of the history of war in the framework of politics found his historical views opposed because of their political impli-cations.

Although he was lauded at his eightieth birthday celebration in 1928 as a fighter for Germany's honor in international politics, few of his countrymen could accept Delbrück's view of domestic war guilt. This was a bad omen for the future of republican Germany.

1918–1919, *DOLCHSTOSS* OR DEFEAT?

German society after World War I had a political cast, a strident tone, and a deadly historical quarrel.[3] The first transition, 1918–1919—from war to peace and from empire to republic—was the most difficult and set the tone for all that followed. We have suggested that the legitimacy of the republic depended on acceptance of a particular historical interpretation of the end of war: did the imperial regime engender its own demise or had domestic forces dealt a crippling blow from within? The domestic war guilt issue focused squarely on the closing months of 1918. Two very different interpretations developed.

The *Dolchstoss* or "stab in the back" legend originated at military headquarters. In July 1918, Ludendorff's aide, Colonel Max Bauer, had drafted a letter to Interior Minister Drews demanding an increase in military pay. The war is not yet won, he wrote; we will win if the homeland no longer stabs the army in the back and if the army, by receiving its due, can maintain trust and confidence.[4] Later that week, at the Düsseldorf Industry Club, Colonel Bauer again blamed the people at home. The War Ministry and chancellor did nothing thoroughgoing; there was a continuous danger at our backs.[5] He complained that the results of this faintheartedness were also evident at the front and found it remarkable that military discipline had held up so long. As the Supreme Command had no direct influence over civilian affairs, it was not responsible for the domestic breakdown.[6]

The final German offensive was crushed by a French attack spearheaded by five hundred tanks. Shaken German armies retreated from their Marne River positions. On August 8, the "German day of mourning," a massive Allied offensive crossed the Somme and penetrated bloodily several kilometers through the forward positions. The retreating armies moved in bewilderment from one position to another in the face of superior numbers, equipment, and esprit de corps. At German headquarters was a mood of sorrow and disbelief. The officers were paralyzed and shocked. As one observer wrote: "They did not want to understand why this was so and therefore they did not." Educated in the belief that success in war depended upon battle and attack, they could not comprehend that the strategic ideas of the Schlieffen School could lead to failure.[7]

Throughout August, with increasing enemy advances, the tension between the illusion of victory and the reality of defeat became an obsession in Ludendorff's mind. He searched for an explanation of the strategic outcome of the war and a way to shift responsibility away from the General Staff and himself. The chief of staff and other officers at headquarters were paralyzed and inactive from mid-July through September; a neurologist was called in. Finally, on October 1, Ludendorff told his staff officers that he had asked the kaiser: ". . . to include in the government those circles whom we have chiefly to thank that things have come so far. We will see these people brought into the ministries. They shall conclude the peace that now must be made. They shall drink the soup they have cooked up for us."[8]

During the following two months this explanation spread through-out conservative circles. Civilians, the Reichstag peace coalition, and those who had supported negotiations were responsible for the military defeat.[9] President Wilson added impetus by suggesting that the Allies might agree to less rigorous terms if they did not have to negotiate with the "military masters and monarchical autocrats." Consequently the government of Prince Max von Baden accepted the suggestion of Mar-shal Foch that civil officials rather than the General Staff negotiate the armistice.

As preliminary armistice exchanges began, Ludendorff rejected the Allied proposals, tried to sabotage the negotiations, and demanded a continuation of the war.[10] This brought about his dismissal and an inter-im command headed by Hindenburg, but with General Wilhelm Groener acting on Hindenburg's behalf. In the confusion of early No-vember, Groener felt that he must safeguard at all costs the one great asset the army, and indeed Germany, still had—the military prestige of Hindenburg. Groener reasoned that Hindenburg must not be identified with the armistice, the peace, or the new republican government.[11]

Following the lead of military headquarters, the civilian supporters of unlimited war aims also took up the "stab in the back." Leaders of the Pan-Germans and Fatherland Party used it to shift responsibility away from themselves to Bethmann Hollweg and the parties of the Liberal Reichstag majority.[12] The collapse of the home front had prevented Hindenburg from winning, they said. The German people had lost faith in the military: terrible stories from the home front had enervated the army.[13] Rumors were circulated in Berlin newspapers and at the univer-sity that defeatism at home had caused military collapse.[14] New Reich Chancellor Friedrich Ebert welcomed guards regiment home to Berlin on the 10th of December, 1918, with the words that no enemy had over-whelmed them.[15] People's Party leader Gustav Stresemann wrote that the war front had held up to the last moment, but the civilians had capit-ulated.[16] The Pan-German *Deutsche Tageszeitung,* in a front-page story entitled, "The German Army Betrayed," attributed to the English general Maurice a statement that civilians had stabbed the German army in the back.[17]

Gradually the *Dolchstoss* legend grew and spread throughout public life. The left and liberals in Germany, especially the Socialists and those related to the munitions strikes in 1917–18, were accused of treason against the state in the waning days of the World War. Those who had favored limited war aims and supported peace negotiations were also implicated. The government of Max von Baden had negotiated a prema-ture armistice, undercutting the German military position. The army was undefeated in the field.

It is not surprising that these men sought to evade association with the outcome of the war. For those with expansionist war aims and conservative political expectations, the actual outcome was an even greater shock than for those, like Delbrück, with more moderate presumptions. The inexplicably large gap separating expectations from outcome, and the suddenness with which this chasm opened, are crucial in the handling of all postwar German strategic and political questions.

Simultaneously a second view of the end of the war was taking form. "How greatly have I erred." With deep sadness Delbrück began his commentary in December 1918.[18] As bad as the situation had been four weeks earlier, he had not given up hope that the front would hold, an armistice be achieved; that a transition could be made to a more responsible government without sharp break with the past. He held faith that Germany's military power would keep the country politically moderate. This hope was unfounded, he now recognized. The proud army which had withstood the whole world for four long years was beaten, morally dissolved, and forced into a virtual capitulation. Even in the worst hours, Delbrück had not envisioned such an outcome.

Trying to explain the events of November 1918, Delbrück turned to the past. The Prussian-German army, he wrote, was created out of the old standing army of Frederick the Great and the noble officer corps, reconstructed after the defeat of 1806, and united with the concept of general conscription. The enormous power that this army developed in 1813, 1866, 1870, and in the World War resulted from the fusion of these two elements: military honor and discipline from the old professional army, and massive national defense power from general conscription and reserve forces. Although they worked well together, a certain tension always remained. Middle-class elements filled the officer corps, yet the sharp separation between officers and men was preserved. The harshness of military discipline was often felt as brutality and endured with difficulty. Middle-class parties overlooked complaints of mishandling of soldiers, as in the Zabern affair, a potential crisis over militarism. But as long as the army remained victorious the system was sacrosanct. The break finally came where Scharnhorst joined the standing army and the army of the people. It was the mutiny of the men, the armed people, against the professionals of the officer corps.

All reports agree that the morale of the army as it began the March 21 offensive was as splendid as it had been during the ebullient march to the front of August 1914. In spite of this the army failed to conquer Arras, Amiens and Ypres. . . . With the entry of the Americans, superior capabilitily passed to our enemies, not only superiority of men but of tanks, airplanes, artillery and munitions.

In the face of this onslaught the damage was so great that finally German power gave out. Then the spirit collapsed. The feelings of the home front might have been one factor, but what could the best morale sent from home do against the increasing power and the inexhaustible strength of the enemy in men and materials?

The campaign and the war was lost not because morale was low; morale was low because the troops began to feel the impossibility of a German success.[19]

If Prince Max had taken over the leadership of the Foreign Office at the end of June, Delbrück asserted, things might have been different. By October, when he became chancellor, General Ludendorff informed him of the collaspe of the army and the necessity for an immediate armistice. If the old regime had requested this, their bankruptcy would have been clear. The prince accepted the possibility that the situation was better than Ludendorff reported, that the troops could still hold out. He had no other choice. He could only exploit his reputation as a man of peace and hope that the armistice request might be taken not as a sign of military weakness but as a consequence of the change of government and the humane view of new leadership. But the enemies were not deceived: they used their military advantages, and then came the final terrible events. Before the conclusion of negotiations, the Social Democratic Party ended the regime and made Germany defenseless.

The military-Pan-German leadership led Germany to this disaster, Delbrück stated, but the Social Democratic Party completed it by using the military catastrophe to gain power precisely when everything depended on holding the remaining strength together.

Delbrück described the November 1918 rebellion which began in the navy. As the officers saw that the coming armistice might bring surrender of German warships to England, they decided to go down honorably and to take the English fleet to the grave with them. Naval history celebrates the idealism of the captain who would rather die with his ship then surrender his flag. The distrust of the sailors, who suspected they might be sacrificed for military honor, already existed. In 1917 Admiral Capelle had reported a very dangerous political fermentation in the navy at Wilhelmshaven. Undoubtedly a systematic revolutionary cultivation of the sailors had already taken place. Preparations for sea battle in the fall of 1918 touched off the powder. The naval mutiny sparked similar actions in the land army. The officers no longer controlled their men.

What did the soldiers want? Delbrück asked if they had suddenly become republicans. His response was negative. Even the Social Democrats were only republicans in theory: few Germans desired a republic; all they wanted was peace, an end to the fighting.

The military mutiny, which itself had nothing to do with the Social Democrats, joined together with the political revolutionaries because both were of accord that a positive program could be established. . . . Hopelessness at the front required peace. To demand and to facilitate peace, one had to demand the abdication of the Kaiser. Abdication meant revolution and revolution at that moment meant our complete lack of an army and the destruction of our situation. . . . The closest historical analogy to the World War for Germany was the Peloponnesian War and the destruction of Athens. . . . How strong, proud and self-assured was Athens under Pericles' leadership at the beginning of the conflict.[20]

This was Delbrück's December 1918 explanation of the revolution. This interpretation, modified in various ways, has become accepted gradually since 1945.[21] During the Weimar period, however, it was aberrant and foreign not only to public opinion but for many German leaders. Delbrück was not fundamentally a republican either before or after 1918. He was a republican by reason, not feeling, whose allegiances were only painfully and never completely torn away from the monarchy and all that it represented. His historical instincts nonetheless convinced him that the war had forced a fateful structural change in the German State.

During the early spring of 1919, Delbrück's thoughts turned repeatedly to domestic war guilt: what factors within Germany had aided foreign pressures? He realized that one reason for Germany's weak moral position was the 1914 war plan and the invasion of Belgium.[22] In May, German Minister of Foreign Affairs Count Ulrich von Brockdorff-Rantzau invited Delbrück, along with Max Weber, Graf Max Montgelas, and Albrecht Mendelssohn Bartholdy, to Versailles to respond to the victor's claim that Germany had started the war and thus should pay reparations.[23] Their memorandum and the Allied response of June 16, 1919, touched off the great international war guilt controversy that raged for several decades. During the summer and fall of 1919, Delbrück publicly and privately expressed his utterly downcast mood. "I see only black, here and for all the world," he wrote.[24]

By late spring of 1919 the first of Erich Ludendorff's three war commentaries had appeared: *My War Memoirs 1914–18*.[25] According to Ludendorff, Germany would have won the war if only the right spirit had united the populace. The French, English, and Americans had backed their leaders, but the Germans had declined to support the will to victory. During most of the war, Ludendorff wrote, the Reich had the choice of triumph or defeat. Suddenly in autumn 1918, a negotiated peace became necessary. Paradoxically, he clearly perceived the deficiencies of men and materials which had existed from spring 1918.

Ludendorff's assertions were historically false, Delbrück responded.[26] The decisive question was whether Germany could have negotiated a peace before 1918. Was everything done to realize a settlement? If a negotiated peace was possible in September and October 1918, he wrote, when the war was lost, it was possible before that loss.[27] Ludendorff sought victory by battle while simultaneously admitting Germany's inability to fight such a war.

In the spring of 1919, in the National Assembly at Weimar, the ruling left had attempted to create a special court to investigate the military defeat. Failing that, it successfully called for a parliamentary investigation of the causes, course, and conclusion of the World War. Hearings began in August 1919, and in November Hindenburg and Ludendorff appeared before the second subcommittee in Berlin. Karl Helfferich had just testified for three days, making front-page news across Germany. Not only did he successfully question the legality of the proceedings, but he intimidated the committee and indicted one of its members, Independent Socialist Oskar Cohn, for accepting money from the Soviet government to revolutionize Germany. Helfferich's barbed thrusts goaded committee members into various unfortunate admissions. Cohn, for example, acknowledged that for him the committee was merely a vehicle to attack the old imperial government.[28]

During the hearings, Hindenburg stayed at Helfferich's house, which was cordoned off by a Reichswehr honor guard and several police detachments; and, according to one historian,[29] Helfferich strongly influenced Hindenburg's presentation.[30] Their arrival at the hearing was preceded by a triumphal motorcade through the streets of Berlin. Although Hindenburg was to read a prepared statement, then Ludendorff to answer questions, they ignored Reichstag procedure.

While the army had fought gallantly until the last minute, Hindenburg said, the nation had proved itself weak and undisciplined. Disintegration of civilian morale had set in even before he and Ludendorff had taken over Supreme Command in August 1916, and was exemplified by the government's rejection of their proposals to concentrate all national forces to terminate the war quickly and favorably. From that moment on, they were uncertain about the home front. Military goals became untenable, operations were bound to fail, and soon the collapse became inevitable. The revolution was only the keystone. An English general said justly that the German army was stabbed in the back. The sound core of the army could not be blamed. Its performance, like that of the officer corps, called for admiration. It was perfectly plain on whom the blame rested. Further proof, if necessary, could be found in the utter amazement of the enemies at their victory. Hindenburg finished by saying that he and Ludendorff had always shared the important decisions.[31] Ignoring questions, he and his chief of staff left the hearing.

Thus the "stab in the back" legend, launched a year earlier within the General Staff, was formally enunciated to the German public at the Reichstag inquiry. The generals spared themselves and their conservative supporters the onus of responsibility and upheld the myth of the undefeated army betrayed at home. In the face of this formidable backing, contrary documentary evidence and expert opinion during the next decade proved less effective.[32]

In a series of articles following this testimony, Delbrück tried to undermine the generals' position. The German military unitedly believed that only the Schlieffen Plan could bring victory in 1914. This belief morally justified the march through neutral Belgium. But the plan failed. Were German forces too weak from the start? Did Germany underestimate Belgian resistance, or the rapidity of English aid, or the defensive tenacity of the French? Or did General von Moltke lack the consistency and willpower to carry out such a plan?

Delbrück delineated a second phase of war leadership under General von Falkenhayn which aimed to follow the idea of Schlieffen to seek a decision in the west, but in an entirely different manner. Falkenhayn had decided against victory by battle. After the first month of the war, Falkenhayn had realized that a military decision like that of 1870 was impossible. Instead he wanted to convince the Western opponents that they could defeat Germany only if they were willing to destroy themselves in the process. By limited battles and diplomacy, the enemy was to be made conscious of Germany's power and, at the same time, of German willingness to negotiate. The best example of this strategy was at Verdun.

Describing Clausewitz's distinction between the strategy of annihilation and that of attrition, Delbrück reminded his readers that many great wars in world history had been fought and won using limited strategy. Verdun aimed to make the enemy use up far greater forces than Germany. The French would be bled to death, not annihilated. This "bleeding out" was a special form of the war of attrition, Delbrück averred. Frederick the Great achieved many of his greatest successes in this way. He did not try for Napoleonic decisions because he had as little power as Falkenhayn in the World War.[33]

Delbrück recognized that it was impossible to compare Ludendorff and Falkenhayn exactly: after Falkenhayn was replaced as chief of the General Staff, Russia left the war and America entered it, fundamentally altering the whole strategic situation. Nonetheless, the difference between the two commanders was clear from a comparison of their strategy for 1915. Ludendorff had urged a great sweep to annihilate the whole Russian left wing far beyond the Kowno-Wilna lines. If a German army appeared there, he reasoned, the Russians would have been forced backwards, and in the process might have been encircled and destroyed. Falkenhayn opposed this: to encircle and destroy the large and well-led Russian army appeared to him utopian. Delbrück pointed out that Russian resistance would have been formidable. In April 1915 the Germans and Austrians together had 1,303,000 men, compared to 1,767,000 for the Russians. With such superior forces, the Russians could not have been annihilated. Ludendorff, Delbrück concluded, overestimated German potential.[34] In all of his plan—the fall campaign of 1915, the Hindenburg program, the peace of Brest Litovsk, the March 1918 offensive—ideals were out of balance with reality. Ludendorff wanted to destroy the enemy, but this was impossible given the means available.[35]

By 1920 it was clear that Delbrück was not entirely alone in these views. In addition to some socialists, he was joined by a few retired combat officers. Writing from their own experience, they emphasized how problematic the outlook for war had been in August 1914. General von Gleich, for example, condemned the enforced uniformity of official military history before 1914 because it resulted in an underestimation of material realities. By focusing on map studies and local tactical exercises, the army failed to consider the economic capabilities of potential opponents. As a result, Germany entered the war with a strategy unsuited to its relative weakness. As soon as German strength was exhausted, collapse became unavoidable. He concluded that the World War was lost before it had begun.[36] Officers who celebrated Ludendorff as a great patriot often could not refrain from asking publicly why the General Staff had failed to supply enough ammunition and supplies in 1918.[37] Others noted caustically that Ludendorff had not only lost the war but was unable to understand the reasons for this catastrophe.[38] "Foreign enemies," as Ludendorff and the conservatives called them, also joined Delbrück's side of the argument. Alphonse Buat, chief of the French General Staff, asserting that material weaknesses had felled the Germans in 1918, feared that Ludendorff had failed even to concentrate his available resources. The basic problem of the German army in spring 1918 had been lack of men, ammunition, and food.[39]

Ludendorff and the conservatives lashed out at their critics, demanding that old soldiers support the honor of the Imperial Army and not allow traitors to tarnish its image. For many conservatives, Ludendorff was *the* symbol of those who had fought for the fatherland,[40] and he thrust himself forward as a patriotic leader. Do not allow, he said, malevolent critics to dishonor the military reputation of Field Marshal von

Hindenburg and of his first quartermaster general. Ludendorff urged his wartime comrades to stop the complaining, bitter judgments, and damaging analysis. He urged them to close ranks under the strong self-control of battle. Germany's enemies continued to fear the old army, he said: they stand amazed at its deeds. Do not criticize its reputation but join together in a common defense against foreign enemies and those Germans who would corrupt us with disparaging analysis.[41]

Other generals who had participated in the World War tried more subtle ways to influence public impressions of the war. Hindenburg, for example, suggested to his former subordinate Wilhelm Groener that a critical history of the 1918 offensive might favor Germany's enemies, cause shame to the officer corps, and convince the fatherland of its defeat.[42] Germany, Hindenburg implied, was better off believing that its army had been undefeated in the field.

THE MILITARY, SOCIETY, AND HISTORY: THE WEIMAR YEARS

We began *War Images* with a discussion of the army in the new German state of the 1870s and the status of history in army and university. These relationships were again important in the 1920s. As Germany had been a new empire in 1871, she was a new republic in 1918. Beyond this, however, much was changed. The wars of unification had been brief, decisive, victorious. The World War was a prolonged, ambiguous defeat with enormous losses. As victory in 1871 fostered political unity, defeat initiated political and social trituration.

In the 1920s as in the 1870s, the army was an important vehicle of political change. Its leaders contributed to the disintegration of the traditional order by failing to support the kaiser in November 1918 and then, shortly thereafter, by making a compact with the head of the new republican government. That no republican army was ever created is an anomaly of Weimar Germany. In the chaos of the early postwar years, many looked to the old army as a traditional institution which had to be preserved in the face of "modernism": the abolition of the monarchy, democratic politics, and socialist tendencies. Admittedly, a few declared that republican Germany needed no army or that the military establishment should be reduced in size and importance. Because Germany's wartime enemies tried to enforce these views in the Treaty of Versailles, however, this was difficult for Germans to accept or advocate. Many saw the military as the symbol of security at a time when their country appeared threatened by enemies at home and abroad.

German society took on ominous militaristic tones. Dispirited and worn-out troops, retiring from the front with arms and equipment, found a homeland in which the old order seemed to have vanished. Parties of the center, supporting the fledgling democracy, clashed against the antirepublican left, which advocated a communist government, and the conservative right, which desired some form of restoration. To achieve their goals, political parties created paramilitary forces. Following the example of the left-wing Spartacists and the conservative Freikorps which bloodily routed the communists from Berlin, each segment of the political spectrum created party militia: the *Stahlhelm, Werwolf,* and the Nazi *Sturmabteilung* on the right, the *Reichsbanner* in the center, and the *Rotfront Kämpferbund* on the left. Members included returned soldiers searching for the Germany they had left behind, for something different and better, or perhaps for the comradeship and excitement of life at the front.

The wholesale entry of military ways into politics was accompanied by a nostalgic longing for a romanticized past—for an idealized wartime unity when conflicts and self-interests had been submerged in the desire for victory. Ernst Jünger's romantic versions of battlefield actions became best sellers. Antimilitarist works, such as Erich Maria Remarque's *All Quiet on the Western Front,* had less public impact. In popular culture as well as politics, the war provided a battleground for conflicting images of the past. By 1933 it was clear that the road to power had been blazed by paramilitary formations to which the government conceded its near monopoly of uniform wearing. Fighting street and beer hall battles, murdering opponents, applying violence, and threatening more, political parties became military societies.[43] Party rhetoric took on the grammar of wartime propaganda as both Nazi and Communist fought the battle for men's minds.

As in the 1870s, when Field Marshal von Moltke had remained aloof, many officers of the 1920s tried to maintain the army as a disinterested instrument of the state, above politics.[44] But ambiguities regarding the lost war were not cleared up, political parties adopted military ways, and the army became inextricably involved. The first republican president made a compact with the old army; his successor was a field marshal, and the last republican chancellor was chief of the General Staff before assuming civil office. Political activism by younger officers was widespread.

A second dimension important to an understanding of the Weimar years is the attitude of professors and officers toward history. For the professoriate, Fritz Ringer has identified a general feeling of cultural malaise and professional dissatisfaction which reached apogee during the 1920s.[45] Defeat and revolution confirmed professorial suspicions that the world was out of sorts. They interpreted the violent political clashes of the day, in which most of them did not participate, as symptomatic of German decadence and moral failure. A general pessimism was pervasive. One is reminded of the letter Delbrück wrote to his wife from Versailles in 1919, in which he saw only black ahead, not only for Germany but for all the world.

German historians in this period have been divided into two groups. The majority were "orthodox conservatives." Such men as Delbrück's wartime antagonists Dietrich Schäfer and Georg von Below had been strategists of annihilation, and from November 1918 they fought the republic, believing that foreign and domestic enemies had combined to destroy their venerated Second Reich. Glorifying the empire and adhering to traditional idealism, for them the strong state continued to be the central, ethical force in the past. Idealism and spiritual values remained the major causative factors in history. They viewed materialism with suspicion and fear; it signified decadence vaguely linked to a lack of patriotism. They opposed critical analysis and other intellectual techniques which undermined traditional sources of social cohesion. In 1921 the conservatives uniformly rejected the Prussian Ministry of Culture's call for educational reform, interdisciplinary programs, and the teaching of useful general knowledge. This was an example of utilitarian present-mindedness. The conservatives sought a purely spiritual engagement with the world.[46]

A much smaller group, called the "modernists," liked the new republic no better than their orthodox opponents did. They were republicans by reason, not by feeling, as Friedrich Meinecke once referred to this group which included himself, Delbrück, Troeltsche, Max Weber, and a few others. This circle, most of whom had favored limited strategic aims during the war, resigned themselves to democracy as a technical necessity of modern times. Two of this group considered historiographically the most novel were Friedrich Meinecke and Otto Hintze. In fact, neither departed very far from tradition. If Meinecke now admitted that the state could no longer be completely identified with ethical considerations, and Hintze called for broad comparative studies interrelating social, political, and economic factors, neither put their ideas into practice.[47]

Hans Delbrück did not become a major intellectual leader among the modernists during these years. His writings continued starkly in contrast to conservative historical orthodoxy, but Delbrück remained an outsider even among modernist historians. Although political pressures now forced Delbrück into his most radical historical position, it was in every respect a continuation of his work before 1918. Delbrück's isolated position of the 1920s resulted not from his historical methods, which separated him from the conservatives, but from the conclusions which resulted from the application of these methods to war and politics, conclusions neither conservative nor modernist could accept.

The professoriate were uneasy in the new political climate. Their disquiet influenced both their pessimistic overall views and their reassertion of traditional methods and forms of history. Little that was fundamentally new developed during the 1920s. Eckart Kehr, Martin Hobohm, and others who broke new paths in the direction of social and economic history were unable to continue in the 1930s, and few survived that decade. Delbrück's recognition as historian did not begin until after 1945.

If the professors remained personally disquieted but professionally uninvolved during the 1920s, the officers had both a personal and a professional stake in the outcome of World War I, and both of these interests received strong institutional support. Though outlawed by the Versailles Treaty, the General Staff and War Academy continued their intellectual role. Staff officers selected by examination were educated professionally in a three-year course of study, with military history central. In the guise of civilian bureaucrats, they investigated the past, prepared for the future, and taught a uniform body of strategic doctrine which again bound history and war planning together. A new quasi-civil agency, the *Reichsarchiv*, perpetuated the tradition and function of the old Military History Section. Following the intellectual pattern established after 1871, officers of the old army celebrated its triumphs and defended its defeat in the World War. More than a thousand volumes, dwarfing anything previously attempted, embodied the patriotic and idealist traditions of the "Prussian" and "Schlieffen" Schools in support of this image.

But the officers were also divided in their loyalties. Although many active and retired soldiers accepted General Staff views, some did not. Foremost among these were combat veterans—company, regimental, or divisional commanders whose war experiences had been far different from those of the staff officers, and whose historical interpretations as a result starkly contrasted to those of the General Staff. Few among this group supported the *Dolchstoss* legend. Having experienced firsthand the dehumanizing brutality of industrial mass warfare, they understood why Germany had lost the war.

NOTES

1   The situation is reflected in numerous court cases during the Weimar period, for example in the case Matthias Erzberger versus Karl Helfferich; cf. Erich Eyck, *A History*

of the Weimar Republic, 2 vols. (New York: Atheneum, 1970), 1:43ff.; Arnold Brecht, *The Political Education of Arnold Brecht* (Princeton: Princeton University Press, 1970), pp. 176ff.; Heinrich Hannover and Elizabeth Hannover-Druck, *Politische Justiz 1918-33* (Frankfurt: Fischer Bücherei, 1966); Reinhard Rürup, "Problems of the German Revolution," *Journal of Contemporary History* 3 (1968): 129ff.; Michael L. Hughes, "Private Equity, Social Inequity: German Judges React to Inflation, 1914-24," *Central European History,* vol. 16, no. 1 (March 1983), 76-94.

2   Family members circulated a petition in 1920-21 asking Delbrück to recant his position with regard to the World War. Later, by about 1925, the leaders of this group came to Delbrück and apologized. Conversation with Frau Helene Hobe, June 1974, Berlin-Dahlem.

3   Peter Gay, *Weimar Culture* (New York: Harper Torchbook, 1968), pp. 6, 80.

4   Joachim Petzold, *Die Dolchstosslegende* (East Berlin: Akademie Verlag, 1963), p. 502; notes of July 2 and July 13, 1918, Bauer Nachlass, Bundesarchiv Koblenz, quoted in Feldman, *Army, Industry and Labor,* p. 502. Cf. Friedrich Frhr. Hiller von Gaetringen, "Dolchstoss-Diskussion und Dolchstoss-Legende im Wandel von Vier Jahrzehnten," in *Geschichte und Gegenwärtsbewusstein: Festschrift für Hans Rothfels,* ed. Walter Besson and Frhr. von Gaertringen (Göttingen: Vandenhoeck & Ruprecht, 1963).

5   Feldman, *Army, Industry and Labor,* p. 502.

6   Bauer to Fleischer, 3 September 1918, quoted ibid., pp. 502-03. The theme of *Dolchstoss* is evident in all of Bauer's writings on the World War. He believed the German Army was "predestined for victory": it must have been stabbed in the back because it could not have been defeated. Cf. Adolf Vogt, *Oberst Max Bauer: Generalstabsoffizier im Zwielicht 1869-1929* (Osnabrück: Biblio Verlag, 1974), pp. 158-70.

7   Testimony of General der Infanterie Mertz von Quirnheim, the president of the Reichsarchiv, 13 November 1923, and Generalmajor von Bartenwerffer, 26 November 1923, typescript in *Nachlass Delbrück,* Fasz. 108, DSB. The point at issue here is the long delay from approximately July 18 to September 28, 1918, between the time when the battlefield situation had definitely turned against Germany and the notification of this from the Supreme Command to the Foreign Office and Reichstag leaders. Although it may be correct that Ludendorff did not want to tell the civil government that the war was lost for Germany, those at headquarters during this period emphasized something more than simply a desire to avoid responsibility, especially during July and August. When Mertz von Quirnheim asked Ludendorff on September 1, 1918, if he had reported the German military situation to the Foreign Office, Ludendorff replied that he had been unable to do so. His state of mind, Mertz said, was like that of a soldier who had returned from a heavy bombardment. Nobody, Mertz wrote, civilian or military, at headquarters during August and September 1918, could have had the slightest doubt that the German military situation had reached a crisis. Anyone who could think and listen, even with the minimum military knowledge, must have come to this conclusion. However, he emphasized, human beings must *want* to undestand before they *can* understand. He suggested that both officers and civilians were in a state of trauma by their realization that the war was lost and that the strategic philosophy of the previous half century, which undergirded it, had failed. Delbrück-Mertz interview transcript, dated 1 June 1922, *Nachlass Delbrück,* Fasz. 120, DSB; letter of Mertz to the chairman of the fourth Subcommittee of Investigation, Berlin, dated 13 November 1923, copy in *Nachlass Delbrück,* Fasz. 108, DSB.

8   Albrecht von Thaer, *Generalstabsdienst an der Front und in der OHL,* ed. Siegfried A. Kaehler (Göttingen; Vandenhoeck & Ruprecht 1958), p. 235.

9   Report of 7 October 1918, quoted in Feldman, *Army, Industry and Labor,* p. 516; cf. Eyck, *A History of the Weimar Republic* 1:33-38.

10   Ritter, *Sword and Scepter* 4:322ff.; Arthur Rosenberg, *Imperial Germany: The Birth of the German Republic 1871–1918,* pp. 232ff.; Fischer, *Germany's Aims,* pp. 618ff.; Andreas Dorpalen, *Hindenburg and the Weimar Republic* (Princeton: Princeton University Press, 1964), pp. 12ff.; Eyck, *A History of the Weimar Republic* 1:36–38.

11   Dorpalen, *Hindenburg and the Weimar Republic,* p. 21.

12   Petzold, *Dolchstosslegende,* p. 40.

13   *Deutsche Zeitung,* no. 546, 26 October 1918, quoted in Petzold, *Dolchstosslegende,* p. 40.

14   Friedrich Meinecke, *Strasburg/Freiburg/Berlin* (Stuttgart: K. F. Koehler, 1940), pp. 254–55.

15   Friedrich Ebert, *Schriften, Aufzeichnungen, Reden* (Dresden: S. Hirzel, 1926), 2:127.

16   *Deutsche Stimmen,* no. 46, 17 November 1918, quoted in Petzold, *Dolchstosslegende,* p. 43.

17   Petzold, *Dolchstosslegende,* pp. 27–28; Fritz Klein, ed., *Deutschland im Ersten Weltkrieg,* 3 vols. (East Berlin: Akademie Verlag, 1970), 3:22–46; Frhr. Hiller von Gaertringen, "Dolchstoss-Diskussion und 'Dolchstoss-Legende' im Wandel von Vier Jahrzenhnten," in Besson & Gaetringen, eds., *Geschichte und Gegenwartsbewusstein, Festschrift für Hans Rothfels.*

18   Delbrück, "Waffenstillstand-Revolution-Unterwerfung-Republik," *PJ* dated 23 November 1918, reprinted in Delbrück, *Krieg und Politik* 3:203–24.

19   Ibid., pp. 207–08.

20   Ibid., pp. 213–14. Cf., Hans Delbrück, *Vor und nach dem Weltkrieg* (Berlin: Otto Stollberg, 1926), pp. 404–70.

21   Cf. Reinhard Rürup, "Problems of the German Revolution"; Koppel Pinson, *Modern Germany* (New York: MacMillan, 1966), pp. 339–91; a slightly different view is put forth by F. L. Carsten, *Revolution in Central Europe, 1918–1919* (Berkeley: University of California Press, 1972).

22   Hans Delbrück, "Die deutsche Kriegserklärung 1914 und der Einmarsch in Belgien," *PJ* 174 (February 19, 1919).

23   He spoke with Bethmann-Hollweg and with Gottlieb von Jagow prior to departure, spent the period May 21 through 27 in France living at Versailles with the German delegation, many of whom, such as his former student Walter Simons, the Commissioner General of the delegation, and Kurt Hahn, he had known for some time. The statement of the four men was contained in the German note of May 24, 1919, which attempted to refute as much of the allied report as had become known by publication in the allied press, to supply additional documentary evidence which they hoped would prove helpful in clarifying the issue of responsibility, and at the same time to induce the Allies to alter their verdict. Cf. Alma Luckau, *The German Delegation at the Paris Peace Conference* (New York: Columbia University Press, 1941), pp. 81–84; Philip M. Burnett, *Reparation at the Paris Peace Conference,* 2 vols. (New York: Columbia University Press, 1940), 2:31ff.; letter of Delbrück to State Secretary von Jagow, 17 May 1919, *Nachlass Delbrück,* Fasz. 119, DSB; letters of Hans Delbrück to Lina Delbrück, quoted in *Lina Delbrück Memoirs,* Part 14, pp. 246–50. Delbrück came away from Versailles in very low spirits. In 1919 Delbrück became involved in the public attempt by the German government to refute the war guilt claims laid upon Germany by the victors. On the one hand he worked on editing the publication of German documents on the outbreak of the war in 1914, along with Walter Schucking

and Graf Montgelas, *Die deutschen Dokumente zum Kriegsausbruch 1914,* 5 vols. (Charlottenburg: Deutsche Verlagesgesellschaft für Politik und Geschichte, 1919). Delbrück also became involved in a controversy with Karl Kautsky over the outbreak of the war as it was presented in this document collection. Cf. Karl Kautsky, *Delbrück und Wilhelm II: Ein Nachwort zu meinem Kriegsbuch* (Berlin: Verlag Neues Vaterland, 1920), and Hans Delbrück, *Kautsky und Harden* (Berlin: Karl Curtius, 1920). In addition, Delbrück was associated with the Zentralstelle zur Erforschung der Kriegsschuldfrage, one of the agencies of the German Foreign Office, whose purpose was to carry forward the German fight against Article 231 of the Versailles Treaty, the war guilt clause, by a series of publications. Cf. Imanuel Geiss, "The Outbreak of the First World War and German War Aims," pp. 71–74 in Walter Laqueur and George L. Mosse, eds., *1914: The Coming of the First World War* (New York: Harper Torchbook, 1966), and Fritz Klein, ed., *Deutschland im Ersten Weltkrieg* 1:19–21. *Nachlass Delbrück,* Folder 49, BAK, contains much documentation dealing with Delbrück's position over 1914, particularly his spirited debate with French historian Alphonse Aulard. A recent assessment of the debate is David E. Kaiser, "Germany and the Origins of the First World War," *Journal of Modern History,* vol. 55, no. 1 (Sept. 1983), pp. 442–74.

24   Delbrück to wife, 24.5.1919. Cf. Delbrück letters to his wife from Warnemünde, September 1919, *Nachlass Delbrück,* DSB, and the following *PJ* essays: "Frieden" *PJ* dated 28 June 1919, "Die Verfassungs-Beratung. Schwarz-rot-gold," 27 July 1919, "Die Regierung Bauer-Noske-Erzberger," 27 July 1919, "War unser Niederbruch unabwendbar?" 27 July 1919; reprinted in Delbrück, *Vor und nach dem Weltkrieg,* pp. 406–35.

25   *Meine Kriegserinerungen 1914–18.* (Berlin: E. S. Mittler, 1919).

26   Delbrück, *Ludendorff, Tirpitz, Falkenhayn* (Berlin: Verlag Karl Curtius, 1920), pp. 1–9.

27   Ibid., pp. 9–19.

28   See Williamson, *Karl Helfferich,* pp. 304–08.

29   Ibid.

30   Dorpalen, *Hindenburg and the Weimar Republic,* pp. 49ff.

31   Ibid., p. 51–52.

32   Ibid., pp. 52–53.

33   Delbrück, *Ludendorff, Tirpitz, Falkenhayn,* pp. 48–50; cf. Martin Hobohm "Delbrück, Clausewitz und die Kritik des Weltkriegs," *PJ* 181 (1920): 203–33, and Moser, *Ernsthafte Plaudereien über den Weltkrieg,* p. 89ff.

34   Delbrück, *Ludendorff, Tirpitz, Falkenhayn,* pp. 50–51. This view of Russian strength has recently been confirmed by the extensive use of Russian sources. Norman Stone, *The Eastern Front 1914–1917* (New York: Charles Scribner's Sons, 1975).

35   Delbrück, *Ludendorff, Tirpitz, Falkenhayn,* pp. 65–70.

36   Generalmajor Z. D. von Gleich, *Die alte Armee und ihre Verirrungen* (Leipzig: R. F. Koehler, 1919), pp. 99–100.

37   Generalleutnant Schwarte, "Ludendorffs Urkundenwerk," *Militär-Wochenblatt,* 24 July 1920.

38   Hauptmann A. D. Willy Meyer, "Ludendorff als Feldherr," *Die Welt am Montag,* 27

December 1920. Cf. Otto Lehmann-Russboldt, *Warum erfolgte der Zusammenbruck an der Westfront?* (Berlin: Verlag Neues Vaterland, 1919), p. 4.

39 General Buat, *Ludendorff* (Lausanne: J. Payot, 1920), p. 32.

40 Major A. D. von Sodenstern, "Ludendorff," *Deutsche Wehr: Militärische Wochenbeilage der Deutschen-Zeitung,* 20 November 1920.

41 General Ludendorff, "Kriegsgeschichliche Studien und Kritik," *Militär-Wochenblatt,* 11 December 1920.

42 Dorothea Groener-Gayer, *General Groener* (Frankfurt: Societäts-Verlag, 1955), p. 24.

43 Alfred Vagts, *A History of Militarism,* p. 458.

44 Craig, *The Politics of the Prussian Army,* pp. 382ff.

45 Ringer, *The Decline of the German Mandarins,* pp. 200ff.

46 Ringer, ibid., pp. 210ff.

47 Iggers, *German Conception of History,* pp. 232ff. Cf. Felix Gilbert's introduction to his edited work, *The Historical Essays of Otto Hintze* (New York: Oxford University Press, 1975), and Bernd Faulenbach, *Ideologie des deutschen Weges: Die deutsche Geschichte in der Historiographie zwischen Kaiserreich und Nationalsozialismus* (Munich: C. H. Beck, 1980).

6 / THE POLITICS OF MILITARY HISTORY, 1921–1929

MILITARY HISTORY IN UNIVERSITY AND ARMY

In the first eighteen months of the peace, Delbrück's political position had separated him from the two constituencies to whom he sought to speak—professoriate and officer corps. Thus it is not surprising that political opposition took intellectual and bureaucratic form following Delbrück's attempts to institutionalize his historical methods in the university and to influence the writing of the official history of the World War in the General Staff.

Mindful of his failure in 1896 to win promotion in military history, Delbrück tried just before his retirement in 1921 to create a chair for military history at Berlin. A lengthy memorandum to the philosophy faculty summarized his professional career and the rationale to continue this work. When he joined the faculty in 1881, his purpose had been to treat the history of war from ancient to modern times, to make a "cross-cut" through world history. Lectures, seminars, and publications of the succeeding forty years had created a unique school of research rooted in a systematic study of the technical aspects of war. This methodology related strategy and tactics to political and economic systems and focused on conceptual and comparative conclusions which crossed the boundaries of ancient and modern history.

Delbrück pleaded that his research went beyond technical military history to its primary value of enriching general historical understanding. The changeover from a barter to a money economy related to new forms of military organization and strategy. Whole epochs, such as the migrations of the Germanic peoples, appeared in a new light through an understanding of the size and configuration of their armies.

For these reasons, Delbrück urged that university lectures and seminars continue his work. He suggested that the appointment could be held either by an officer who had practical understanding of current military techniques in addition to sufficient historical education, or by an historian with adequate knowledge of military ways. Recalling the officers' arguments against him in the 1880s, Delbrück cautioned against the illusion that an experienced soldier with an historical education would have it any easier than a painter or an architect who tried to be-

Hans Delbrück
1925

come an academic teacher of art history: the study of military history was not preparation for practical military service. Although the military officer and the military historian naturally shared many things, their goals differed, and military history in the university was no substitute for technical study in the War Academy. This was an important distinction because Article 177 of the Versailles Peace Treaty forbade educational institutions from focusing on military affairs. Military history in the university, Delbrück said, was not militaristic: it was an auxiliary science for constitutional, economic, and social history. Finally, Delbrück proposed Martin Hobohm, his long-time assistant at Berlin and a vehement fighter against the Pan-Germans during the war, for appointment to this new chair.[1]

At the time of this appeal, though his career spanned four decades, eleven published volumes, and several hundred articles and essays, Delbrück's historical work had very limited acceptance in the German scholarly world. The seventy-five doctoral dissertations from his seminars, 1885–1919, were all on ancient, medieval, or modern war. None of their authors became well known as a military historian.[2] A few, such as Peter Rassow, entered academic life but researched in other areas. Others, like Otto Haintz, Emil Daniels, Siegfried Mette, and Konrad Molinski, associated for a time with the *Preussische Jahrbücher*. Daniels and Haintz completed volumes five and six of the *History of the Art of War*, published in 1928 and 1932.[3] No officer who had attended Delbrück's lectures or participated in his seminars went on to high command or to fame as a military historian. Although Delbrück's interpretations influenced the Swedish and perhaps the Japanese General Staff, Delbrück's students were not allowed to teach at the Berlin War Academy.[4]

The philosophy faculty commission considering Delbrück's memorandum, dominated by conservatives such as Pan-Germans Eduard Meyer, Theodor Schiemann, and Michael Tangl, and led by Delbrück's wartime opponent Pan-German Vice Chancellor Dietrich Schäfer, rejected it. The technical specialists—both conservative and moderate—agreed that an auxiliary science such as military history was superfluous: any general historian could master it. The Pan-Germans celebrated the appointment of a high officer for military history lectures in the university as highly desirable but inappropriate, and not at that time feasible. The moderate professors, as they had in the 1880s, questioned the need for civilians to study military history—this was best left to the officers and War Academy. They were against introducing the study of war into the university, a civilian sphere of activity. One member apparently voted against it in deference to an entente protest. Even Meinecke, Delbrück's close colleague, neighbor, and friend, voted against him.[5]

In addition, the commission turned down Delbrück's nominee, Martin Hobohm, for appointment to the faculty. It would be a contradiction, they implied, to appoint a military historian who opposed the General Staff interpretation of war.[6] Why did the faculty not accept Hobohm's scholarship, Delbrück asked in a letter to the Prussian Minister for Art, Science and Education? Politics played an important role: Hobohm's writings against the Pan-Germans were decisive.[7] Two years later, after many appeals to the ministry and the state secretary, Delbrück was able to get the title "associate professor" for Hobohm—but without tenure and without compensation *(nichtbeamteter ausserordentlicher Professor)*.

Thus Delbrück failed to convince a majority of his professional colleagues that the scientific study of armies and society was a legitimate historical discipline. He was to have no better success with the officers of the General Staff.

In 1919 a new institution was formed to carry on the work of the outlawed Military History Section of the General Staff. Known as the Reichsarchiv, its setting in the former Potsdam War Academy building symbolized its purpose, membership, and activities. Ostensibly established to collect and house the documents of the German Reich (1871–1918), to research, publish, and lecture on Reich history, in fact its main mission was to write the official history of the World War. It was headed by General Mertz von Quirnheim, aide to Hindenburg in the final months of the war and, some say, the real author of Hindenburg's memoirs. Ludendorff's wartime liaison officer to the Reichstag, Colonel Hans von Haeften, directed the research division. Karl Ruppert, formerly of the Great General Staff, was its chief of personnel and *éminence grise*. Although nominally a department of the Ministry of the Interior, in reality the Reichsarchiv was closely connected to the Troop Office (formerly the Great General Staff) and the War Ministry. Of its sixty-five members, thirteen were civilian, fifty-two active or retired officers. The Interior Ministry constantly put pressure on the Reichsarchiv to appoint more conservative opponents of the republican government.[8]

In the summer of 1920, an historical advisory commission was appointed to the Reichsarchiv. To this belonged Professors Hans Delbrück, Hermann Goetz, Gustav Meyer, Friedrick Meinecke, and Hermann Oncken. It was dominated, however, by officers and bureaucrats, including the state secretary in the Ministry of the Interior and former German Nationalist Theodor Lewald as president; Prussian State Archivist Paul Kehr; Generals Mertz von Quirnheim, Hugo Freiherr von Freytag-Loringhoven, Karl von Borries and, after 1925, Hermann von Kuhl and Wilhelm Groener. From the start, the Reich Ministries of Interior and Foreign Affairs feared the publication of documents from their archival files which would reveal the imperialist and aggressive policies of the Reich government prior to 1918. Such publication, they realized, would further weaken their government in the eyes of the victorious powers and hinder the revival of German national power in Europe. So strongly did they hold this view that the Foreign Office forbade the Reichsarchiv from using various documents. Such a task had to await Fritz Fischer forty years later. Both ministries had grave reservations about the Reichsarchiv writing a political description of the war and revealing the frictions among German policy makers. Against this official bureaucratic pressure from long-tenured government officials still loyal to the monarchy, came opposite-side pressure from the representatives of the Weimar coalition parties. These men, many of whom were liberal and socialist, and had been elected in 1919 as a result of the new ultrademocratic constitution, had different fears. Because of the composition of the Reichsarchiv, they feared that an expanded history of the World War— including discussion of political, economic, and social aspects in an enlarged conceptual framework, would turn out to be an apology for Pan-German annexationist policies and a direct attack against the republican government.

The result of the tactical maneuvering between these two groups and the two sets of concerns represented was that both stepped back. Neither wanted or allowed a political and economic history of the war and its immediate causes. Therefore, by default, the Reichsarchiv was allowed to go ahead with a purely military-technical presentation—exactly what the General Staff had been doing before 1914.[9]

From the start, the majority in both the Reichsarchiv and Historical Commission sought to limit the World War history to the traditional General Staff study—a description of single battlefield actions excluding political, economic, or social influences, published as a bureaucratic work without individual author responsibility. A few members of both Archive and Commission, with Hans Delbrück their spokesman, opposed this approach by proposing directly opposite policies.[10]

Archive President Mertz tried vainly to remain neutral between the dominant conservatives and the handful of moderates. His attempt to publish Martin Hobohm's extended social and economic introduction to the series was denied. Officers and conservative professors saw the civilians, especially the left liberal historians, as aliens in their midst, and this antagonism was returned: Veit Valentin and Ludwig Bergstrasser feared political censorship. The Foreign Office urged the employment of more civilians to avoid the impression abroad that the Archive was merely a continuation of the Military History Section of the old General

Staff. The Army Ministry argued that indeed it was a continuation and should act as such. Officers pleaded that Germany needed an "official" history of the war to respond to the French official history. The political purposes of the Prussian School were about to be revived: as one of the ruling majority stated in the Reichsarchiv debate over methods and philosophy of history, "The war was fought by the old army and therefore its history should be written by members of the old army."[11] This position won out.

Reichsarchiv publications began in 1925 and several series resulted: seventeen volumes of *The World War 1914–18;* a series entitled, *The Great War in Detail,* projected at thirty-three volumes; and more than a thousand *Memoirs of the German Regiments.*[12] All were bureaucratic histories, limited to description of single battlefield actions. These tomes, like the General Staff series on the wars of Frederick the Great, continued the Prussian, patriotic tradition.[13] They supported a uniform, single-purpose interpretation of war.

An important goal of Reichsarchiv publications was the creation of Graf Schlieffen as a national hero. His war plan truly "exemplified the spirit of the General Staff," it was an "infallible blueprint for victory" which had become "watered down," mainly by General von Moltke the younger before the war and by General von Falkenhayn during the war.[14] Although apologists for the Schlieffen Plan had emerged as early as 1915,[15] not until 1920 did they begin to support publicly their position. In that year three of his closest associates detailed Schlieffen's strategic legacy.[16] A second and a third series óf writings followed.[17] Members of the old "Schlieffen School" maintained close personal relations, exchanged letters, and "approved" of each other's manuscripts.[18] In 1922 Field Marshal von Mackensen was elected president of the newly formed Schlieffen Association.[19] The most important goal of Reichsarchiv publications, however, was to maintain Schlieffen's influence over current war planning.[20]

Although it is difficult to generalize for all German strategic ideas of the 1920s, at least during the years when Hans von Seeckt was chief of the Army Command (1919–1926), two trends seem clear, and these in various ways duplicate developments which we have described for the years prior to 1914. First of all, the small Versailles Treaty army of 100,000 preserved the "spirit of the offensive." Staff exercises, war games, and General Staff trips of this period were predicated not on the basis of actual army size but on the theoretical existence of a much larger force. Such a relationship between present war plans and future army expansion, as one officer wrote, encouraged more "confidence and imagination" in the solution of operational problems. Secondly, the corollary to this larger army was its employment in the flank attack and envelopment of enemy forces, a common answer to a variety of tactical problems.[21]

It is not surprising, therefore, to find members of the Schlieffen School depicting the opening phase of the World War in terms of a brilliant idea which had been imperfectly executed. General Groener gave the keynote to this approach. He feared that the great didactic purpose of Schlieffen's ideas would be lost on the younger generation, and lamented that the "great symphony—the Schlieffen Plan—could only be attempted once and that the conductor had bungled it."[22]

By 1922 it was becoming clear to Delbrück that he would be unable to convince either professors or officers that his historical methods and the conclusions derived from them were legitimate. Although it may not have been a conscious decision on his part, having failed with the technical experts, Delbrück turned increasingly to the public forum, attempting directly to influence popular opinion with his interpretation of the World War. This uphill fight he ultimately lost. Not only conservative politicans, officers, and those who had held important positions during the war, but broad segments of German society supported the treacherous *"Dolchstoss"* legend. The myth of the "November Criminals" and the "stab in the back" was preached from church pulpits and inscribed in school and university textbooks.[23]

As the aging historian took his historical method, and with it the prestige of the university, into the public forum, the lines between historian and publicist blurred and sometimes disappeared. In popularizing the strategic debate, a certain vulgarization took place. In attempting to gain public acceptance, Delbrück jeopardized the support of many of his moderate colleagues because his image of the World War often appeared to them indistinguishable from that of socialists, communists, and even Germany's wartime enemies. Close friends, such as Friedrich Meinecke, found it impossible to support him publicly.[24] Conservative professors, rightist publicists, officers, and bureaucrats attacked him viciously. The whole spectrum of modern popular media and interest-group propaganda methods—fueled by war guilt and the most disastrous inflation experienced within a two-year period by any country in modern world history—were used by his opponents. Few people came to his defense.

THE PUBLIC DEBATE, 1921-1929

In contrast to the debate over methods of military history in university and Reichsarchiv, fought out in private and professional meetings, the controversy over the results of these methods—the historical image of the World War—was a bitter, protracted public debate on the front pages of partisan newspapers, in pamphlet literature and memoirs, and before Reichstag Committee investigations and courtroom trials. It became an important cause célèbre of the Weimar period. Monarchical politics and military establishment were formally on display, and so were many of the officers, nobles, and high bureaucrats of the old empire. The dikes of secrecy appeared breached. Palace gossip would become matters of public record. The German public waited for the flow of official secrets.

To explore the question of domestic war guilt—who or what had lost the war for Germany—the National Assembly had in August 1919 created the first Reichstag investigative committee in German political history.[25] We have already described Hindenburg's testimony before its subcommittee in November of that year. Before the fourth subcommittee, which focused on the collapse of 1918, the conflicting positions of Delbrück and his military opponents were forcefully highlighted.[26] Colonel Bernhard Schwertfeger, General Staff liaison officer, General Herman von Kuhl, close advisor to Ludendorff in 1917–18, Professor Delbrück, and others testified as expert witnesses during the six-year-long hearings. Even before the proceedings began, the Reichswehr Ministry issued a private warning appeal asking for a narrow, restricted focus on minor issues. German historical writing, in its "deadliest hour," would be poorly served by anything else. At issue were Germany's honor in the world community as well as feelings of shame by the German people. This warning had little impact on participants: under this public pressure, each side laid bare its argument, unadorned, but few in Germany were listening or were able to understand.[26]

Legal responsibility for Reich decisions in war and peace, Colonel Schwertfeger testified, was bound up ideally in the relationship between the kaiser and his two main advisors, the chief of the General Staff and the chancellor. In theory, each presented the strongest case possible, and the kaiser decided between them.[27] Schwertfeger admitted, however, that from the time of Schlieffen on, the kaiser had gradually given up responsibility for military decisions to the "technical experts." This became all the more true after 1914. By 1917, with the replacement of Bethmann Hollweg, the balance tipped absolutely in favor of the military technicians. From then on, Schwertfeger contended, the kaiser abdicated not only his military role but his political power as well—the officers even selected the chancellor.[28]

As for the strategy of 1918, Schwertfeger conceded that the Supreme Command was fully aware of deficiencies in soldiers, gasoline, food, clothing, and munitions. Considering the overwhelming superiority of

Germany's west-front enemies, the officers concluded that only a crushing attack could win the war:

> Therefore the Supreme Command built its plans around the magic power of the offensive, that most confident Germanic way of war. . . . Indeed, in the whole army the decision to attack was seen as an end to the unbearably long war of position. . . . If the wartime situation by that time had developed so that political viewpoints were virtually excluded, this was Germany's fate and not the guilt of individual personalities.[29]

General von Kuhl, who, we will recall, helped plan it, testified that the 1918 spring offensive was the last best chance for Germany to win the war.[30] He admitted that the Supreme Command misjudged the strength and arrival time of United States forces. It had estimated that half a million Americans would arrive and that they would not immediately enter the front lines.[31] In reality, seven U.S. divisions were in France by March, and two million men had arrived by November 1918. Kuhl admitted that this had been decisive, but he contended that the Supreme Command had correctly sought a decision before substantial American forces had become engaged.[32]

What material and human resources were available for this "decision"? Kuhl acknowledged that

> there were extreme and general scarcities of men, food and supplies. From a reserve on paper of one million men, less than ten percent were actually fit for combat duty. Many divisions were inducting men forty-one years of age and older and those who were fathers of more than four children. Horses were scarce and food for horses was unavailable anywhere.

> Nevertheless we concluded that a defense could only make our position weaker. The course of the war up to that time had demonstrated that the defensive battle . . . with its difficult moral pressure and terrible bodily suffering was more difficult and brought more suffering than an attack. . . . There was only one opinion in the whole army: to undertake the heaviest attack as soon as possible rather than to wait weakly in our trenches.

> Was the army capable of such a great attack? The briskness and joy of the attacking troops in 1918 made unforgettable impressions on everyone who saw them. Considering everything the Supreme Command reached the only conclusion it could: Germany had to attack . . . even our enemies expected it. The war could only end with a victory of weapons by one side or the other. If the attack failed, then the war was lost.[33]

The hearing room fell silent as Kuhl finished his testimomy with these fateful words.

In defending their strategy, the officers repeatedly stressed that civilians could not really understand the military operations of the World War. One had to examine the daily operations maps and study the military science works of both German and enemy generals. This task was exceedingly complex for the trained officer and virtually impossible for anyone else. Civilian Reichstag committee members agreed, voicing publicly their reluctance to judge strategic questions.[34]

Hans Delbrück's testimony followed that of Schwertfeger and Kuhl, and he originally presented his views as a commentary to their statements, believing the officers' own testimony had condemned them and that his own case needed little further explication. The officers hotly disputed this, wanting it publicly understood that the three statements were separate and hoping that they would also be viewed as different. In content, the testimonies of the three were very similar. Delbrück's conclusions, however, were diametrically opposite.

Delbrück's main points were that the German offensive of 1918 was (1) not in tune with the political war aims of the German government, particularly with reference to Belgium; (2) that end and means were out of balance, given the strategic attempt to annihilate the enemy in the face of severe shortages of men, supplies, horses, and food; and (3) that a sustained breakthrough by German troops in 1918 was impossible and foolhardy, considering the enemy failure during the two previous years to break through using superior numbers of men and better equipment. He concluded by laying guilt for the German defeat on Erich Ludendorff and commenting that it was a fundamental error to assume that Ludendorff spoke for the entire army. Delbrück felt that most soldiers would have welcomed a negotiated peace, an armistice without shame. Ludendorff had played a malicious game with the future of Germany to satisfy his own personal ambition. If General Ludendorff had been brought to trial for mutiny in July 1916, Germany might have been saved.[35]

Although Delbrück emphasized specific guilt and responsibility, committee members focused on narrow technical details: they wanted only to establish the facts. As its composition changed twice because of elections, the committee gradually lost its original purpose. In 1926, after six years of testimony, the majority could reach no definite conclusion as to the responsibility for the German military defeat of 1918. The minority resolution, written by Communists, Independent Socialists, and Social Democrats, rendered a verdict which not only quoted Delbrück's testimony but fundamentally agreed with it.[36]

The testimony presented before the fourth subcommittee was not widely circulated. Many in the Reichstag did not want the document published, and it appeared finally in one incomplete edition during the years 1925–29. As soon as Herman Goering became Reichstag president in August 1932, he prevented a new edition, and copies of the old one were used as scrap paper.[37]

However, portions of the testimonies of Schwertfeger, Kuhl, and Delbrück had been released earlier—in 1923 in a book issued by Reimar Hobbing, a publisher famed for controversial subjects. The officers, realizing that their statements, if understood from Delbrück's point of view, might be fatal to the General Staff, prefaced their testimonies with an indictment undercutting the validity of the entire book. They reminded readers that many historical sources for the World War were not yet available. The largest part of the war archives was still closed, especially those of the foreign enemies. To understand complex military operations it was necessary to know the thinking of the commanders and to understand the situation as it had appeared at the time. Documents for this purpose were lacking.

In addition to insufficient sources, the officers remonstrated that observers were too close to the war for objective historical evaluation. Military critics were caught up in party politics. One side sharply attacked the statements of the other. Political agitation made clear and unbiased judgment impossible.[38] For these reasons, the officers contended that final conclusions on wartime military operations could be made only with great reservation. An objective historical assessment was impossible.

Delbrück could hardly disagree with such sentiments, for they formed an important part of his own historical methods. However, the officers need not have worried. There is no indication that many Germans read the testimonies or that, having done so, they sided with Delbrück against the wartime commanders. Support for Delbrück's position in the *Sozialistische Monatshefte* only hardened conservative opinion against him.[39]

Public debate over the World War climaxed in the years 1923–1925, filled as they were with assassinations, the Ruhr occupation, a ruinous inflation, and attempts by right and left to seize power by force. Leading the debate were Ludendorff and Delbrück.

Ludendorff's most detailed defense of his wartime actions appeared in *War Strategy and Politics: An Outline of the History of the World War.*[40] In this work, five main themes, by this time well known, stand out. According to Clausewitz and Schlieffen, the only true form of strategy and the highest goal of war under all circumstances and conditions was the annihilation of the enemy.[41] The march through Belgium implementing this concept was an unavoidable strategic necessity and failed only because General von Moltke's "will to victory" was too weak; the retreat of the Second Army in early September 1914 robbed the Reich of victory.[42] General von Falkenhayn's failure was due to false strategic ideas of attrition. Verdun, carried out under this erroneous concept, was a catastrophe. Had the strategy of annihilation been employed continuously, it would have successfully ended the war.[43] In spite of weak domestic morale, symbolized in the Reichstag peace resolution, by the spring of 1918 the power relationships were more favorable than they had been in 1914, and Germany had no choice but to attack. This succeeded: by June 2 the enemy generals themselves were admitting defeat. Along with this, the Supreme Command told the Reich chancellor to open a "peace offensive."[45] But the morale of the home front did not hold; the Social Democrats, pacifists, and defeatists led to Germany's downfall.

Delbrück's response was *Ludendorff's Selbstporträt*.[46] He accused Ludendorff of fatally altering the Schlieffen Plan, of misunderstanding Clausewitz, and of destroying the German Empire by following a strategy of blind idealism in the face of insurmountable material realities.

Military critics, Delbrück wrote, faulted the operation plan of 1914 because it stretched out the German army to encompass two-thirds of Alsace and parts of the Swiss border, whereas in Schlieffen's original idea the army was extended only as far south as Strasbourg. Only Ludendorff defended this change, called by Hindenburg a "watering down." He had good reason to, Delbrück emphasized, for he himself was chief of the operations section at the time. Delbrück asked what the reason was for such a change.

Ludendorff himself said that he had wanted to protect Baden and overrun the French in Alsace, hoping for a nice partial victory at the start of the campaign. In choosing this course, Ludendorff fell into a fundamental error of strategic thinking: he forgot Clausewitz's dictum that beginning success was nothing, final success everything. Worse yet, an initial success, such as Alsace, that reduced the chance of final victory, was really a failure.

General von Moltke had told Reichstag delegate Matthias Erzberger in January 1915 that he thought it a mistake from the outset to attack in the west: Germany should have gone first against the east, smashed the Russian steamroller, while defending in the west. Moltke, the responsible chief, did not say why he failed to carry out this view. Surely the kaiser would not have opposed Moltke if his operations sections had supported him. The opposition to Moltke's plan, Delbrück concluded, must have come from Ludendorff. The general believed that to attack in the west and defend in the east was natural and obvious because "decision-seeking" actions against Russia were so lengthy that the General Staff could neither hold out in the west long enough for a victory against the Russians, nor protect Germany's industrial areas along the French border crucial for war production.

The mistake, Delbrück wrote, was Ludendorff's emphasis on "decision-seeking" operations. A "decision" against Russia—in the sense of total annihilation—was very difficult if at all attainable. Delbrück believed that there had been three possibilities. The German army could have driven back the Russians temporarily, then turned west. The French, meanwhile, might have been held up by the strongly fortified positions along the Metz-Strasbourg line or provoked the odium of world opinion by crossing neutral Belgium. Another possibility was to stretch the German flank to the sea, going beyond Mezieres and Maubeuge. However, a third option was decided upon: to extend the attack on the left flank to the Swiss border. This decision took the soul out of the Schlieffen Plan, for its central point was the strengthening of the right wing and the withholding of the left. This modification divided the German army more evenly over the front. It was too difficult to attempt victory in Lothringen and southeastern France, on the extreme left wing, and then to shift troops behind and across, north and west two hundred miles to the right flank. At this point, the plan itself contained fundamental faults.[47]

Recent historians have concluded that in its general lines the ratio between right wing and left was not essentially altered from Schlieffen to Moltke. Nonetheless, the lack of concentrated strength in the First, Second, and Third flanking Armies and the difficulties of rearranging logistics to support the rapidly moving northernmost divisions were crucial in the failure of the attack.[48] However, the opening of the war was less important for Delbrück; in his view, the more essential mistakes were made in 1918.

If Ludendorff desired victory in spring 1918, what were the available means, Delbrück asked? If he wanted a great decision, he failed to concentrate all his forces in the west to this end: hundreds of thousands of men remained on the eastern front, in Finland, the Crimea, and the Caucasus. Either he had to bring all available power to the west for a battle of annihilation or, if German power was insufficient, then he had to try for a limited action accompanied by diplomatic efforts to achieve a negotiated peace. The sine qua non for such a strategy was the declaration of an independent Belgium, a declaration which Ludendorff repeatedly refused to allow the Foreign Office to make. There were many indications, Delbrück averred, that between July 1917 and July 1918 such a declaration would have found the enemy receptive.

The offensive launched on March 21, 1918, failed because of basic shortages of men and materials in the German army and because of the technology and the terrain of the battlefield. Although the campaign initially achieved some tactical success—by dint of good luck in attacking the break point between the French and British armies where it was most difficult to bring up reserves—it soon slowed and halted after enormous losses, without achieving any strategic objectives. Delbrück repeated Ludendorff's own statements that the German army lacked adequate munitions, food supplies, horses, and gasoline. By spring 1918, restoration of railroad lines to support a swiftly moving attack was impossible. The battleground had been bitterly contested for four years. Everything was destroyed. The attack miscarried not so much because of enemy resistance but because of inherent impossibilities on the German side.

After the first attack was halted, Ludendorff launched two others in different places. They also failed. No political moves to negotiate an end to the war accompanied these failures because Ludendorff was blind to the relationship between strategy and politics. Delbrück asked why Ludendorff continued this murderous assault after the first action clearly had shown its hopelessness. It was said that he reckoned further attacks "by chance" might accomplish a breakthrough. Ludendorff hoped for a deus ex machina: namely, for the sudden domestic collapse of a western power in the manner of the Russian Empire. Was this strategy or was it the illusion of a man without feelings of responsibility?[49] Delbrück concluded:

> To justify the failure of the great offensive and the final military collapse the accusation was put forth that Social Democratic underminings cut the sinews of the attack and deprived Germany of victory. . . .

> The army fought bravely and flawlessly. Although there were some attempts to poison morale by the independent Socialists and communists . . . although thousands of desertions weakened the front troops . . . the army, with the exception of a very few, fought on faultlessly until the last. The weakening of fighting power resulted from the terrible losses, the enormous exhaustion, the poor supplies and the military failure to achieve anything more than local tactical successes. . . . The decisive factor was not the lack of German will to fight but the ever increasing power on the enemy side. Ludendorff wanted a great victory to bring peace yet because of German weaknesses he himself expected no more victories. . . .

Why and how did this in no way hopeless situation end in a complete collapse of mutiny and revolution? . . . The military collapse was not the result of the revolution, the revolution was the result of the collapse. The bonds of loyalty in Germany broke as the troops lost hope, as the fall and collapse of Bulgaria and Austria-Hungary isolated Germany and Ludendorff's sudden armistice demand made known to all the world that for Germany the war was lost. . . .

If one condemns the treason of the mutinied army, one must not forget that the first mutiny was that of the commander, Ludendorff, who left the service of the Kaiser because he could not abide the Kaiser's politics. . . . Ludendorff changed the defensive war into a war of conquest, he did not understand the strategic requirements of the war and by his resistance to the king and government brought on the revolution which finally buried the German Reich.[50]

In 1917–18 a debate had occurred among the Entente Powers over what kind of strategy should be adopted for the duration of the war. Delbrück described this English wartime dispute, hoping the German public would compare it to their own situation.[51]

He noted that in early 1918 the British held two contrasting views over the continuation of the war. One, advocated by the English chief of staff, General Robertson, was that England should fight on as before, despite very great losses. Robertson's argument was that when all the Germans were dead, there would still be some Englishmen and Frenchmen alive, and the Allies would have won!

The other view, supported by Lloyd George and General Wilson, was to remain on the defensive in France in 1918, but to deal an offensive blow against Turkey in Syria. If they could succeed in Syria, Turkey would be broken and that would be a blow to the whole Central Alliance. They were confident of the strength of their defensive in France. In spite of a double superiority in numbers and continued attacks, the English and French had failed to break through the German lines. Therefore, they reasoned that Germany, with fewer men, could not succeed in breaking through their lines. In 1919, when the masses of Americans arrived, the entente could mount a final offensive. In the meantime, to maintain the defensive lines, Lloyd George wanted a unified command at Versailles. The Allies feared that Germany might attack and overwhelm one segment of the line and that a general reserve under the control of a war council with overall view of the front would enable them successfully to carry out a strategy of attrition. Lloyd George named General Wilson as the English member of this council.

General Robertson was enraged at this decision. Colonel Repington, the English military critic, shared Robertson's views and scathingly condemned the new strategic plan, the unitary reserve, and the war council in the *Morning Post* of 11 February 1918. Repington sneered at the idea of seeking the decision on a secondary campaign field instead of in France, and hoped that the House of Commons would overthrow Lloyd George and General Wilson. Prime ministers and other civilians, Repington wrote contemptuously, have occupied themselves in teaching soldiers how and where to make war! He was unconcerned that England's enemies might come to know her war plans. Lloyd George brought charges against Repington, only incidentally mentioning the Syrian campaign and thus concealing its importance. Repington was convicted and fined, the House of Commons supported Lloyd George, and General Robertson was relieved.[52]

Here was a striking comparison between civil-military relations in England and in Germany. The English put down the intrigue of the officers and adhered to the strategy of attrition. In Germany the generals won out and the strategy of annihilation was pursued to the grave of Imperial Germany.

Throughout his discussion, Delbrück repeatedly tried to separate Ludendorff from Hindenburg, placing much less responsibility on the latter, knowing well that an attack against the venerable field marshal would only inflame angry public opinion. Ludendorff bound himself and all strategic decision-making inseparably to the aged field marshal.

Naturally Delbrück's image of the strategy and politics of the World War from the vantage point of 1923 was limited by inadequate sources and by closeness to the events. For example, he failed to criticize Ludendorff's blindness to the use of mechanized forces, especially tanks, and other effective counterweapons. By the summer of 1918 the Allies' offensives included as many as four or five hundred massed tanks. Nonetheless, by using the war memoirs of German, French, and English participants, he pieced together a reasonably objective interpretation which stands up remarkably well, especially in its essential point that a lack of men and material ultimately brought the German attack to the ground in 1918.[53]

Ludendorff's Self Portrait was widely read—going through ten printings and two editions in less than a year—and provoked a response reminiscent of the attacks against Delbrück in the 1880s. Delbrück, Ludendorff wrote, was acting like the enemy foreigners, slandering his war leadership to destroy him as a national rallying point.[54] Officers and Pan-Germanists noted that Delbrück was not an historian but a publicist and "maker of false hypotheses."[56] He was no expert *(Fachmann)*[56] but only a strategist of the chair *(Kanzel-Stratege)* who lacked that "instinctive" understanding of military affairs which came from practical experience and technical training.[57] War on paper was very different from war in reality.[58] These arguments are familiar, having been leveled against Delbrück's historical interpretations before 1914.[59]

The socialist support of Delbrück was the most sensitive, not only because the socialists agreed with him, but because this undoubtedly made it more difficult for his conservative opponents and moderate supporters to appreciate his arguments. If Ludendorff, noted the *Sozialistische Monatshefte*, had only abandoned the attack and combined the strategy of attrition and annihilation, if it would not have given victory, at least it would have averted defeat. The legend of Ludendorff had to be destroyed because it arose from a militarism which could no longer stand in the way of Germany's future.[60] Philip Scheidemann's use of Delbrück's conclusions in a Reichstag speech brought the response that Delbrück was not a military specialist: his opinions could not be used as valid judgment.[61]

Delbrück made one final attempt to delineate the nature of the lost war before the German public. In the months preceding the Reichstag elections of May 1924, a series of vicious articles appeared in the conservative Munich *South German Monthly* advocating the "stab in the back" interpretation of the end of the World War and attacking the treasonous actions of left and liberals.[62] As a result, the publisher of the *South German Monthly*, Paul Crossman, was taken to task by Martin Gruber, editor of the Social Democratic *Munich Post*, as a "falsifier of history."[63] Crossman brought suit for libel. The trial, conducted in Munich, lasted nearly a month and made daily headlines all over Germany.[64] Lawyer Max Hirschberg and Hans Delbrück prepared Gruber's defense. Their goal was to clarify the *Dolchstoss* question and to make a sudden and decisive impact on public opinion.[65] The fundamentals of their position were that (1) the military superiority of Germany's opponents and the political inadequacies of German leadership had defeated the German army; (2) the revolutionary activities of domestic radicals had only a relatively meaningless impact on the army; (3) the Social Democratic leadership remained patriotic to the end of war and did its utmost to oppose the militant revolutionaries of the extreme left; (4) the Social Democratic leaders neither planned nor carried out the revolution, but only became involved at the last moment to try to avoid chaos. During the trial, the latter part of this position became self-evident, and the opposition lawyer, Graf Pestalozza, withdrew the broad claim that *Dolchstoss* had been committed by Social Democracy in general, limiting the accusation only to the radical left.

The official judgment, however, confounded Delbrück's attempt at clarification. The presentation in the *South German Monthly*, admitted the judge, was partly incorrect and in error. Incorrectness and error, however, were also found in other historical presentations. The World War lay too close for complete and certain historical research: historical objectivity was impossible. Therefore, the deficiencies in the presentation of the *South German Monthly* could not be considered consciously false. Historical arguments, such as Delbrück's testimony, were incomplete and therefore inadmissible. Testimony as to the truth or falsehood of the *Dolchstoss*, which was useful for historical research, was of marginal value in civil lawsuits.

Gruber was found guilty of slander and fined.[66] Delbrück was attacked as senile, a turncoat, and a party fanatic.[67] His claim to expertise was denied: he held no important position during the World War.[68] One wonders how closely Delbrück and his position were associated in public opinion with the general summary of the case presented in the December 21, 1925, issue of the Donau News *(Donau-Zeitung)*. The *Dolchstoss* trial, this report claimed, ended with a judgment against the *Munich Post*, its communist supporters, and all Social Democracy. No criminal guilt was spoken of, only a dangerous moral guilt. Summary of the matter went like this. Bethmann Hollweg was brave and extraordinary, but not a statesman. He did not know what to do in this difficult period. The Kaiser was weak and well meaning, but lacked courage and understanding. The German people were left leaderless and in this crisis lost confidence in their government. So the Independent and Left Socialists *(Spartacists)* tried to take the lead, but they knew no fatherland. They wanted revolution and feared victory, for victory would have preserved the old form of the state.[69]

Delbrück's own perception of all of this was prophetic. The trial, he wrote, was a duel between military representatives of the old Reich and civilian supporters of the new republic. The officers and their supporters on the right displayed a shocking intellectual and moral attitude, fanatic and full of hate. Except for a few, they were so dogmatic and zealous that if these people ever came to power again Germany's fate was sealed.[70]

Ten years after the revolution of 1918, the Weimar Government published a retrospective historical view,[71] describing its origins as a time of Germany's deepest misery. A decade of domestic struggles had so radically distorted perspectives that the only interpretation universally acceptable was the thesis that the revolution had been a clash with bolshevism, and its eventual defeat. The Weimar Reich rested not upon the revolution but upon the continuity of German history preserved in spite of it.[72] Ironically, Ludendorff's chief, *Reichspräsident* Paul von Hindenburg, at Delbrück's eightieth birthday celebration in 1928, which was attended by many of the elite from Germany's governmental, business, military, and intellectual circles, presented him with the *Adlerschild des Reiches*.[73] He was called the "rector of German historians" for his fight against international war guilt claims. But few could understand or support his indictment of domestic military treason. When Delbrück died in July 1929, it was evident that he had failed to gain many adherents, either for his methods of military history or the conclusions produced in their most striking application, his analysis of the World War.

Soon after 1933, the legend of the "stab in the back" was elevated to the status of historical truth. But this only slightly exaggerated the views held by large segments of German society before 1933. As for strategic thinking, by the early 1930s the Schlieffen School so completely dominated German military thinking that the General Staff exercise of winter 1935 was a replica of the exercise of 1893. On 15 March 1935, at the close of the exercise, Schlieffen's final remarks were quoted verbatim:

> . . . it is only twenty-two years since that time when the idea of the offensive from first to last thrilled everybody. The weapons of war have changed, but the fundamental laws of strategy remain the same and these laws point to one thing; that one cannot be victorious over the enemy without attacking. I am thankful to those gentlemen who have preserved the idea that one must attack in such a way as to practically annihilate him.

Appended to this were these words: "This conclusion speaks for itself. It is beyond doubt that this fundamental idea is also absolutely correct today."[74]

NOTES

1   "Denkschrift über einem Lehrstuhl für Kriegsgeschichte," *Nachlass Delbrück*, Faszikel 22, DSB. Martin Hobohm, Delbrück's candidate for this position, was born in 1883, had received the Berlin philosophy faculty prize for his essay "Angaben Machiavellis über das Kriegswesen"; from this prize essay grew a dissertation, on the basis of which he was promoted at Göttingen, and finally a two-volume work, *Machiavellis Renaissance der Kriegskunst*, 2 vols. (Berlin: K. Curtius, 1913). In 1913 he had habilitated at Berlin. His *Antrittsvorlesung* was a comparison between the strategy of Torstensons and Frederick the Great. He also served as an assistant at the Berlin Zeughaus, a museum of military history at that time. For many semesters he served as Delbrück's assistant. From May 1915 he headed the Zentralstelle für Auslandsdienst, an office created by the German Foreign Ministry but also supported with private contributions, to fight against Pan-German propaganda with publications of its own. By July 1916 the Pan-Germans began their own attack against the office and Hobohm. In early 1917 he was inducted into the army and sent immediately into combat—possibly, Hans Schleier notes, as a result of the "good relations" between the Pan-Germans and

the military authorities. Badly wounded, Hobohm nonetheless returned to the Zentralstelle in fall 1917 and began to prepare a book-length treatise against the Pan-Germans. Cf. Hans Schleier's long biographical essay in his *Die bürgerliche deutsche Geschichtsschreibung der Weimarer Republik*, pp. 531–58.

2   Cf. the list of dissertations, *Nachlass Delbrück*, Fasz. 38, DSB.

3   The Daniels volume probably owes something to Delbrück's lectures on the war of 1870–71, nearly eight hundred pages of which are to be found in the *Nachlass Delbrück*, Fasz. 83, BAK. Daniels' work in turn influenced the writing of the standard account in English, Michael Howard's *The Franco-Prussian War* (New York: Collier Books, 1969), p. xii.

4   Otto Haintz, "Delbrück, Karl XII und der schwedische Generalstab," in Daniels and Ruhlmann, *Am Webstuhl der Zeit*, pp. 63ff.; Konrad Molinski, "Der historiker Delbrück," in Ferdinand J. Schmidt, Konrad Molinski, and Siegfried Mette *Hans Delbrück. Der Historiker und Politiker* (Berlin: Otto Stolberg, 1928), pp. 44ff. Another foreigner influenced by Delbrück's ideas was the military historian and general staff officer Ishiwara Kanji of the Imperial Japanese Army. Cf. Mark R. Peattie, *Ishiwara Kanji and Japan's Confrontation with the West* (Princeton: Princeton University Press, 1975), pp. 30, 32. Thanks to Professor John Killigrew, my colleague at Brockport, for this information.

5   "Kommissions Report-Antrag Delbrück," no date, one page typed, *Nachlass Delbrück*, Fasz. 22, DSB.

6   *Nachlass Delbrück*, Fasz. 22, DSB, contains most of the documents for this. See also letters of Delbrück to Hobohm, 4.3.1920; Hobohm to Solf, 1.2.1920. In 1913, at his initial appointment to the faculty, Hobohm had wanted to create a new form of instruction, the colloquium, or what was called in German a *repetitorium*, a form of instruction which stood between the lecture and the seminar. The faculty did not like this: they considered it presumptuous and tactless for a junior faculty member to make such a suggestion. They suspected him of wanting to create a "cramming institute" *(Einpauk-Anstalt)* to earn more money. They raised questions about Hobohm's preparation (he had not attended enough lectures) and about the initial faculty vote in the matter of his appointment, in which there had apparently been some abstentions. To Delbrück this was a carefully orchestrated attack by Hobohm's political opponents, Dietrich Schäfer, Wilhelm Schulze, and other Pan-Germanists.

7   Letter of 1921, seven typed pages, *Nachlass Delbrück*, Fasz. 22, DSB. The faculty considered Hobohm's published book, *Machiavellis Renaissance der Kriegskunst*, one of the foundations of Delbrück's fourth volume of the *History of the Art of War*, as insufficient. To counter this, Delbrück had collected letters attesting to its value from Friedrich Meinecke, Max Lenz, Max Lehmann, Gustav Roloff, Walter Goetz, Hermann Oncken, and others. Hobohm's opponents used an unfavorable review by Gustav Fueter, a *Privatdozent* in Switzerland, in the 1914 *Historische Zeitschrift* 113:578. Why, wrote Delbrück to the minister, is such testimony on behalf of the scientific importance of Hobohm's work not accepted? I must unfortunately suggest, he concluded, that party politics plays a role in this. Lehmann, Goetz, and Hobohm are known as sharp fighters against the Pan-Germans. Fueter was a vehement Pan-German. That two of the witnesses supporting Hobohm are also known as Pan-Germans does not seem to make a difference. Hobohm's political activities, his writings against the Pan-Germans were decisive in this matter, Delbrück concluded. Delbrück letter of 1921 to the Minister für Kunst, Wissenschaft und Volksaufklarung, *Nachlass Delbrück*, Fasz. 22, DSB. Cf. Delbrück's criticism of the 1914 review in *Geschichte der Kriegskunst* 4:117–18. There were at least two faculty commissions and several votes, at least one of which was close—four to three against Delbrück. In appealing directly to the minister and under-state secretary, Delbrück argued that it was

always difficult to create something new in a faculty, especially if it was comprised of old men who were completely devoid of understanding of the new directions in the field of history. He emphasized that they would not be continuing anything from past tradition—Delbrück himself held no professorship *(Lehrauftrag)* in military history—but creating something entirely new. Even Franz Mehring had often praised his work, Delbrück noted. This meant that even after his own death, his methods and approach, having been accepted, would continue and the university should join in this scholarly and scientific effort. Through it all, Hobohm's position remained tenuous. Finally, in 1923 Hobohm was given a nontenured associate professorship *(nichtbeamteter ausserordentlicher Professor)*, but without any essential change in his legal status or his material remuneration. In addition to this, Hobohm became involved in a lawsuit with Professor Georg von Below. Below was a vehement Pan-German. Hobohm, together with another Delbrück student, Paul Rohrbach, published a critical examination of Pan-German politics from the 1890s to 1918: *Die Alldeutschen* (Berlin: H. R. Engelmann, 1919). Originally assembled when the authors were members of the press bureau of the German Foreign Office (Zentralstelle für Auslandsdienst), Berlin, the report grew from 178 pages in 1916 to a full book by 1919. Cf. Hans Schleier, *Die bürgerliche deutsche Geschichtsschreibung der Weimarer Republik* (Berlin: Akademie Verlag, 1975), pp. 541ff. As a result of newspaper articles Hobohm wrote, he and Below got into a lawsuit. Hobohm lost the suit on a technicality and had to pay costs and print a retraction of one of his previous statements regarding Below. Cf. the court record (Amtsgericht 7, Freiburg/Berlin, 20 January 1921), *Nachlass Delbrück*, DSB. The lawsuit was being tried while Delbrück was trying to win Hobohm a place on the Berlin faculty. Another young historian who got into trouble for opposing the Pan-Germans during the war was Veit Valentin. For his critical *PJ* review of a book by Graf Ernst zu Reventlow in August 1916, Valentin was attacked by the *Prorektor* of Freiburg University, Professor Georg von Below, Alfred von Tirpitz, and others. After much acrimony, the matter ended with the Freiburg faculty revoking Valentin's *venia legendi*, his right to teach in a university. Cf. *Perspektiven und Profile: Aus Schriften Veit Valentins*, ed. Will Schaber (Frankfurt/m: Waldemar Kramer, 1965), pp. 16–25. Cf. letters of Hobohm and Rohrback to Delbrück, August–November 1916, *Nachlass Delbrück*, folder 43, BAK.

8 Karl Demeter, *Das Reichsarchiv: Tatsachen und Personen* (Frankfurt/Main: Bernard & Graefe, 1969); Schleier, *Die bürgerliche deutsche Geschichtsschreibung der Weimarer Republik*, pp. 128ff.; Craig, *Politics of the Prussian Army*, p. 398; Heinrich Aschenbrandt, *Kriegsgeschichtsschreibung und Kriegsgeschichtsstudium im Deutschen Heere* (Königstein, Germany: USA Army, Historical Division, 1952). Hans Delbrück memorandum dated 24 November 1920, *Nachlass Delbrück*, Fasz. 119, DSB. Letter of Paul Kehr to Delbrück, undated, *Nachlass Delbrück*, Fasz. 119. Letter of Hans Rothfels to author, Tübingen, 13 August 1974; letter of Bernard Schwertfeger to Delbrück, 27 September 1920, *Nachlass Delbrück*, Fasz. 119, DSB. Herman von Kuhl, "Brauchen wir eine amtliche Geschichte des Weltkrieges?" *Deutsche Zeitung*, 9 December 1923; minutes of various Reichsarchiv meetings plus letters and memorandum regarding its purpose and internal organization, especially Hobohm's letters to Delbrück, are contained in *Nachlass Delbrück*, Folders 50 and 51, BAK.

9 Schleier, *Die bürgerliche deutsche Geschichtsschreibung der Weimarer Republik*, pp. 130–35. Craig, *Politics of the Prussian Army*, pp. 396ff.; Gorlitz, *History of the German General Staff*, p. 219.

10 Cf. Martin Hobohm's critique of Reichsarchiv research, contained in a series of letters and notes to Delbrück 1921–23, especially Hobohm's memo "Wachsende Krisis im Reichsarchiv" of March 11, 1923. "The purpose of this work is to describe the military actions in minute detail," Hobohm wrote on March 23, 1923, *Nachlass Delbrück*, BAK Folder 50. There was a controversy over whether to include Hobohm's extended introduction to the first volume of *The World War, 1914 to 1918*. This essay,

a copy of which seems unavailable today, apparently contained the following chapters: 1, The Situation at War's Outbreak, Foreign Politics, Domestic Politics, Economics; 2, The German and Allied Military: An Overview of Strength and Mobilization Plans; 3, The German Transportation System and Its Military Importance; 4, The German Economic System and its War Mobilization; 5, The Mobilization of the Spirit. Ultimately this was completely rejected, *Nachlass Delbrück*, folder 51, BAK. In its place were patriotic and brief introductions written by the two men charged with final proofreading for each volume. For example, Generalmajor a. D. Rudolf von Borries and Professor Dr. Alois Schulte wrote, in their joint statement introducing volume 1, that the book was "a memorial to the fighting and bleeding army" and "in honor of German dead whether they lay at home or had been buried abroad." *Der Weltkrieg 1914 bis 1918* (Berlin: E. S. Mittler, 1925–), 1: x.

11   Schleier, *Die bürgerliche deutsche Geschichtsschreibung den Weimarer Republik*, p. 133. Herman von Kuhl, "Brauchen wir eine amtliche Geschichte des Weltkrieges?" *Deutsche Zeitung*, 9 December 1923. There were other tensions as well. For example, Dr. Paul Kehr, Prussian state archivist, argued from the start that the functions of archive and institute should be separated, as had been the custom in the Prussian State Archives. Letter of Kehr to Delbrück, undated, *Nachlass Delbrück*, Fasz. 119 DSB.

12   Ritter, *Sword and Scepter* 3:499–505; Fischer, *Germany's Aims*, p. 640. Joachim Petzold, in *Deutschland im Ersten Weltkrieg* 3:22ff., notes that volumes eleven through eighteen were published in the period 1933–44 by the new Forschungsanstalt für Kriegs-und Heeresgeschichte, led by Hans von Haeften. Cf. Erich Murawski, "Die amtliche deutsche Kriegsgeschichtsschreibung über den Ersten Weltkrieg," in *Wehrwissenschaftliche Rundschau* 9 (June 1959): 513–31.

13   Cf. especially Gerhard Ritter's criticism in *Sword and Scepter* 3:504; Schleier, *Die bürgerliche deutsche Geschichtsschreibung der Weimarer Republik*, pp. 128ff.

14   Wallach, *Dogma der Vernichtungsschlacht*, pp. 310ff.

15   Hans Kania, *Graf Schlieffen der Chef des grossen Generalstabes als Vorbereiter des grossen Krieges* (Potsdam, 1915), p. 22.

16   Wilhelm Groener, *Politik und Kriegführung* (Stuttgart: Chr. Belser, 1920); General von Freytag-Loringhovan, *Generalfeldmarschall Graf von Schlieffen* (Berlin: E. S. Mittler, 1920); General Herman von Kuhl, *Der deutsche Generalstab in Vorbereitung und Durchführung des Weltkrieges* (Berlin: E. S. Mittler, 1920).

17   Oberst Max Bauer, *Der grosse Krieg in Feld und Heimat* (Tübingen: Osiandersche Buchlandlung, 1921); Oberst Wilhelm Foerster, *Graf Schlieffen und der Weltkrieg* (Berlin: E. S. Mittler, 1921); Rudt von Collenburg, "Graf Schlieffen und die Kriegsformation der deutschen Armee," *Wissen und Wehr* 8 (1927); General Herman von Kuhl, "Graf Schlieffen und der Weltkrieg," *Wissen und Wehr* 4 (1923), and "Graf Schlieffens Cannae," *Militär-Wochenblatt* 59 (1924); Hugo Rochs, *Schlieffen* (Berlin: E. S. Mittler, 1926).

18   Wallach, *Dogma der Vernichtungsschlacht*, p. 310ff.

19   Ibid., p. 311.

20   Ibid., p. 312.

21   Post, *Civil-Military Fabric of Weimar Foreign Policy*, pp. 204ff.

22   Groener-Geyer, *General Groener*, p. 227.

23   Koppel Pinson, *Modern Germany*, 2nd ed., (New York: MacMillan, 1966), p. 414; Frederick Spotts, *The Churches and Politics in Germany* (Middleton, Conn.: Wesleyan University Press, 1972), p. 7.

24   After World War II, Meinecke repeatedly stated that Delbrück had been correct. Meinecke wished he had strongly supported him. Conversation with Frau Helene Hobe, a neighbor of Meinecke after the Second World War, July 1974, Berlin-Dahlem.

25   Dr. Ludwig Herz, "Der parlamentarische Untersuchungsausschuss, Sein Ziel und seine bisherigen Ergebnisse" (Berlin: Fortschritt-Verlag der Hilfe, 1920). Cf. Eugen Fischer-Baling, "Der Untersuchungsausschuss für die Schuldfragen des ersten Weltkrieges," pp. 117–37 in Alfred Hermann, ed., *Aus Geschichte und Politik: Festschrift zum 70. Geburtstag von Ludwig Bergstraesser* (Düsseldorf: Droste, 1954); cf. Delbrück's own description of the report of the Fourth Subcommittee, to which he gave testimony, "Die Katastrophe von 1918 nach dem Bericht des parlamentarischen Untersuchungsausschusses," unpublished memorandum with Delbrück's corrections, *Nachlass Solf*, Folder 99, BAK. Dr. Albrecht Philips, the president of the Fourth Subcommittee, "Die Ursachen des deutschen militärischen Zusammenbruchs 1918," *Memelländische Rundschau*, 28 July 1925; the proceedings in full were published as Deutschland, Nationalversammlung, *Das Werk des Untersuchungsausschusses* 4. Reihe, "Die Ursachen des Deutschen Zusammenbruchs im Jahre 1918," 12 vols. (Berlin: 1925–29), hereinafter cited as *U.A. 4. Reihe.*

26   Hans Schleier, *Die bürgerliche deutsche Geschichtsschreibung der Weimarer Republik,* pp. 556–61. This appeal was sent to Martin Hobohm, who showed it immediately to Delbrück. Hobohm was originally appointed the expert witness to the Fourth Subcommittee; however, he provoked such antagonism from committee members and other witnesses that in May 1921 he resigned and Delbrück took his place. Hobohm was caught between the same forces as Delbrück: the officers saw him as a civilian and the professors questioned his scientific competence; however, he had an extremely unstable personality and lacked Delbrück's reputation and experience, not to mention academic position and bureaucratic connections.

27   Testimony of Colonel Bernhard Schwertfeger in *U.A. 4. Reihe* 1:118ff.; cf. Reichstag, *Beilage zu den Stenographischen Berichten über die öffentlichen Verhandlungen des Untersuchungsausschusses* (4. Unterausschuss) "Ursachen des Zusammenbruchs" (Berlin: Reimar Hobbing, 1923), pp. 1–7, hereinafter *Ursachen des Zusammenbruchs.*

28   Schwertfeger testimony, *U.A. 4. Reihe* 1:124–49.; cf. *Ursachen des Zusammenbruchs,* pp. 13–19.

29   "Das unsere Westgegner in der Gesamtausrüstung, in der Ausstattung mit Flugzeugen und Tanks, besonders aber mit Bekleidungsgegenständen, Munitionen und vor allein Lebensmitteln uns erheblich überlegen waren, wurde gewissenhaft in Rechnung gestellt. Trotzdem erhoffte die oberste Heeresleitung den Sieg und baute hierbei auf die Zauberkraft der Offensive, dieser germanischem Wesen vertrautesten Kampfform." *Ursachen des Zusammenbruchs,* p. 72.

30   Reichstag, 12 Ausschuss, *Beilage zu den Stenographischen Berichten über die öffentlichen Verhandlungen des Untersuchungsauschusses.* "Ursachen des Zusammenbruchs," testimony of General der Infanterie Herman von Kuhl.

31   Ibid., pp. 184ff.

32   Ibid.

33   Ibid., pp. 206–17.

34   Testimony of General Wetzell, 10 November 1923, typescript in *Nachlass Delbrück,* Fasz. 108, DSB; *U.A. 4. Riehe* 1:191ff.

35   Ursachen des Zusammenbruchs, testimony of Professor Hans Delbrück, pp. 218–41; for the split between the staff officers and the combat officers, see Karl Rohe,

Das Reichsbanner Schwartz-Rot-Gold (Düsseldorf: Droste, 1966), pp. 126ff.; *U.A. 4 Reihe,* 1:153.

36 Albrecht Phillips, "Die Ursachen des deutschen militärischen Zusammenbruchs 1918," *U.A. 4. Reihe* 1:27–32. Fischer-Baling, "Der Untersuchungsausschuss," pp. 125–26.

37 Fischer-Baling, "Der Untersuchungsauschuss," pp. 125–26; *U.A. 4. Reihe* 27–32.

38 Hobbing, *Ursachen des Zusammenbruchs,* p. x.

39 For example, Schützinger, "Der Fall Ludendorff," *Sozialistische Monatshefte,* no. 11, 1924; cf. General von Zwehl, "Demokraten und Sozialisten über den militärischen Zusammenbruch 1918," *Preussische Neue Kreuz Zeitung,* 30 July 1925; Wolfgang Foester, *Der deutsche Zusammenbruch 1918* (Berlin: Verlag von R. Eisenschmidt, 1925); General von Kuhl, "Die Ergebnisse des Untersuchungsausschusses über den Zusammenbruch 1918," *Militär-Wochenblatt,* 25 August 1925.

40 *Kriegsführung und Politik: Ein Abriss aus der Geschichte des Weltkrieges* (Berlin: E. S. Mittler, 1923).

41 Ibid., pp. 1–10.

42 Ibid., pp. 71–76.

43 Ibid., pp. 91ff.

44 Ibid., pp. 108ff., 206ff.

45 Ibid., pp. 218ff.

46 Hans Delbrück, *Ludendorff's Selbstporträt* (Berlin: Verlag für Politik und Wirtschaft, 1922).

47 *Ibid.,* pp. 40–45. cf. Wilhelm Marx, *Die Marne-Deutschlands Schicksal?* (Berlin: E.S. Mittler, 1932); pp. 14–23; Moser, *Ernsthafte Plaudereien über den Weltkrieg,* pp. 35ff.

48 Wallach, *Dogma der Vernichtungsschlacht,* pp. 132ff., the most recent examination of this, concludes that the Schlieffen plan was not watered down. Hermann Gackenholz argued that Moltke's ideas were not only independent of Schlieffen's, but contrary to his in terms of the operations for the south. Cf. Hermann Gackenholz, *Entscheidungen in Lothringen 1914; der Operationsplan des jüngeren Moltke und seine Durchführung auf dem linken deutschen Heeresflügel* (Berlin: E. S. Mittler, 1933); cf. Larry H. Addington, *The Blitzkrieg Era and the German General Staff, 1865–1941* (New Brunswick, N.J.: Rutgers University Press, 1971), points up the logistical difficulties of the Schlieffen Plan, pp. 14–22; Martin van Creveld, *Supplying War: Logistics from Wallenstein to Patton* (Cambridge: Cambridge University Press, 1977), pp. 109ff.

49 Delbrück, *Ludendorff's Selbstporträt,* p. 58.

50 Ibid., pp. 59–64.

51 Ibid.; cf. Paul Guinn, *British Strategy and Politics 1914 to 1918* (Oxford: Clarendon Press, 1965), pp. 278ff.; Ernst L. Woodward, *Great Britain and the War 1914–18* (London: Methuen, 1967), pp. 322–31. See also C. A. Court Repington, *After the War: A Diary* (London: Constable & Co., 1922), pp. 261–63.

52 Guinn, *British Strategy and Politics 1914 to 1918,* pp. 281–89; Woodward, *Great Britain and the War 1914–18,* pp. 322–31; Delbrück, *Ludendorff's Selbstporträt,* pp. 49–51. On Repington, see W. Michael Ryan, "The Invasion Controversy of

1906–1908: Lieutenant-Colonel Charles à Court Repington and British Perceptions of the German Menace," *Military Affairs* 44 (February 1980):8–12.

53   Cf. Cyril Falls, *The Great War* (New York: Capricorn Books, 1959), pp. 331ff.; C. R. M. F. Cruttwell, *A History of the Great War* (Oxford: Clarendon Press, 1936), pp. 506ff. Correlli Barnett, *The Swordbearers: Studies in Supreme Command in the First World War* (London: Eyre & Spottiswoode, 1963), pp. 269–331; Even B. H. Liddel-Hart, who in 1928 could hardly put up with Falkenhayn's limited strategy while characterizing Ludendorff as "perhaps the greatest of all among the leaders of the War of 1914–1918," could see the material difficulties in the German offensive of spring 1918; cf. his *Reputations: Ten Years After* (Boston: Little, Brown & Co., 1928), pp. 203–04.

54   General Erich Ludendorff, "Mein doppeltes Gesicht," *Münchner Neueste Nachrichten*, 21 November 1922.

55   "General Buat oder Hans Delbrück," *Königsberger Blätter: Sonntagsbeilage der Königsberger Allgemeinen Zeitung für Wissenschaft, Kunst und Unterhaltung*, 9 April 1922.

56   Ibid.; "Delbrück contra Ludendorff," *Hamburger Nachrichten*, 5 March 1922; Dr. Wildgrube, "Delbrücks Selbstporträt," in the *Preussische Neue Kreuz-Zeitung*, date missing, *Nachlass Delbrück*, Fasz. 121, folder 2, DSB.

57   General von Zwehl, "Oberst Bauer gegen Professor Delbrück," *Preussische Neue Kreuz-Zeitung*, 5 November 1922.

58   Dr. Wilhelm Spiekernagel, "Hans Delbrück als Kriegsgeschichtsschreiber," *Hamburger Nachrichten*, 16 January 1921; cf. General Freiherr von Freytag-Lorinhoven, "Warum können wir nicht zu einer einheitlichen Auffassung über den verlorenen Krieg gelangen?" *Volk und Wehrkraft: Wehrbeilage der Zeit*, 5 April 1922.

59   General Alfred Kraus "Zwei Kriegsbücher," *Deutschlands Erneuerung: Monatsschrift für das Deutsche Volk* 6 (February 1922): 109–18.

60   Herman Schützinger, "Hindenburg und Ludendorff," *Sozialistische Monatshefte* 18 (1922).

61   *Berliner Börsen Zeitung*, 22 February 1922; *Die Neue Zeit*, 31 March 1922 and 7 April 1922.

62   "The Dolchstoss," *Süddeutsche Monatshefte*, April 1924; and "The Consequences of the Dolchstoss: New Documents," *Süddeutsche Monatshefte*, May 1924. Another example of the bitterness of political strife during these years is detailed in Annelise Thimme, "Der 'Fall Tirpitz' als Fall der Weimarer Republik," in Imanual Geiss and Bernd Wendt, eds., *Deutschland in der Weltpolitik des 19. und 20. Jahrhunderts* (Düsseldorf: Bertelsmann, 1974) pp. 463ff.

63   And other things such as an "untruthful mercenary writer" a "business patriot," and a "political Shylock." Martin Gruber, "The Dolchstoss Lie Book," *Münchner Post* of April 25, 27–28, and 29, 1924.

64   Cf. court proceedings, Amtsgericht München, Abteilung Strafgericht, copy from President Frank to Delbrück, dated Munich 9 December 1925, *Nachlass Delbrück*, BAK.

65   Ewald Beckmann, *Der Dolchstoss-Prozess in München* (München: Süddeutsche Monatshefte, 1925), pp. 7, 12–14. Independent Socialist Party, *Der Dolchstoss-Prozess in München: Eine Ehrenrettung des deutschen Volkes* (München: G. Birk, 1925), pp. 272ff.

66   Copy of court record, *Nachlass Delbrück*, BAK.

67   "Hans Delbrück, der Historiker," *Münchner Neueste Nachrichten*, 9 November 1925.

68   Colonel a. D. Gadke, "Nochmals der Dolchstoss," *Steglitzer Anzeiger*, 12 January 1926.

69   "Die Wahrheit aus dem Dolchstossprozess," *Donau-Zeitung*, 31 December 1925.

70   Delbrück to Wilhelm Solf, 19 December 1925, *Nachlass Solf*, Bundesarchiv, Koblenz.

71   *Zehn Jahre deutsche Geschichte 1918–1928*, quoted in Reinhard Rürup, "Problems of the German Revolution 1918–19," *Journal of Contemporary History*, III (1968) p. 110.

72   Reinhard Rürup, ibid., p. 110.

73   Since orders of merit and nobility were abolished under the republic, this was an honorary decoration created by Reich President Frederick Ebert in 1922. Granted by the German chief of state, it was awarded seventy times between 1922 and 1944.

74   Wallach, *Dogma der Vernichtungsschlacht*, pp. 316ff.

7 / HISTORY, WAR, AND SOCIETY

GENERAL

We began this book with a conflict over the military strategy of Frederick the Great and the interpretation of Clausewitz in the 1870s. Parties in the dispute were members of two bureaucratic elites in a Central European kingdom which had just elevated itself to the position of dominant partner in a new empire, which was also a new nation. Armies and war had been of central importance in the evolution of the kingdom, as they were instrumental in the creation of the nation. The dispute over eighteenth-century strategy revealed a unique image of the military past in the minds of the next generation, those who, by and large, had not experienced war. Frederick the Great, Napoleon, and Moltke had all used the same strategy, although the conditions of war in which each lived had changed. The questions raised by the controversy, however, were of wider interest for the relationship of the two royal bureaucracies, for the developing concept of specialization of labor in the society, and as an example of the enigma of strategic studies in modern history. Who was the professional in dealing with the military past, the historian or the soldier? What was the legitimate way to know about the military past, by knowledge or by experience? How was war planning to be accomplished in an era of rapid technological change?

History was a central concern to both bureaucratic elites. As it was a *Geisteswissenschaft* within the university and a dominant form of knowledge in the development of German higher education, history was also important in the General Staff. Each group institutionalized the study of the past with specialized methodology, lectures, seminars, practical laboratory exercises, and the publication of books and journals. Prior to about 1880, the university and the General Staff had divided military history between them, the former dealing with what they understood as the humanistic framework of war, that is, mainly with its political causes and consequences; the latter with what they called the technical study of war, with tactics, battles, and leaders.

There was good reason for such a division of labor, for underlying these two kinds of military history was a fundamental difference in the role of each bureaucracy in state and society. For the professors, history was unique epochs in the relatively far distance, the reconstruction of a vanished past understood on its own terms. The fifty-year rule separated

165

Hans Delbrück
1928

these men from present and future. But for the officers, history was didactic: studied and written in terms of its relationship to the desired image of the army in society, to practical military training and, above all, to future war planning. This central theoretical issue separated the Delbrück and Schlieffen approaches to war. Historical reconstruction, to understand the past, and policy making, to appraise military performance and draw lessons for the future, although related in various ways, are two different intellectual approaches to organized violence.

By 1890, two men had set out to solve particularly difficult problems within the academic and military bureaucracies. Delbrück, by no means in a position of authority, wanted to create a new specialty within the historical profession. Schlieffen, chief of the General Staff and war commander designate of the Imperial German Army, had to fashion an operational plan for the million-man army. Delbrück's quest was a speculative adventure, Schlieffen's problem a preemptive order. During the following twenty-four years, each man's work brought him closer to the professional field of the other, so that on the eve of the Great War a kind of reversal had taken place. Delbrück, the historical realist, alarmed by the increasingly hostile international climate and by rising conservative nationalism at home, turned his thinking to current defense policy. Schlieffen, the military idealist, confronted by material-logistical problems which no military planner ever faced before, and lacking war experience, increasingly looked to an image of the past.

Both men faced a fundamental problem in human knowledge, defined in its military context as planning for future war, a social phenomenon which cannot be simulated because of its relationship with death. Neither historian nor war planner recognized the full impact of the era of rapid technological change in which he lived. By the summer of 1914 neither was very close to reality.

World War I was the acid test for Schlieffen's war plans as it was for Delbrück's historical methods. The war in actuality differed greatly from the war image, a situation which became completely clear only at the very end. Neither the application of Schlieffen's operational legacy nor the employment of Delbrück's empirical criticism succeeded in this novel and unexpectedly brutal experience. Schlieffen's ideas, taught for so long within the military education system, ultimately led to a misinterpretation of German successes and a misunderstanding of German failures. Delbrück's work as empirical critic was equally ineffective. The Second Reich went down to defeat.

The peace which followed was terrible for both victor and vanquished, and images of the First World War were at the center of controversy virtually until the outbreak of the Second. Forces in German

university life and in the German army which were unwilling to legitimize the scientific study of military history in the 1880s, were unable to
do so in the 1920s. Delbrück, who sought to make a bridge between the
two approaches to war, had failed.

WESTERN MILITARY EXPERIENCE

Was this controversy unique? A number of major conflicts over social
science methods in German academic life raged in the decades before and
after the turn of the century. This was not true for questions of military
strategy. Military-political debates began in Prussia in the early 1860s
with the liberals contesting against the conservatives over military conscription, a constitutional crisis of the first magnitude which was finally
resolved as a consequence of the victories over Austria and France. Debate continued over military bills during the Second Reich; however, the
discussion rarely revealed military thinking on strategic questions. Even
the Zabern affair of 1913 did not become a serious revelation of army life
or the military mind. During the Second World War the strategic issues
reemerged: a war of annihilation was planned and carried out in Poland,
the Lowlands, and France, but failed in Russia, where a war of attrition
set in after initial successes.

In France, strategic planners before 1914 were subject to many of the
same fears as Schlieffen, and as with him, their most important military
writers, such as Ferdinand Foch and Ardant Du Picq, discovered
Clausewitz and carried forward a one-sided interpretation from which
they concluded that a strategy of annihilation was the legitimate and
correct way in war. There were intense parliamentary discussions over
military bills in the Third Republic, but no real public debate over strategic planning.

British strategic thinking was completely transformed in the decades
prior to 1916. However, little of this was in the public forum: professional soldiers largely carried it out. Even in the United States some
disagreement over strategy occurred prior to the World War, but no public debate. America feared no invasion from either Canada or Mexico,
and two great oceans insulated her from European or Asian involvement. Therefore, the climate of politics and military thinking was quite
different in this country, particularly when compared with Germany.

SOCIOLOGICAL PERSPECTIVES

When this study first began, it seemed to be accessible using methods
of the sociology of knowledge, particularly the possibility of Karl Mann-

heim's "detached perspective" gained when, within the same society, two socially determined modes of interpretation come into conflict and, in criticizing one another, render each other transparent—allowing the outlines of the contrasting modes of thought to be discovered.[1] To a limited degree, our analysis conforms to this approach. We have identified two modes of thought, the historical and the policy making or the academic and the military, which conflicted, thereby revealing the assumptions of each more clearly. Yet the analysis cannot be understood primarily in terms of social or professional types or modes of thought. Officers such as Generals von Caemmerer and von Schlichting understood Delbrück, while historians such as Johannes Kromayer and Dietrich Schäfer did not.

Other approaches to the debate from this perspective can be obtained by grouping together such elements as the participants, their use of media, and their institutions. For example, the controversy may be analyzed geographically. In the first period (1878–1914) it centered in Berlin, or more generally, in Prussia. The issues concerned the historical evaluation and strategic views of two Prussian officers, one a king, the other a general. After 1914, and especially following 1918, the focus of debate shifted from the eighteenth century to the World War. As the issues became national in scope and political in impact, the discussion extended throughout Germany.

In terms of participants, not more than a dozen men engaged in the debate before the World War. After 1914 the debate expanded considerably. Initially, the small number of the debaters reflects the fact that the issues, mainly historical and theoretical, were esoteric and interested only a limited professional group. They seemingly had no practical or future impact on most Germans. Following 1918, World War strategy became a matter of intense public discussion as the aftermath of the war was felt by Germans everywhere. In both periods, however, many of the most prominent military writers in Germany were involved.

The number of participants and the geography of the conflict both relate to the nature of the publications which carried the debate. In the first period, four main journals published most of the discussion: the *Preussische Jahrbücher*, the *Militär-Wochenblatt*, the *Zeitschrift für Preussische Geschichte und Landeskunde*, and the *Historische Zeitschrift*. In addition, several of the protagonists published books or pamphlets, mainly through Berlin publishing houses. The General Staff publisher, E. S. Mittler, for example, carried the discussion in seven books of this period. The limited editions of most German publishers and the small circulation of the journals indicate probable narrow dimensions of the debate. Most likely none of the journals exceeded the eighteen hundred copies per month circulation of the *Preussische Jahrbücher*—the most popular of the journals in which the debate appeared. The other journals were written for narrower, more specialized audiences. Estimating influence on this basis is most difficult. Assuming that the *Militär-Wochenblatt* was sent to regimental headquarters and higher-ranking military groups, a large number of officers beyond its numerical circulation number could have read it. After the World War the situation changed dramatically. A much wider range of publications carried the debate—daily and weekly newspapers of international reputation, a wide variety of special interest pamphlets, books, and political clubs and meetings in Hamburg, Vienna and Munich, Paris and London, as well as in Berlin. Likewise, the discussion lost much of its scholarly overtone: both sides aimed at influencing political opinion. A popularization and vulgarization of the debate took place.

A final influence on the number and kind of participants was the institutional setting. In both periods the orginators of discussion were a small elite: officers from the Great General Staff, professors in the War Academy and University of Berlin. Both elites lectured. Delbrück filled the largest lecture hall at Berlin, which could hold two hundred students, and a War Academy class was about one hundred officers before the war. Thus it is possible that a large number of students heard one side of the debate or the other. After World War I, the issues extended well beyond these institutions, and the discussion was carried by an expanded group of the same kind of participants, plus a wide variety of political commentators and parties, special interest groups, the legal system, government bureaucracies, and elected assemblies such as the Reichstag.

INTELLECTUAL AFFINITIES

A body of ideas existed which constituted the materials of Delbrück's thought when he began to study history. We have identified various aspects of Hegel and Ranke in particular which seem important. Delbrück's military history was characterized by a "longitudinal" framework, as he often called it, which encompassed all of Western civilization. A particular moment in time was always considered as part of, or in relationshp to, this larger view. Delbrück's history was comparative: commanders, logistical problems, weapons were seen in pairs or outlined against each other. One military problem or situation illuminated another. Delbrück, like Spengler, Toennies, Weber, and many of his generation, was fascinated by universals. Like Hegel and Goethe, both essential in his education, Delbrück seldom lost the larger humanistic perspective. From Ranke, Delbrück carried forward a concern for historical realism and an understanding of the rigorous, explicit use of eyewitness primary accounts—often used against each other to find out "what really happened."

As one of the founders of the scientific study of armies and society, Delbrück was profoundly indebted to several types of research, especially to the new and developing social sciences and to technical military treatises. But he offended conventional practitioners by attempting to provide a new technical language to deal with military history, intuiting that military history could not become a rigorous science until it acquired a new way to communicate findings. Without such a language, general syntheses similar to those in the physical sciences would be impossible. Delbrück was obviously fascinated by his contemporaries' attempts to use quantitative measurement. In time he became equally interested in the possibility of introducing and comparing exact technical data on war machines, logistical systems, and weapons. Obviously his confrontation with the officers in the 1880s forced him to be careful and correct in citing military techniques, some of which he was then familiar with from his own wartime and reserve experience. Delbrück recognized that quantitative arguments would most strongly support his historical images. From that time until the World War, his historical narrative relied more and more on the viewpoint of bourgeois materialism and less on qualities associated with the Prussian School or German idealism. This tendency became sharply more pronounced during the war and reached final form during the 1920s. Ironically, as Delbrück came more under the influence of materialism and realism, his ties with experience faded. Thus, after 1914 his own lack of current military experience plus a radical shift to empirical criticism left his work vulnerable on the very grounds which he had often said were essential to good military history: the comparative technical data of war.

All his life, Delbrück stood on the middle ground, with the military criticizing him as an outsider who presumed to read the law to the officers in their own domain, and university colleagues rejecting the study of war as intellectually illegitimate. Delbrück antagonized both officers and professors by departing from the dominant idealist tradition which his opponents, though differing in many other ways, were surprisingly united in upholding. The Schlieffen School of strategy, created within the General Staff and the Prussian School of history, originated within the university, shared much common ground. Both were rooted in German idealism and inspired by the forces of German nationalism. In substantial measure, then, Delbrück belongs to the next generation of German and European scholarship.

GERMAN SOCIETY IN AN AGE OF CHANGE

One interpretation of Delbrück's life is that he was an historian who tried to put his profession into practice. The difficulty of doing so in the German society of that era has often been remarked upon, and we may recall Max Weber's conviction about science and politics quoted at the start. Another commentator has said that the tragedy of German liberalism was that its proponents, like Frederick Naumann and Hans Delbrück, did not feel themselves qualified political specialists. In the rapidly modernizing Second Reich it was unthinkable that a man became involved in anything for which he was not technically qualified. The German respect for the specialist stood above everything else.[2] As Delbrück lamented during the closing days of the war, Germany had many specialists, but none trained for politics.

Delbrück himself appeared as a generalist to his contemporaries because he united technical competencies from two fields to form a new specialty. The technical methods he used had been developed within institutions which enjoyed protected royal status, even a kind of legal exclusivity. It is well known that soldiers and scholars represented two leading institutions in Prussian-Germany. The officer corp and the university were central pillars of the industrial feudal state. Within each bureaucracy the headquarters, so to speak, was centered in Berlin: for the officer corps the Great General Staff, for the university system the Friedrich Wilhelm University on Unter den Linden. As the General Staff established the paradigm in strategic matters, both in Prussia and for the armies of the federal states, the University of Berlin established it for German higher education. All of this has received much attention. Both officers and professors have been portrayed as members of closed, almost caste systems, inward-turned officials of the royal bureaucracy. Each system had its own values, traditional rites of passage, closeness to the throne, and unique attitude toward society. Little or no mutual relationship has been suggested. As commentators have noted the unparalleled isolation of mature scientific communities, so we tend to apply this kind of exclusivity to these two counter-elites, and not without good reason. But our research suggests that a limited interaction did occur between members of the two leading Prussian institutions: they crossed at exactly that point where one might expect conflict, namely over theories of knowledge resulting from specialization of labor.

Both professoriate and officer corps were reaffirming long-held dominant positions during this period. Although their methods were ultimately for different purposes, the institutionalized division of labor tended to protect theoretical positions once they were staked out. This became evident in the 1890s when Delbrück unwittingly touched upon one of the sensitive pillars of the military educational system—its dependence on particular historical images in support of war planning. Once this had been done, it indirectly threatened the reputation of the military in society and directly undermined the authority of the army in military history questions, an authority which in peacetime was clearly one of its claims to legitimacy. In addition, Delbrück, the bourgeois academic, revealed the ignorance of the noble officers. In 1900 this situation was bad enough in the eyes of the officers. After 1918 it became virtually intolerable, when a lost war undermined the major traditional justification of the military. Thereafter the controversy was no longer a matter of historical methods or criticism of traditional Prussian heroes; it was a matter of honor and legitimacy—the honor of the army and the legitimacy of the traditional political system and its leadership.

DELBRÜCK'S LIFE

The major unifying theme to all of this is Hans Delbrück. His life was devoted to the critical study of armies and society during two periods when this was most difficult—1871–1914 and 1914–29. Into a tradition of scholarship centering on library research and seminars, with resultant narrow specialization of period and topic, Delbrück brought Rankean empirical explicitness—the mud, grease, and iron of battlefield and supply wagon, and Hegelian conceptual affinities. He compared Greek, Roman, Swiss, and Prussian soldiers. Against the idealism and nationalism which dominated historiography, whether in university or General Staff, Delbrück's realism and materialism were discordant.

Two of the major themes of Delbrück's life treated in this essay, the debate over methods of military history and the attempt to institutionalize modern military science, reached denouement during the formative period of new nations: the empire of 1871 and the republic of 1918. After 1871 the military experience was too successful, after 1918 too catastrophic, to encourage the critical study of military history on a broad scale. The third major theme, the shift from historian of war to empirical critic of military operations, ties together the two parts of Delbrück's life as it unites his two quite different professions. It is ironic that in the only major European state created and destroyed in less than a century by war, Delbrück was one of a very few whose primary professional concern for over fifty years was military history.

In October 1919, after they returned from the Versailles Peace Conference, Max Weber wrote to Hans Delbrück suggesting that they collaborate in creating a new university research institute. Its purpose was to study military science. Weber's main concern, following what must have been lengthy conversations with Delbrück, was that military history had to be studied in a fundamentally different way than in the past: the approach had to be new "from the ground up."[3] Weber died eight months later. The institute failed to materialize, and soon the study of military history was expurgated from the one German university in which it then existed.

If his historical methodology and conclusions set Delbrück apart from the officers and professors before 1914, this was even more true thereafter. Delbrück led a double life within the university and as a publicist. Although this weighed against him professionally, the tension between both of these lives enriched his work. Historian and political commentator were not in direct conflict with each other until the World War. Even then, his striving for historical reality did not conflict openly with his sense of political legitimacy until nearly the end. The lost war meant the passing of Delbrück's world and the creation of a severe tension between his search for historical clarity and his sense of political equity. This tension is well symbolized in the epitaph which he wrote for his gravestone:

Veritatem colui
Patriam delixi.[4]

NOTES

1 Karl Mannheim, *Ideology and Utopia* (New York: Harcourt Brace & World, 1936), pp. 265ff.

2 Frederick C. Sell, *Die Tragödie des deutschen Liberalismus* (Stuttgart: Deutsche Verlags-Anstalt, 1953), p. 364.

3 Wolfgang J. Mommsen, *Max Weber und die deutsche Politik 1890–1920*, 2nd ed. (Tübingen: Mohr, 1974), p. 351.

4 "I sought the truth.
   I loved my country."

Bibliographic Essay

Hans Delbrück (1848–1929), military historian, editor of the *Preussische Jahrbücher,* and professor of history in the University of Berlin, is a figure whose life reaches across Prussian-German history with unusual breath and depth, whose personal and professional relationships describe a broad matrix of interstices through Imperial and Weimar society. Delbrück deserves a full-scale biography, for he is a major figure in Prussian-German history who remains largely unknown. Let us suggest the nature and extent of the sources, and secondly, what work remains to be done.

PRIMARY SOURCES

I. BOOKS

Delbrück's published work comprises twelve volumes as follows. His dissertation, *Über die Glaubwürdigkeit Lamberts von Hersfeld* (Bonn: Carl George, 1873), a critical examination of the eleventh-century German chronicler Lambert von Hersfeld, long accepted as credible by historians, was one of the first dissertations in the philosophy faculties of German universities written and defended in German rather than in Latin, reflecting the high tide of national feeling which prevailed at the time. *Das Leben des Feldmarschalls Grafen Neidhardt von Gneisenau* (Berlin: Georg Stilke, editions of 1882, 1896, 1907, and 1920) remains the classic scholarly biography. Even though begun by Georg H. Pertz, it was very much Delbrück's work by the second and third editions. His work in military history comprises six volumes: *Die Perserkriege und die Burgunderkriege: Zwei kombinierte kriegsgeschichtliche Studien* (Berlin: Georg Reimer, 1887); *Die Strategie des Perikles erläutert durch die Strategie Friedrichs des Grossen* (Berlin: Walther & Apoland, 1890); *Geschichte der Kriegkunst im Rahmen der politischen Geschichte* (Berlin: Georg Stilke, 1900–20). The latter appeared in four volumes as follows: Volume 1 *Das Altertum,* Greek and Roman military ways, was originally published in 1900, revised in 1907 and again in 1921. Volume 2, entitled *Die Germanen,* dealing with the fall of the Roman Empire, the Germans, the Byzantines, and the beginning of medieval warfare, was issued initially in 1903 and revised in 1921. Volume 3, *Das Mittelalter,* encompassing roughly the period from Charlemagne to the fifteenth century, was published in 1907 and revised in 1923. Volume 4, *Neuzeit,* dealing with the Renaissance, the wars of religion, eighteenth-century and Napoleonic warfare, was published in one edition of 1920. These volumes, recognized as the pioneering work in the field, established the modern view of the study of war and trace the interrelationships between armies and society from the Greeks to Napoleon. The work was reissued in German in 1962–66 by Walter de Gruyter, Berlin, and was translated into Russian in the period 1936–39 by the People's Commissariat for Defense and the State Publishing House, Moscow. An English translation is currently under way by Colonel Walter J. Renfroe of the United States Military Academy, West Point, under the aegis of the Greenwood Publishing Company, Westport, Connecticut. Volumes 1, 2, and 3 have been published. A fifth volume in this series, dealing with wars of the mid-nineteenth century, was published in 1928 by Emil Daniels, and a sixth, dealing with the wars of the late nineteenth century, was published by Emil Daniels and Otto Haintz in 1932. These latter works continue the Delbrück tradition and methods, since both Daniels and Haintz were his students, but they cannot be called Delbrück's work. *Numbers in History,* (London: University of London, 1913) contains two lectures Delbrück delivered at the University of London in October 1913 which summarize his historical methodology with examples drawn from various works, particularly his research in English military history and his usage of comparative demography in criticism and reconstruction. *Regierung und Volkswille* (Berlin: Georg Stilke, 1914) contains the substance of a series of lectures Delbrück presented at Berlin on government, in particular the theory and practice of the German government of that day. *Bismarcks Erbe* (Berlin: Ullstein, 1915), commissioned as a popular biography, is really a scholarly essay combining Delbrück's own reminiscences of Bismarck and Frederick III with a wartime plea for rational politics, for political dominance over military decision-making, and for the balance of power. Delbrück's final work was his *Weltgeschichte,* 5 vols. (Berlin: Georg Stilke, 1925–29), which dealt with the history of Western civilization from the Greeks and Romans to 1888. Delbrück strongly focused on Germany in most of these volumes, and the final volume provides a commentary of sorts on the first four decades of his own life. He wrote this after retiring from the university, basing it on lecture notes from the four-semester series in "world history" delivered at Berlin beginning in 1896.

II. ARTICLES

A second category of primary sources is Delbrück's published articles. These fall into several groups. At various times Delbrück wrote lengthy essays which were separately published as pamphlets. Included here are

Die Polenfrage (Berlin: Herman Walther, 1894), a fifty-page essay which outlined Delbrück's position regarding the historic relationship between Prussia and Poland and suggested that Germanization policies were harmful to this relationship; *Kautsky und Harden* (Berlin: Karl Curtius, 1920), a fifty-page pamphlet drawn from two lengthy *Preussische Jahrbücher* essays which criticized both of these journalists from the historical point of view and supported Delbrück's image of the outbreak of World War I; and *Ludendorff's Selbstporträt* (Berlin: Verlag für Politik und Wirtschaft, 1922), an eighty-page critical analysis of Erich Ludendorff's strategy and politics during the World War embedded in a critical review of various war memoirs.

The largest collection of individual essays are his writings in the *Preussische Jahrbücher*, which he coedited with Heinrich von Treitschke from 1883 to 1889, and thereafter edited himself until 1919. An important part of these writings is his monthly political commentary, approximately three hundred sixty essays (1889–1919) dealing with various aspects of German domestic and foreign politics. A third category of work in the *PJ* is his reviews, averaging one or two per issue. These are an important source, for Delbrück seldom limited himself to a simple criticism: he usually added his own views or compared several works written on a single topic. He was a wide ranging commentator on everything from the feminist movement, the Christian Social Congress, Germanization policies in Prussian Poland and Schleswig, to the Dreyfus Affair, socialism, the Krüger Affair, naval politics, and much else.

A fourth category of essays comprises those which appeared in journals other than his own. Delbrück's earliest published work is in the *Zeitschrift für Preussische Geschichte und Landeskunde*, and a few of his essays appear in the *Historische Zeitschrift* before 1914. During World War I his essays appeared in various periodicals created to support his views and those of the *Mittwochabend*. After 1919, with the selling of the *PJ*, he continued for a time to write for it, and his essays were carried in a number of journals such as the *Archiv für Politik und Geschichte*. Selections from his *Preussische Jahrbücher* essays were collected and published as independent volumes: *Historische und politische Aufsätze* (Berlin: Georg Reimer, 1886, second edition, 1907); *Erinnerungen, Aufsätze und Reden* (Berlin: Herman Walther, 1902, third edition, 1905); *Krieg und Politik*, 3 vols. (Berlin: Georg Stilke, 1917–19); and *Vor und nach dem Weltkrieg* (Berlin: Otto Stollberg, 1926).

III. UNPUBLISHED MATERIAL

A third category of sources is to be found in two collections of Delbrück papers: the main collection in the Deutsche Staatsbibliothek, Ber-

lin, DDR, and a second but still important assemblage in the Bundesarchiv, Koblenz, BRD. Delbrück was an inveterate saver of papers,
correspondence, and printed materials during his lifetime. Most of this
he organized himself; the rest was ordered by his wife after 1929 and by
his nephew, Peter Rassow, professor of history at Köln, 1946–62. The
result is a rich collection covering many aspects of life in Imperial and
Republican Germany. Let us briefly describe each collection.

At the death of his wife, Lina Thiersch Delbrück, in 1944, the largest
part of Delbrück's papers, comprising professional, political, and personal documents, plus a voluminous correspondence, was given to the
Deutsche Staatsbibliothek, where his neighbor and close friend for over
forty years, Adolf von Harnack, had been the general director. This
Nachlass is located in the Handschriftenabteilung, Literaturarchiv, Unter den Linden 8, Berlin, DDR.

The Nachlass contains 155 separate parts and is organized into ten
main sections, as follows. Part I, files 1–13, contains articles, newspaper
clippings, telegrams, and work pertaining generally to Delbrück's personal and professional life. Part II, files 14–24, deals with his university
life and includes details on university business matters, the calling of
various professors to Berlin, discipline investigations, petitions, notes
on the creation of institutes, special candidates for degrees, the list of
Delbrück dissertations, and so on. Part III, files 25–33, comprises published and unpublished essays on politics. Included are folders on Delbrück's membership on the German Versailles Delegation (1919), a list
of Mittwochabend members, and papers dealing with Delbrück's relationship to the publisher of the Preussische Jahrbücher. Part IV, files
34–71, encompasses small essays and pieces of writing intended for publication or as outlines for research on such topics as the Treaty of Versailles, Leopold von Ranke, and the war guilt question. Manuscripts of
Delbrück's published books are not included. Part V, files 72–85, is made
up of lecture notes for courses of lectures Delbrück gave at various times
at the University of Berlin. Among the more interesting ones are the
following: very lengthy (several hundred pages) lecture notes on the
"War of 1870–71," which probably form the basis for Emil Daniels' volume 5 of the Geschichte der Kriegskunst; "Selected Chapters on Strategy
and Tactics"; "War as a Cultural Factor"; "Class Conflict in World History"; "Concerning the Economic Conditions of the Peoples in its Inter-
relationship with their War Constitution and Ways of War." Part VI,
files 90–95, contains reviews and criticism of Delbrück's published
works. Delbrück systematically saved reviews and commentary for all of
his work beginning in 1890. The varied reviews from little-known academic journals and local newspapers show the wide readership, if not

understanding, of his works among the literate German public: university professors, secondary school teachers, government officials, newspaper writers and publicists, and various officers' groups in Prussia and among the federal states. A separate folder relates to each published volume. *Part VII* consists of articles, essays, and book reviews Delbrück collected for use and reference in his lectures and publications. Delbrück read widely and habitually clipped out articles and saved them for future use, often with his own annotations. *Part VII* is broken down into seven categories: military history, the World War, nationalism, general history, constitutional and party history, social and economic history, and miscellaneous. *Part VIII* is made up of Delbrück's *Briefkonzeptbücher:* twenty eight-by-twelve notebooks filled with drafts of letters Delbrück sent out. From the early 1900s on, Delbrück employed a secretary who lived in his large family house, and from 1917 on she used a typewriter. These letter drafts include a brief paragraph of contents, a date, and an address; they comprise the years 1898–1917. Many of these letters are referred to in his wife's memoir of Delbrück's life, *Lina Delbrück Memoirs.*

Part IX contains fifteen hundred letters Delbrück sent out between 1868 and 1929, and *Part X* more than twenty-five thousand letters he received during the period 1872–1929. Included in the latter collection are, for example, professors Adolf Bauer (Graz), ten letters (1887–1900); Julius Beloch, four letters (1908–14); Ernst Bernheim, four letters (1895–98); Karl Diehl, eight letters (1896–1903); Bernhard Erdmansdorffer, nine letters (1888–98); Joseph Fuchs (gymnasial professor), seventeen letters (1894–1914); Bruno Gebhardt, seven letters (1894–99); Otto Haintz (Delbrück student), twelve letters (1916–29); Martin Hobohm, fifty letters (1907–28); Theodor Heuss, twelve letters (1909–1923); Ernst Jäckh, eight letters (1908–24); Karl Lamprecht, twenty-one letters from 1894; Max Lehmann, forty letters (1883–1927); Max Lenz, forty letters (1883–1927); Erich Marcks, fifteen letters (1894–1921); Adolf Matthaei (art historian and professor, Kiel), thirty-five letters (1896–1919); Friedrich Meinecke, eighteen letters (1893–1929); Siegfried Mette (Delbrück student), thirty-five letters (1915–29); Konrad Molinski (Delbrück student), twenty-eight letters (1915–29); Theodore Mommsen, seven letters (1890–1900); Friedrich Naumann, fifteen letters (1895–1925); Karl Neumann (art history professor, Göttingen), thirty letters (1894–1918); Herman Oncken, thirty-five letters (1897–1928); Friedrich Paulsen, seven letters (1891–1908); Hugo Preuss, ten letters (1901–24); Paul Rohrbach (Delbrück student), thirty-five letters (1895–1928); Gustav Roloff (Delbrück student), forty letters (1895–1929); Albert von Ruville (historian, professor in Halle), sixteen letters (1895–1908); Ferdinand J.

Schmidt (Delbrück student), five letters (1920–24); Richard Schmidt (professor of history at Greifswald), seventeen letters (1887–1925); Gustav Schmoller twenty-two letters (1894–1917); Max Sering, nineteen letters (1894–1920); Heinrich von Treitschke, forty letters (1884–95); Ernst Troeltsch, nine letters (1895–1919); Adolf Wagner, fifteen letters (1894–1915); Max Weber, eight letters (1895–1919); Egmont Zechlin, eleven letters (1923–29). Although much of this correspondence is merely polite exchange, some of it is worth further study, especially the correspondence with those regular and long-time correspondents. For example, much of it originated in 1894, the year of Delbrück's first strong statement against Prussian Germanization in Poland.

Other correspondence of potential significance is that from Reichschancellor Prince Bernhard von Bülow, fifteen letters (1898–1922); Herman Fürst von Hatzfeld, twenty letters (1889–1928); Graf Paul von und zu Hoensbroech, twenty-five letters (1893–1919); Joseph Koscielski, eight letters (1893–99); Prinz Max von Baden, eight telegrams, five letters (1917–27); Graf Max Montgelas, seventy letters (1919–29); his publisher Georg Reimer, eighteen letters (1886–1907); Georg Graf von Schlieffen, thirty letters (1912–16); Anna Gräfin von Schlieffen, geb. Roberts-West, thirty-five letters (1914–19); his publisher Georg Stilke, fifty-five letters (1910–29); Rudolf von Valentini, eighteen letters (1900–25); Kaiserin Friedrich Victoria, wife of Kaiser Friedrich III, twenty-five letters (1872–1900); Berlin publisher Theodor Wolff, nineteen letters (1907–29).

A second collection of papers is in the Bundesarchiv, Koblenz, BRD. Like those in the DSB, these papers were originally organized in folders by Delbrück himself, and they comprise documents which had been in the hands of Delbrück's nephew and student Peter Rassow, professor of history at Köln University after 1945. At his death in 1962 his widow, Hildegard Rassow, gave them to the Bundesarchiv. A small section comprises documents given by Frau Helene Hobe, Delbrück's daughter, since 1965.

The Koblenz *Nachlass* contains sixty-four separate folders, ordered pretty much as Delbrück left them, in six parts. *Part I*, folders 1–23, contains a variety of materials focusing on Delbrück's political writings and the controversies they provoked in the years 1881–1929. Included here are various newspaper articles written by Delbrück, with his marginal comments; material on several court cases (Maximillian Harden vs. Delbrück, 1898; Major A. D. von Tiedemann-Seeheim vs. Delbrück, 1902–04); materials dealing with working-class conditions, with Bismarck's plan for a *"Staatsstreich,"* with voting and tax reform; censored articles of Delbrück's, 1915–18; and material over the controversy provoked as a result of the consideration of Delbrück's *Vor und nach dem Weltkrieg* for use as a primer in Prussian secondary schools. *Part II,* folders 24–31, includes documents dealing with the formal organization and scientific institutes of Berlin University and the creation of new research institutes, for example an Academy of German Literature at Weimar, and an Institute for Economic Research at Leipzig. *Part III,* folders 32–37, contains newspaper articles and letters relating to Delbrück's interest in Germanization policies in Poland and North Schleswig, and his interests in German foreign policy in the Near East and Asia. *Part IV,* folders 38–46, relates mainly to Delbrück's World War I activities, in particular the question of German war aims, the problem of Poland, his fight against the Pan-Germans and Fatherland Party. Contained herein is a collection of wartime pamphlets supporting the war aims of right and left plus material on the "Büro Hobohm," created to fight against the conservative war aims movements in 1915, and on Delbrück's own fight against the Fatherland Party. *Part V,* folders 47–60, contains documents on the war guilt questions and Delbrück's post-1918 involvement in war guilt controversies; material on the Historical Commission for the Reichsarchiv, on the Reichstag Committee to Investigate World War I, and on the Munich *Dolchstossprozess. Part VI* contains handwritten biographical sketches of Delbrück's grandfather, Leopold von Henning (1781–1866), and parents Berthold (1817–1868) and Laura Delbrück (1826–1911). *Part VII* includes various materials donated by Frau Helene Hobe since 1965 relating to Friedrich Althoff, Delbrück's Reichstag candidacy in 1887, and his proposed appointment to Leipzig in 1889–94.

An interesting aspect of both archival collections is Delbrück's habit of writing notes on odd pieces of scrap paper, letters, and printed articles. Thus, one finds in Berlin, for example, sprinkled throughout his lecture notes, wedding and engagement announcements from friends, relatives, and students; advertisements from all types and kinds of Berlin businesses; receipts for purchases and sale of stocks and bonds; and formal invitations to attend various court, university, and political functions. This not only indicates Delbrück's Prussian parsimoniousness but may allow historians to reconstruct some of the social and economic context of his life. Librarian Horst Wolf of the Handschriftenabteilung, Literaturarchiv, Deutsche Staatsbibliothek, is preparing a complete catalogue of the Delbrück *Nachlass*. In Koblenz, Delbrück's marginal comments provide a running commentary on book reviews, articles, and clippings.

After Delbrück's death, his wife prepared two lengthy essays which incorporate her own memoirs of her husband's life, quotations from

Delbrück's family, from his letters, from her letters to her parents, and from his publications. The first of these is *Hans Delbrück in Briefen*, which covers the years 1848 to 1880, 134 pages. The second is entitled *Hans Delbrück's Leben für seine Kinder aufgezeichnet*, referred to above as *Lina Delbrück's Memoirs*, and covers his entire life up to 1919 in fourteen volumes and many hundreds of pages. The Bundesarchiv, Koblenz, has a copy of the latter work. Frau Hobe has written a brief essay, *Einige Erinnerungen an meinen Vater Hans Delbrück*, which describes the five years 1919–25, during which she served as his secretary.

IV. PUBLISHED PRIMARY ACCOUNTS OF DELBRÜCK'S LIFE

A fourth category of sources is the published memoirs and autobiographies of those who knew Delbrück. Foremost among these are memoirs of Agnes von Zahn-Harnack, the wife of Delbrück's closest friend, Adolf von Harnack, and his neighbor in Berlin from 1907 on, *Adolf von Harnack* (Berlin: Walter de Gruyter, 1951); Martin Hobohm, his student aid in lectures during the war and assistant editor of the *PJ*, wrote a very sensitive brief rendering on the occasion of Delbrück's seventieth birthday, *Hans Delbrück, der Siebzigjährige* (Berlin: Georg Stilke, 1918); the Delbrück *Festschrift* of 1928, edited by his students Emil Daniels and Paul Rühlmann, *Am Webstuhle der Zeit* (Berlin: Reimar Hobbing, 1928), which includes essays by Daniels, Rühlmann, Wilhelm Groener, Ernst Buchfinck, Graf Max Montgelas, Paul Röhrbach, Otto Haintz, Gustav Roloff, Otto Becker, Peter Rassow, Walter Simons, Ludwig Herz, and Konrad Lehmann; a second work by three younger students of the same year, *Hans Delbrück: Der Historiker und Politiker* (Berlin: Otto Stolberg, 1928), with essays on Delbrück's philosophy of history by Ferdinand J. Schmidt, on his historical work by Konrad Molinski, and on his work in politics by Siegfried Mette. Others who knew him and who have described his life and work include Johannes Ziekursch, "Hans Delbrück," in the *Deutsches Biographisches Jahrbuch*, 1929 volume; Peter Rassow, in his brief but excellent "Hans Delbrück als Historiker und Politiker," originally presented in the historical seminar of Köln University in November 1948 and published in *Die Sammlung*, 1949; and Theodor Heuss, in a perceptive essay in *Deutsche Gestalten: Studien zum 19. Jahrhundert* (Tübingen: Rainer Wunderlich, 1951).

V. SECONDARY WORKS

Although references abound in the secondary literature dealing with Imperial Germany, few scholars have examined Delbrück himself, and those who have (1) deal with only one segment of his life, (2) are relatively brief, and (3) base their study on only a single portion of his original work. Thus, for example, Annelise Thimme's fine basic study, *Hans Delbrück als Kritiker der Wilhelminischen Epoche* (Düsseldorf: Droste, 1955), describes the development of his political ideas prior to 1914, based primarily on Delbrück's essays in the "Politische Korrespondenzen" section of the *Preussische Jahrbücher.* Gordon Craig, "Delbrück: the Military Historian," in E. M. Earle, ed., *Makers of Modern Strategy* Princeton: Princeton University Press, 1943), an excellent brief study, deals with Delbrück's work in military history on the basis of his published books. Richard H. Bauer, "Hans Delbrück," in Bernadotte Schmitt, ed., *Some Historians of Modern Europe* (Chicago: University of Chicago Press, 1942), reprinted in S. William Halperin, *Essays in Modern Europe Historiography* (Chicago: University of Chicago Press, 1970), is a general account based mainly on secondary sources. Hans Schleier, "Treitschke, Delbrück und die *Preussische Jahrbücher* in den 80er. Jahren des 19. Jahrhunderts," in *Jahrbüch für Geschichte,* vol. 1 (1967), describes the economic and personal relationships undergirding the *PJ* on the basis of the Treitschke and Delbrück *Nachlässe* in the Deutsche Staatsbibliothek. Hans Schleier, "Hans Delbrück, Ein politischer Historiker zwischen Preussenlegende, amtlicher Militärgeschichtsschreibung und historischer Realität," in *Jahrbüch für Geschichte,* vol. 12 (1979), 378–403, an overall evaluation of Delbrück by one who has looked thoroughly at the Delbrück *Nachlass* in the DSB and written on the period and institutions of Delbrück's life. Two of Delbrück's students have been perceptively described. Walter Mogk discusses Paul Röhrbach's ideas, activities, and writings in German foreign relations from the 1890s to 1914 in his *Paul Röhrbach und das' Grössere Deutschland': Ethischer Imperialismus im Wilhelminischen Zeitalter, Ein Beitrag zur Geschichte des Kulturprotestantismus* (München: Wilhelm Goldmann Verlag, 1972). Hans Schleier provides a good biographical sketch of Martin Hobohm in *Die bürgerliche deutsche Geschichtsschreibung der Weimarer Republik* (Berlin: Akademie Verlag, 1975). There are three unpublished dissertations dealing with Delbrück: Gertrud Gut, "Studien zur Entwicklung Hans Delbrück als politischer Historiker," Freie Universität, Berlin, 1951; Hans-Alfred Steger, "Deutsche Weltpolitik bei Hans Delbrück 1895–1918," Universität Marburg, 1955; Arden Bucholz, "Hans Delbrück: Military Historian," University of Chicago, 1972.

Work on German historians and historiography of this period has treated Delbrück as a unique but marginal figure, largely, one suspects, because of the difficulty of integrating his political life with his intellectual work, of dealing with a monarchist who at times opposed the imperial regime, and with a bourgeois materialist who wrote military history.

Thus, for example, Hans-Heinz Krill, *Die Rankerenaissance: Max Lenz und Erich Marcks: Ein Beitrag zum historische-politischen Denken in Deutschland* (East Berlin: Akademie Verlag, 1962); Joachim Streisand, *Die bürgerliche deutsche Geschichtsschreibung von der Reichseinigung von oben bis zur Befreiung Deutschlands vom Faschimus,* vol. 2 of *Studien über die Deutsche Geschichtswissenschaft* (East Berlin: Akademie Verlag, 1965); Heinrich Ritter von Srbik, *Geist und Geschichte vom Deutschen Humanismus bis zur Gegenwart,* 2 vols. (Münich: F. Bruckmann, 1950); Georg Iggers, *The German Conception of History* (Middletown, Conn.: Wesleyan University Press, 1968); Charles E. McClelland, *The German Historians and England* (Cambridge: Cambridge University Press, 1971); Hans Ulrich Wehler, ed., *Deutsche Historiker,* 5 vols. (Göttingen: Vandenhoeck & Ruprecht, 1971–72).

Aside from Annelise Thimme's and Gorden Craig's, the three most perceptive attempts to treat Delbrück deal with him during the World War in the context of the German university professors as a group, and in doing so, each work encounters the problem that Delbrück was both methodologically and politically a *rara avis.* He fits into generalizations regarding the German professoriate as a whole only with great difficulty and some distortion. Thus, Hans Gatzke, *Germany's Drive to the West* (Baltimore: Johns Hopkins Press, 1950) accurately assesses Delbrück's general position within the war aims movement; Fritz Ringer, *The Decline of the German Mandarins* (Cambridge: Harvard University Press, 1969) places Delbrück within the "modernist" group of professors; and Klaus Schwabe, *Wissenschaft und Kriegsmoral* (Göttingen: Musterschmidt, 1969) accurately describes Delbrück as the leader of the movement for a negotiated peace; however, none of these works adequately relates Delbrück's philosophy of history or his political ideas to his main contributions to historical knowledge, his work in military history.

There are several areas which need further research. A full-scale examination is needed of his political life and activities from the 1860s, and of the formation of his political ideas through Weimar Reich. Such an examination would have to account for his relationship to Kaiser Friedrich III, his parliamentary activities in the 1880s, his controversies with the Prussian cultural and interior ministers in the 1890s over Germanization programs in Prussian Poland and Schleswig, his place in the politics of Berlin University, and his work in German national politics during and after the World War. Secondly, a full-scale biography should attempt to integrate his scholarly and his political work with his family and personal relationships. The sources for such study are abundant. Delbrück is a figure whose life and work deserve to be restored to the German era in which he played so important a part.

INDEX